Congregational Prayer

صلاة الجماعة للأستاذ صالح بن غانم السدلان

Dr. Saalih ibn Ghaanim al-Sadlaan

Translated by Abu Rumaysah

2000

Congregational Prayer
By Dr. Saalih al-Sadlaan
Translated by Abu Rumaysah

Published by:
Al-Basheer Company for Publications and Translations
10515 E. 40th Ave. Suite #108
Denver, CO   80239-3264
U.S.A.
www.al-basheer.com

(Note: Not affiliated with Basheer Publications)

Printed in U.S.A.

Cover Design by Ahmed Ali Ansari, Al-Basheer Graphics

ISBN 1-891540-10-6 $15.00 softcover

Table of Contents

Publisher's Introduction

In the name of Allah, Most Compassionate, Most Merciful. All praises are due to Allah; we praise Him; we seek His help; we seek His forgiveness; and we seek His guidance. We seek refuge in Allah from the evil in our souls and the badness of our deeds. For whomever Allah guides, there is none to lead him astray. And for whomever He allows to go astray, there is none to guide him. I bear witness that there is none worthy of worship except Allah, for whom there is no partner. And I bear witness that Muhammad is His servant and Messenger. O believers, have *taqwa* [fear] of Allah according to His right and die not save as Muslims. O mankind, have *taqwa* of your Lord, the One who created you from one soul and created from it its mate and from them spread forth many men and women. And fear Allah from whom you demand your mutual rights and [do not cut] familial ties. Surely, Allah is ever an All-Watcher over you. O believers, have *taqwa* of Allah and always speak the truth. He will direct you to do righteous deeds and will forgive you your sins. And whoever obeys Allah and His Messenger has indeed achieved a great achievement.

To proceed: Verily, the truest speech is the Book of Allah. The best guidance is the guidance of Muhammad. The worst affairs are the innovated ones. Every innovated matter is a heresy. And every heresy is a going astray. And every astray act is in the Hell-fire.

It is with great pleasure that we present this English translation of Dr. Saalih al-Sadlaan's *Salaah al-Jamaah* or *Congregational Prayer*. We are certain that it is the most extensive coverage of this topic in English. Indeed, its topic is one that is long overdue in the English literature.

We would like to express our thanks to Dr. al-Sadlaan for his permission to translate this and his other excellent works. We also must thank our capable translator, Abu Rumaysah, for his efforts and sacrifice. Abu Rumaysah also added some notes to the text, which are marked off by brackets followed by the abbreviation, "Trans." Finally, we would like to thank Br. Jamaal al-Din Zarabozo for reviewing and correcting the translation. He has also added a few notes when the author himself did not point out weakness in some hadith. His notes are marked off by brackets, followed by his initial "JZ." May Allah reward all who contributed to this work with a great reward.

Homaidan al-Turki
President,
Al-Basheer Company
Jan. 30, 2000

About the Author

The author of this work is Abu Ghaanim Saalih bin Ghaanim Abdullaah as-Sadlaan. He was born in Buraydah, al-Qaseem Province, Saudi Arabia, in the year 1362 A. H. He began his pursuit of knowledge by memorizing the Noble Qur'aan under the auspices of his father. His father, who was a scholar in his own right, is considered to be the first of his teachers. Under him, he studied *Aqeedah* ("creed"), the laws of inheritance, hadeeth and grammar. He was them admitted into the Riyadh School for Memorizing the Qur'aan.

He continued his studies at al-Imaam Muhammad bin Sa'ud Islamic University and completed his intermediary studies in the year 1381 A. H. In the year 1386 A. H., he acquired a degree in *Sharee'ah* from the University. In the same year he began to teach at the Wizaarah al-Ma'aarif. In the year 1391 A. H., he acquired a Master's Degree in Fiqh. His thesis was entitled *al-Shuroot fee an-Nikaah.*

In the year 1395 A. H., he received a doctorate in Fiqh in the Faculty of *Sharee'ah*. His thesis was entitled, *an-Niyyah wa Atharuhaa fee al-Ahkaam ash-Shar'iyyah.* Currently, he is a teacher in the Department of Fiqh in the School of *Sharee'ah* at Muhammad ibn Saud Islamic University.

The author has studied under and benefited from many of the noble scholars. From the most famous and skilled of his teachers are: His father, ash-Shaykh Ghaanim as-Sadlaan (may Allah have mercy upon him); Shaykh Muhammad bin Ibraaheem Aali-ash-Shaykh (may Allah have mercy upon him), under whom he studied *Aqeedah*, *Hadeeth* and *Fiqh*; his eminence, Abdul-Azeez bin Baaz (may Allah have mercy upon him), under whom he studied *Aqeedah* and *Fiqh*; Shaykh Muhammad al-Ameen ash-Shanqeetee (may Allah have mercy upon him) under whom he studied *Usool* and *Tafseer*; Shaykh Abdur-Razzaaq al-Afeefee (may Allah have mercy upon him), under whom he studied *Usool*, *Tafseer* and *Hadeeth*; Shaykh Manaa' al-Qattaan, under whom he studied *Tafseer* and *Usool*; Shaykh Abdul-Azeez bin Muhammad bin Daawood; Shaykh Abdul-Azeez Zaahim; Shaykh Saalih bin Fawzaan al-Fawzaan;

Shaykh Naasir at-Tareem; Shaykh Abdullaah bin Jibreen; and Shaykh Muhammad bin Abdur-Rahmaan bin Qaasim.

By the grace and mercy of Allah, a number of the Shaykh's books have been translated into English and published by Al-Basheer Company. These works include *Marital Discord (al-Nushooz)*, *Words of Remembrance and Words of Reminder*, *The Fiqh of Marriage in the Light of the Quran and Sunnah* and *Fiqh Made Easy*.

Translator's Preface

Indeed all praise is due to Allah. We praise him, we seek His help, we seek His forgiveness and we seek refuge with Him from the evil of our souls and the evil of our actions. Whomsoever Allah guides, none can misguide and whomsoever Allah leaves to stray, none can guide. I bear witness that there is none worthy of worship save Allah, the One Who has no partner; and I bear witness that Muhammad is His servant and Messenger.

The best speech is the speech of Allah and the best guidance is the guidance of Muhammad (peace be upon him). The worst of all matters are those newly introduced (in the religion). Every newly introduced matter is an innovation and every innovation is a going astray. All going astray leads to Hellfire.

To proceed...

The following is a translation of the book *Salaatul Jamaa'ah: Hukmuhaa wa Ahkaamuhaa* by Shaykh Saalih bin Ghaanim as-Sadlaan, may Allah preserve him. This book was chosen to be translated for a number of reasons:

(1) The absence of a book in English that comprehensively deals with the topic at hand.

(2) On each of the issues discussed, the Shaykh has briefly presented the views of the various *madhhabs* of *Ahlus Sunnah wal Jamaa'ah*. He has done so without going into too much technical detail, such that the reader is left understanding why a particular *madhhab* held a certain stance but without getting confused.

(3) On each of the issues, the Shaykh has presented what he sees to be the strongest opinion based upon the evidences.

(4) The Shaykh has highlighted common errors that many people fall into when praying and warned against them.

I ask Allah that He make this action sincerely for Him, to make it of benefit to myself and the Muslims, and to forgive me my errors for they are all from me.

Recommended Books to be Read Alongside This One

Below are a list of books that I feel complement this book and when studied would give the reader a more complete understanding of the essential topic of *salaat* (prayers), based upon the Qur'aan and Authentic Sunnah.

The Prophet's Prayer Described – Muhammad Naasir al-Deen Al-Albaanee

The Prayer: Its Effect in Increasing Eemaan and Purifying the Soul – Al-Awaayishah

The Three Abandoned Prayers – Adnaan Arour

The Friday Prayer – Jamaal al-Din Zarabozo

The Night Prayers – Al-Albaanee/Muhammad Jibali

Some Translation Conventions Used in This Book:

Aalim/ Ulemaa	Scholar/Scholars
Haafidh/Huffaadh	Hadeeth Master/Hadeeth Masters
Faqeeh/ Fuqahaa	Jurist/Jurists
Fard Ayn	Individual obligation
Fard Kifaayah	Communal obligation
Khawf	Reverential fear
Khushoo`	Reverence and humility
Madhhabul Hanafiyyah...	The chosen opinion of the Hanafee/(...) School
Al-Madhhab `inda Maalikiyyah...	The chosen opinion of the Maalikee/(...) School
Al-Mukhtaar `inda Hanbaliyyah...	The preferred opinion of the Hanbalee/(...) School
Muhaddith/Muhadditheen	Scholar of Hadeeth/Scholars of Hadeeth
Mukallaf	Legally responsible person
Qawl ash-Shaafi`ee...	The opinion of ash-Shaafi`ee/(...)
Raghbah	Fervent desire
Rahbah	Dread
Rajaa`	Hope and longing
Riwaayah `inda Shaafi`iyyah...	A reported opinion of the Shaafi`ee/ (...) School

English References Used in the Footnotes

Sahih al-Bukhaaree [9 vols., Muhammad Muhsin Khan, trans., Kitab Bhavan]

Sahih Muslim [4 vols., Abdul Hamid Siddiqi, trans., Kitab Bhavan]

Sunan Abu Dawud [3 vols., Prof. Ahmad Hasan, trans., Kitab Bhavan]

Muwatta Imaam Malik [Prof. M. Rahimuddin, trans., Sh. Muhammad Ashraf publishers]

Abu Rumaysah
3/19/1999

Author's Introduction

All praise is due to Allah. Peace and blessings be upon the most noble of the Prophets and Messengers, our Prophet Muhammad, and upon his family and all of his Companions.

The intelligent person is left with no doubt that the actions of worship performed in the religion have the same position as the foundations of a building; indeed, they are of the same position as that of the soul flowing through the limbs. The concern of the Legislator with the actions of worship reached such a level that He joined them with the foundations of belief, to the point that the Prophet (peace be upon him) said, as Muslim and others recorded,

إِنَّ بَيْنَ الرَّجُلِ وَبَيْنَ الشِّرْكِ وَالْكُفْرِ تَرْكَ الصَّلاةِ

"Indeed between the person and the polytheism and the disbelief is the leaving of the prayer."[1] The basis for this statement is found in the Noble Qur'aan:

فَإِنْ تَابُوا وَأَقَامُوا الصَّلاةَ وَعَاتَوُا الزَّكَاةَ فَإِخْوَانُكُمْ فِي الدِّينِ

"So if they repent and establish the prayer and give the *zakaah,* they are your brothers in the religion" [*at-Tawbah* (9):11].

Hence, Allah made brotherhood in the religion dependent upon establishing the prayer and giving the *zakaah,* and not merely dependent upon articulating the testimony of faith and abandoning opposition.

Certainly, the acts of worship are the signs and outward expressions of belief. The extent of the clarity of the belief in the soul of man and the extent to which faith is alive in his heart will determine how firm he is in enacting the commands of Allah.

The peak of worship and the most important action of worship is the prayer. It is one of the obligations of the religion, one of the pillars of the *Sharee'ah* and represents a

---

[1] *Saheeh Muslim* [Eng. Trans. 1/48 no. 146].

comprehensive set of regulations encompassing the whole of Islam. It is the second pillar of Islam which actualizes, in feeling and in deed, the first pillar: the testimony that none has the right to be worshipped save Allah and that Muhammad is the Messenger of Allah. The rest of Islam comes as a result of the person's performing the prayer. For this reason, the best action the Muslim can perform and the one that brings him closes to Allah is the prayer. The Prophet (peace be upon him) said,

$$اسْتَقِيمُوا وَلَنْ تُحْصُوا وَاعْلَمُوا أَنَّ خَيْرَ أَعْمَالِكُمْ الصَّلَاةُ وَلَنْ يُحَافِظَ عَلَى الْوُضُوءِ إِلَّا مُؤْمِنٌ$$

"Remain steadfast but [know that] you will not [always] be able to. Know that the best of your actions is the prayer and that none preserves performing the *wudu`* except for a believer."[1]

Having a love for the prayer, eagerly going to perform it, performing it in the most complete and perfect way both inwardly and outwardly is an indication of the amount of love of Allah and desire to meet Him that one has in his heart. Turning away from the prayer, being lazy in performing it, being lethargic in going to it, seeing it as something difficult to perform, praying it individually and not in congregation without a valid excuse are signs of the heart devoid of the love of Allah and its not desiring that which is with Him. Al-Hasan, may Allah have mercy upon him, commented upon the saying of Allah,

$$فَخَلَفَ مِنْ بَعْدِهِمْ خَلْفٌ أَضَاعُوا الصَّلَاةَ وَاتَّبَعُوا الشَّهَوَاتِ فَسَوْفَ يَلْقَوْنَ غَيًّا$$

"But after them there followed a posterity who missed (or became lax in) the prayers and followed their lusts. Soon they will face destruction" [*Maryam* (19): 59], by saying, "They deserted the mosques, busied themselves with everyday affairs

---

[1] *Musnad Ahmad* (5/276-277).

and clung to the delights of this world and sins. We seek refuge with Allah from that."[1]

So if this is the case of those who stopped performing the prayer in congregation, what would be the case of the one who abandons the prayer deliberately? Abu al-Dardaa` said,

أَوْصَانِي أَبُو القَاسِمِ أَنْ لا أَتْرُكَ الصَّلاةَ مُتَعَمِّداً، فَمَنْ تَرَكَهَا مُتَعَمِّداً فَقَدْ بَرِئَتْ مِنْهُ الذِّمَّةُ

"Abu Al-Qaasim [the Prophet (peace be upon him)] enjoined me to never leave the prayer deliberately, for the one who leaves it deliberately is absolved of protection."[2]

The obligatory prayers are repeated every day and night five times at the appropriate times for them. Preserving these times is like the servant continually responding to the call of Allah and his giving thanks for the favors that Allah perpetually bestows upon him. Allah said,

فَاذْكُرُونِي أَذْكُرْكُمْ وَاشْكُرُوا لِي وَلا تَكْفُرُونِ

"Remember Me and I will remember you, give thanks to Me and do not be ungrateful" [*al-Baqarah* (2):152].

The Subtle, the All-Aware has completed the ease of performing them by obligating them in congregation, for indeed gathering together for the actions of worship is one of the ways to make those actions easier. Allah made the outcome of preserving the prayers to be the excellence of religion, the rectification of faith and a swift reward—all of which make it very pleasing to the believers and make them praise Allah for obligating it upon them. Allah said,

---

[1] *al-Jaami` li-Ahkaam al-Qur`aan* (11/123) by al-Qurtubee.

[2] Reported in the *Sunan* of ibn Abee Haatim. [Allah knows best, but this is probably a typographical error in the Arabic text of this work. Ibn Abee Haatim is not known for having a collection of hadith entitled *Sunan*. Furthermore, no one seems to ascribe this hadith to any of ibn Abee Haatim's works. In any case, this hadith has been recorded in a number of collections of hadith with different contexts. The recording by ibn Maajah, however, has been graded *hasan* by al-Albaani.—JZ]

إِنَّمَا يَعْمُرُ مَسَاجِدَ اللَّهِ مَنْ آمَنَ بِاللَّهِ وَالْيَوْمِ الآخِرِ وَأَقَامَ الصَّلاةَ وَآتَى الزَّكَاةَ وَلَمْ يَخْشَ إِلاَّ اللَّهَ فَعَسَى أُولَئِكَ أَنْ يَكُونُوا مِنْ الْمُهْتَدِينَ

"The mosques of Allah shall be visited and maintained by such as believe in Allah and the Last Day, establish the regular prayers and pay the *zakaah* and fear only Allah. It is they who are expected to be upon true guidance " [*al-Tawbah* (9):18].

When you come to know this, then know that many books and pamphlets have been written concerning the congregational prayer, its mannerisms, its ruling, its regulations, its benefits and warning from being lax with regards to it. All of these fulfil the purpose for which they were written. However, none of them deal with the topic as a whole in a comprehensive way, as they are works on different topics scattered about here and there. For this reason I decided to gather together in one book the various topics and issues concerning the congregational prayer and resolve most of its issues in the light of the Qur'aan and Sunnah. I have mentioned the opinions of the Jurists in many of the issues—discussing the evidences for each opinion, determining the strongest opinion and clarifying the reason behind this based on what is clear to me.

Another reason behind my writing on this subject is that it has been made possible for me to travel to many of the Muslim lands, Arab and non-Arab, as well as other lands, either visiting them or being summoned there for *da`wah* to Allah upon clear and definite knowledge. During these visits, I saw strange things and objected to many innovations, errors and evils that many of the Muslims were performing in their prayers. They were doing these either out of inherited ignorance, blind following, introducing innovations in the religion, or thinking that they had performed *ijtihaad* when *ijtihaad* has no place in the actions of worship—neither in introducing new actions of worship nor in altering existing ones or by adding to them or decreasing them, no matter how much things have changed or times have progressed. For this reason, I have discussed these matters and have made warnings about them throughout this book.

We ask Allah, the Most High and Omnipotent, that He guide us to and make us conform to the truth and enacting it, indeed He is the One Who Hears and Responds. Peace and Blessings be upon our Prophet Muhammad and upon his family and Companions.

Hoping for the forgiveness of his Lord,
Saalih bin Ghaanim as-Sadlaan
Beginning of Ramadaan, 1412 A. H.

Congregational Prayer

The Meaning of "*Salaah*" in the Language and in the Terminology of the *Shareeah*

The Meaning of "*Salaah*" in the Language

"*Salaah* (صَلَاةٌ) is the singular for the obligatory *Salawaat*. It is a noun that is placed in the position of the infinitive. One says: 'I prayed a *salaah*,' he does not say, 'I prayed *tasliyyah*.' *Salaah* from Allah means His Mercy and from the servant it means supplication and seeking forgiveness."[1]

The Meaning of *Salaah* in the Terminology of the *Sharee`ah*

It refers to an action consisting of specific pillars and known *adhkaar* (specific words) that have to meet specific conditions and is performed at set times. Or, it refers to a set of sayings and actions that are commenced by the opening *takbeer* and completed with the *tasleem* along with the presence of the intention.[2]

The Meaning of *al-Jamaa`ah* in the Language

"In the language, *al-Jamaa`ah* (الْجَمَاعَة) is derived from *jam`*. *Jam`* means to gather together what was dispersed or to join something by bringing together its various parts. It is said, 'I gathered it and it gathered (*jama`tuhu fajtama`a*).' *Al-Jamaa`ah* refers to a number of people who have gathered together for a single purpose. It is also used to refer to things

---

[1] *Basaa`ir Dhawee at-Tamyeez fee Lataa`if al-Kitaab al-`Azeez (3/434).*
[2] *al-Qaamoos al-Fiqhee Lughatan wa Istilaahan* (p. 216) of Sa`dee Abu Jaib with slight alteration.

15

other than people, so, for example, it is said, 'The *jamaa`ah* (group or set) of trees and the *jamaa`ah* of plants.' With this meaning the word can be applied to a collection of anything."[1]

The Meaning of *al-Jamaa`ah* in the Terminology of the *Sharee`ah*

"The meaning of *al-Jamaa`ah* in the terminology of the jurists is applied to a number of people... Al-Kaasaanee said, '*Al-Jamaa`ah* is derived from the meaning of *al-ijtimaa`* and the least number that can be considered a *jamaa`ah* is two—an Imaam and a follower.'"[2]

The Meaning of *Salaatul Jamaa`ah*

"[*Salaatul Jamaa`ah* refers to] the prayer of the follower being linked to and following the prayer of the Imaam while meeting specific conditions. When there occurs a command to perform *salaah* or a ruling linked to it in the *Sharee`ah*, it is understood to refer to the legislated *Salaah*."

Prayer can be obligatory, such as the five daily prayers, or it can be recommended, such as the set sunnah prayers or supererogatory prayers. It can be disliked, such as praying the prayer that is obligatory at the current time behind one who is making up a missed prayer or vice-versa. It can also be forbidden, such as the case when one prays a prayer behind someone and the order and mannerism of that prayer is different, such as prayer of the Eclipse behind one praying the *Fajr* prayer.[3]

---

[1] *al-Mawsoo`ah al-Fiqhiyyah* (15/280).
[2] *Badaa`i as-Sanaa`i fee Tarteeb ash-Sharaa`i* (1/156) of al-Kaasaanee.
[3] *al-Yaaqut an-Nafees fee Madh-hab ibn Idrees ash-Shaafi`ee* (p. 45). by Sayyid Muhammad ash-Shaatiree. [Refer to the chapter, "Repeating the Prayer in Congregation" for a detailed discussion concerning this and the position that Shaykh Sadlaan deems to be the strongest. – trans.]

The Evidence for the Legitimacy and Legal Standing of the Prayer

It is clear that the obligatory nature of the obligatory prayers is established via the Book, the Sunnah and consensus.

As for the Book, the verses concerning it are many; these include Allah's saying,

وَمَا أُمِرُوا إِلاَّ لِيَعْبُدُوا اللَّهَ مُخْلِصِينَ لَهُ الدِّينَ حُنَفَاءَ وَيُقِيمُوا الصَّلاةَ وَيُؤْتُوا الزَّكَاةَ وَذَلِكَ دِينُ الْقَيِّمَةِ

"And they have been ordered only to worship Allah sincerely, making the religion for Him and to establish the prayer and give the *zakaah*. That is the upright religion" [*al-Bayyinah* (98):5].

As for the Sunnah, there are also many *ahaadeeth* concerning this. For example, al-Bukhaaree, Muslim and others report from Abdullaah bin Umar bin al-Khattaab that he heard the Messenger of Allah (peace be upon him) saying,

بُنِيَ الإِسْلامُ عَلَى خَمْسٍ شَهَادَةِ أَنْ لا إِلَهَ إِلاَّ اللَّهُ وَأَنَّ مُحَمَّدًا رَسُولُ اللَّهِ وَإِقَامِ الصَّلاةِ وَإِيتَاءِ الزَّكَاةِ وَالْحَجِّ وَصَوْمِ رَمَضَانَ

"Islam is built upon five pillars: the testimony that none has the right to be worshipped save Allah and that Muhammad is the Messenger of Allah, establishing the prayer, giving the zakaah, performing Hajj and fasting the month of Ramadaan."[1]

As for the consensus, ibn Hubairah said in *al-Ifsaah*, "They [the scholars] have unanimously agreed that the prayer is one of the pillars of Islam and that there are five obligatory prayers during the day and night... They have also agreed that the obligation is never lifted with regards to the legally responsible, mature, sane men. They have been enjoined with it until the time of their death or the commencement of the matters of the Hereafter."[2]

---

[1] Reported by al-Bukhaaree [Eng. Trans. 1/17 no. 7] and Muslim [Eng. Trans. 1/9 no. 18-21].

[2] *al-Ifsaah `an Ma`aanee as-Sihaah* (1/100) of ibn Hubairah al-Hanbalee.

The Position of the Prayer in Islam

Prayer has a great standing, elevated above the other actions of worship; indeed, it has a great position in Islam, a position which no other act of worship holds. The prayer is the pillar of the religion, without which the religion itself cannot be established. Allah said,

$$إِنَّ الصَّلاةَ كَانَتْ عَلَى الْمُؤْمِنِينَ كِتَابًا مَوْقُوتًا$$

"Indeed prayer has been prescribed upon the believers at fixed times" [*an-Nisaa* (4):103].

Prayer is the pillar of every religion. It takes precedence over other acts of worship since it arises as one of the necessary implications of faith. Every messenger and prophet has enjoined its practice and encouraged its performance. This is due to its having a great effect in nurturing the souls and in drawing one close to Allah. There is nothing that can correct the soul, strengthen it and make it desire the virtuous actions and noble manners more than prayer.

There occurs in the words of Abraham (peace be upon him) while supplicating to his Lord,

$$رَبِّ اجْعَلْنِي مُقِيمَ الصَّلاةِ وَمِنْ ذُرِّيَّتِي$$

"O my Lord! Make me one who is devout and steadfast in prayer and [also of] my progeny..." [*Ibraaheem* (14):40].

Allah said with regards to Ismaa'eel (peace be upon him),

$$وَكَانَ يَأْمُرُ أَهْلَهُ بِالصَّلاةِ وَالزَّكَاةِ وَكَانَ عِنْدَ رَبِّهِ مَرْضِيًّا$$

"He used to enjoin his family to prayer and to give *zakaah* and he was well pleasing in the Sight of his Lord" [*Maryam* (19):55].

Allah said while addressing His Prophet Moses (peace be upon him),

$$إِنَّنِي أَنَا اللَّهُ لا إِلَهَ إِلاَّ أَنَا فَاعْبُدْنِي وَأَقِمِ الصَّلاةَ لِذِكْرِي$$

"Indeed I am Allah, there is none worthy of worship save Me; so worship Me and establish the prayer for my remembrance" [*Taa Haa* (20): 14].

The angels called to the mother of Jesus (peace be upon him), as is stated in the Quran,

يَامَرْيَمُ اقْنُتِي لِرَبِّكِ وَاسْجُدِي وَارْكَعِي مَعَ الرَّاكِعِينَ

"O Maryam, stand devoutly before your Lord, prostrate and bow along with all those who bow" [*Aali Imraan* (3): 42].

Jesus (peace be upon him) mentioned the favors bestowed by Allah saying,

وَجَعَلَنِي مُبَارَكًا أَيْنَ مَا كُنْتُ وَأَوْصَانِي بِالصَّلاةِ وَالزَّكَاةِ مَا دُمْتُ حَيًّا

"He made me blessed wherever I may be and enjoined upon me prayer and *zakaah* for as long as I live" [*Maryam* (19):31].

Allah took the covenant from the Children of Isra`eel. Among the most important aspects of that covenant was the prayer,

وَإِذْ أَخَذْنَا مِيثَاقَ بَنِي إِسْرَائِيلَ لَا تَعْبُدُونَ إِلاَّ اللَّهَ وَبِالْوَالِدَيْنِ إِحْسَانًا وَذِي الْقُرْبَى وَالْيَتَامَى وَالْمَسَاكِينِ وَقُولُوا لِلنَّاسِ حُسْنًا وَأَقِيمُوا الصَّلَاةَ وَعَاتُوا الزَّكَاةَ

"And when We took the covenant from the Children of Israa`eel, (saying): Do not worship anyone save Allah, be dutiful and good to the parents, relatives, orphans and homeless, and speak to people in a good way. Establish the prayer and give the *zakaah*" [*al-Baqarah* (2):83].

Allah, the Exalted, said while addressing our Prophet (peace be upon him),

وَأْمُرْ أَهْلَكَ بِالصَّلاةِ وَاصْطَبِرْ عَلَيْهَا لا نَسْأَلُكَ رِزْقًا نَحْنُ نَرْزُقُكَ وَالْعَاقِبَةُ لِلتَّقْوَى

"Command your family to perform the prayer and be constant in doing so. We do not ask sustenance of you; rather We provide you with sustenance and the end is for the God-fearing" [*Taa Haa* (20):132].

Definitely, prayer is the peak and pillar of Islam. It is the connection between the servant, who acknowledges his position as servant and who is sincere to himself, and his Lord

Who nurtures him—the One Who nurtures the whole of creation by His grace and beneficence. The prayer is the sign of the servant's love for his Lord, his acknowledging of Allah's favors and his giving thanks for His beneficence.

The prayer is the action that truly distinguishes the believer from the disbeliever as proven by the Prophet's (peace be upon him) saying,

الْعَهْدُ الَّذِي بَيْنَنَا وَبَيْنَهُمْ الصَّلَاةُ فَمَنْ تَرَكَهَا فَقَدْ كَفَرَ

"The covenant between us and them is the prayer, whoever leaves it has committed disbelief."[1]

Know that whoever is lax in performing the prayer will be even more so lax with regards to any other act of worship. In fact, he has severed all connection between himself and his Lord, as was stated by the Rightly Guided Khaleefah of the Messenger of Allah, Abu Bakr as-Siddeeq. He wrote to his governors, "Know that your most important affair in my eyes is the prayer. Whoever fails to perform them is more likely to fail to perform other actions of worship. Know that there are actions due to Allah during the day that He will not accept during the night and there are actions due to Allah during the night that He will not accept during the day."[2]

Ibn Abu Shaybah reports in his *Musannaf* from Zayd al-Haarith that when death approached Abu Bakr, he sent for Umar so that Umar could succeed him. The people exclaimed, "Are you putting one who is harsh and severe in authority over us? If he is put in authority over us, he will surely become harsher and more severe. What will you say to your Lord when you meet Him having left Umar in charge of us?" Abu Bakr said, "Are you trying to make me afraid of my Lord? I would say, 'O Allah I have left the best of Your creation in charge of them.'" Then he sent for Umar and said, "I enjoin upon you a bequest that you must preserve. Indeed, Allah has a right during the day that He will not accept during the night and

---

[1] Reported by at-Tirmidhee (no. 2623) and an-Nasaa`ee (1/231-232) with a *saheeh* chain.
[2] *Majmoo` Fataawaa* (22/40) of ibn Taymiyyah.

Allah has a right during the night that He will not accept during the day..."[1]

Shaykh al-Islam ibn Taimiyyah, may Allah have mercy upon him said, "As for the actions of the day that Allah does not accept during the night and the actions of the night that Allah will not accept during the day, they are the prayers of *Dhuhur* and *Asr* for it is not permissible for a person to delay them until the night... In general, there is no work that can lift the obligation from a person to pray the prayer at its time such that the person would delay the prayers of the day to the night and the prayers of the night to the day. Rather it is necessary to perform them at their appointed times."[2]

Umar bin al-Khattaab used to write to his governors in outlying regions, "Indeed the most important of your affairs in my eyes is the prayer. Whoever preserves them has preserved his religion and whoever misses them will be even more likely to miss performing anything else. There is no portion of Islam for the one who leaves the prayer."[3]

Hence, every person who treats the prayer as something inconsequential has treated Islam as inconsequential. In fact, the portion of Islam a person has is proportional to the extent that he preserves the prayer and his desire for Islam is the same as the desire he has for the prayer. So beware of meeting Allah while you possess no respect for Islam. For indeed, in reality, the respect for Islam that you have in your heart is like the respect you apportion to the prayer in your heart. It is reported from the Prophet (peace be upon him) that he said, "The prayer is the pillar of the religion."[4]

Do you not know that when the pillar of the tent is removed, the tent collapses and neither its ropes nor pegs are of any avail? The same applies to the prayer in Islam.[5]

---

[1] *Musannaf* (14/527 no. 18902).

[2] *Majmoo` Fataawaa* (22/38-39).

[3] *Kitaab as-Salaah wa Hukm Taarikihaa* (pp. 403-404) by ibn Qayyim al-Jawziyyah.

[4] From the hadeeth of Mu`aadh reported in the *Musnad* of Ahmad (5/231) with the words, "The peak of the matter is Islam and its pillar is prayer."

[5] Taken from the book *as-Salaah* by Imaam Ahmad bin Hanbal (p. 356).

The Position of the Prayer Among the Other Acts of Worship

The prayer was the first obligation to be instituted in Islam after the testimony of faith. For ten years in Makkah, the Messenger (peace be upon him) called to *tawheed* (Islamic monotheism) and forbade *shirk* (associating partners with Allah). When the correct belief became instilled in the hearts of the Muslims and they had complete faith in the *Tawheed* of Allah, Allah obligated upon the Prophet (peace be upon him) and upon the Muslims the five daily prayers. The Prophet (peace be upon him) prayed the obligatory prayers for three years before he migrated to Madeenah. In order to impress upon the Muslims the importance of prayer and the great position accorded to it that is not shared by any other action of worship, Allah obligated it upon the Prophet (peace be upon him) directly, without any intermediary, by addressing him on the Night of Ascent.[1]

This great favor that Allah bestowed upon his beloved (peace be upon him) on the night of the greatest connection was a reward for the sincere servitude that he had established—a level that had not been reached by any other who came before him and that will not be reached by anyone who comes after him. This is why the prayer was the joy of the eye of the Messenger of Allah (peace be upon him). It was the prayer that he would resort to whenever a matter concerned him. It used to be his avenue of relief from anything that worried him. This is why he said to Bilaal,

يا بلال أرحنا بالصلاة

"O Bilaal, comfort us with the prayer."[2]

---

[1] The prayers were obligated on the Night of Ascent but there is a difference of opinion concerning when this occurred. The closest opinion to the truth is that this occured after the tenth year of the Ministry of the Prophet (peace be upon him) and before the Migration. To see the other opinions on this issue refer to *Fath al-Baaree* (7/203) and *al-Bidaayah wa an-Nihaayah* (3/119). Refer also to the hadeeth concerning the Ascent in *Saheeh al-Bukhaaree* [Eng. Trans.5/143 no. 227].

[2] Abu Daawood [Eng. Trans. 3/1388 no. 4967, 4968] and Ahmad (5/364, 371) with a *saheeh* chain.

The prayer was among the last things he reminded us to adhere to, among the many things he told us to adhere to. During the last moments of his life, he said,

الصَّلاةَ الصَّلاةَ وَمَا مَلَكَتْ أَيْمَانُكُمْ

"The prayer, the prayer! And what your right hands possess."[1]

Therefore, the prayer is the beginning as well as the furthest portion of Islam. The proofs for the great position that the prayer holds include the fact that it is most often mentioned in the Qur'aan. Sometimes it is mentioned alone, sometimes it is mentioned alongside *zakaah*, other times alongside patience, and at yet other times with sacrifice. Sometimes it is used to begin and end a list of righteous actions.

Furthermore, the obligation of prayer is general to both men and women, to the slave and freeman, to the rich and poor, to the resident and traveler, and to the healthy and sick. The first action that will be judged on the Day of Judgment is the prayer and it is the last action to be lost before the servant's religion is lost. It is the pillar of the religion such that the religion cannot be established without it, as occurs in the hadeeth,

رَأْسُ الأَمْرِ الإِسْلامُ وَعَمُودُهُ الصَّلاةُ وَذِرْوَةُ سَنَامِهِ الْجِهَادُ

"The peak of the matter is Islam, its pillar is the prayer and its summit is jihaad."[2] Whenever the pillar has fallen, the religion has gone. Refuge is sought with Allah [from that evil end] for the prayer manifests the servitude to Allah, the Magnificent and Exalted.

The prayer has been ordained in the manner that is the best and most complete form of worshipping the Creator, the Blessed and Exalted. It includes the glorification by the limbs, from the articulation of the tongue to the movements of the hands, legs, head and senses. Every part of the body has its portion of humbling itself before Allah in this great action of worship. Not only this but the inner aspects also have their

---

[1] Ahmad (6/290, 311, 321).
[2] Tirmidhee (5/12 no. 2616) and he said that it was *hasan saheeh*.

share. The heart also performs the servitude obligatory upon it. The prayer includes praising and extolling, glorifying and *tasbeeh* and *takbeer*, testifying to the true testimony and standing before Allah in a state of humility and submission. One stands in the state of a slave and one who has no real control over his affairs. The servant seeks to humbly draw closer to Allah through reciting His Speech; then he bows his back in submission and *khushoo'* to Him. Then he straightens again in order to prepare himself for an act of humility greater than the bowing: the prostration. He places his head, the most noble part of his body, on the ground in a state of complete submission and *khushoo'* before his Lord, humbling himself before His Greatness such that his heart is in a state of being in complete need of Him and his body is in a state of total humility.

The servant continues moving between these states until he is about to complete his prayer. He sits in the state of *tashahhud* glorifying his Lord, sending *salaam* and *salaah* upon His Messenger (peace be upon him) and imploring Allah for His bounty and Mercy. So what is there that can possibly be better than this act of worship? What more complete way is there of worshipping Allah? What way is there that is more noble than this in displaying one's servitude to Allah?[1]

---

[1] Refer to *Miftaah Daar as-Sa'aadah* (p. 384).

The Wisdom behind the Legislation of Congregational Prayer

From among the lofty qualities of the Islamic *Sharee`ah* is that it has legislated that many acts of worship be done in congregation, becoming tantamount to an Islamic convention. The Muslims gather so that they may keep in contact with each other, come to know each other, seek advice from one another, seek help in removing any difficulties that they may be in and discuss various issues with each other. This contains great benefit and many desirable points which cannot be enumerated, such as teaching the ignorant, helping the needy, softening the hearts and manifesting the greatness of Islam. The heavenly revelation endorses this understanding for when it prohibits and commands it does not direct this prohibition to any specific individual but to the congregation as a whole. Allah says,

يَاأَيُّهَا الَّذِينَ ءَامَنُوا ارْكَعُوا وَاسْجُدُوا وَاعْبُدُوا رَبَّكُمْ وَافْعَلُوا الْخَيْرَ لَعَلَّكُمْ تُفْلِحُونَ وَجَاهِدُوا فِي اللَّهِ حَقَّ جِهَادِه

"O you who believe! Bow, prostrate and worship your Lord. Perform the good so that you may be successful and perform Jihaad in the way of Allah as it should be done" [*al-Hajj* (22):77-78].

When a Muslim stands before Allah, intimately conversing with Him and humbling himself before Him, he does not speak as an individual, separate from his brethren. Rather, he speaks as one part of a united, connected whole. He says,

إِيَّاكَ نَعْبُدُ وَإِيَّاكَ نَسْتَعِينُ

"It is only you we worship and it is only Your Aid we seek" [*al-Faatihah* (1):5]. He does not say, "It is only You I worship and it is only Your Aid I seek." Then he asks Him from His goodness and guidance but he does not ask for himself only, instead he says,

اهْدِنَا الصِّرَاطَ الْمُسْتَقِيمَ صِرَاطَ الَّذِينَ أَنْعَمْتَ عَلَيْهِمْ غَيْرِ
الْمَغْضُوبِ عَلَيْهِمْ وَلَا الضَّالِّينَ

"Guide us to the Straight Path. The Path of those whom You have guided, not the path of those who have earned Your Anger nor those who have gone astray" [*al-Faatihah* (1):6-7].

The congregational prayer is one of the greatest means to remove social differences and racism based upon one's color, race or land... Through the congregational prayer, Muslims attain mutual love, respect and brotherhood. This is through the elders becoming known and thereby respected, the poor and needy becoming known and thereby helped, the scholars becoming known and thereby asked, and the ignorant becoming known and thereby taught.

From the benefits of the congregational prayer is that the one who does not pray becomes known. Therefore, his action can be rejected and objected to. The one who is lazy with respect to prayer can be known and therefore warned.

In addition, the very fact of Muslims gathering together in the mosques desiring what is with Allah and hoping for His Mercy is a cause for the descent of the Mercy and Blessings of Allah, the Mighty and Magnificent.

In sum, performing the prayer in congregation spreads unity, mutual love and brotherhood among the Muslims and it makes them as one unified rank. It inculcates among them mutual mercy and softness of hearts and, likewise, it nurtures them into becoming organized, disciplined and punctual.

The History of The Legislation of Congregational Prayer

Congregational prayer was sanctioned in Mecca after the prayer had been made obligatory, but it was not obligatory to pray in congregation. After Allah, the Mighty and Magnificent, obligated the five daily prayers on the Night of Ascent, He sent Jibreel (peace be upon him) the next morning to teach the Prophet (peace be upon him) the times and mannerisms of performing the prayer. Jibreel (peace be upon him) did this by leading the Prophet (peace be upon him) in prayer on two occasions by the House (Kaabah). On the first occasion, he prayed *Dhuhur* when the sun had passed the meridian. Abdur-Razzaaq reports in his *Musannaf* from ibn Juraij that Naafi` ibn Jubair and others said, "When the Prophet (peace be upon him) awoke the day after the Night of Ascent after the sun had passed the meridian, it was none but Jibreel descending who awoke him and this is why this occasion was called the first. He was ordered to call out, 'The prayer in congregation.' So the people gathered together and Jibreel prayed with the Prophet (peace be upon him) and the Prophet (peace be upon him) prayed for the people. The first two *rak`ah*s were lengthy and the last two were short. Then Jibreel sent *salaam* to the Prophet (peace be upon him) and the Prophet sent *salaam* to the people. The same was done for *Asr*. Then Jibreel descended at the beginning of the night and he called out, 'The prayer in congregation.' Jibreel prayed with the Prophet and the Prophet (peace be upon him) prayed, lengthening the recitation in the first two *rak`ah*s and reciting loudly and shortening the last two. Then Jibreel sent the *salaam* to the Prophet (peace be upon him) and the Prophet (peace be upon him) sent *salaam* to the people."[1]

---

[1] *Musannaf Abdur Razzaaq* (1/454 no. 1773), Book of Prayer under the chapter: What occurs with regards the obligation of prayer. [This narration found in *Musannaf Abdir Razzaaq* has the following chain: Abdul Razzaaq on the authority of ibn Juraij who said: Naafi ibn Jubair and another (or others) said, "In the morning after the night of Ascencion..." This chain has two defects to it. First, Naafi ibn Jubair is a trustworthy narrator but he is from the generation of the Followers. In other words, there is no way that he could have heard this information directly from the Prophet (peace be upon him). Hence, the chain between Naafi and the Prophet (peace be upon him) is broken. Second, ibn Juraij is Abdul Malik ibn Abdul Azeez ibn Juraij. Although ibn Juraij is acceptable in some of his narrations, he was known for committing the worst kind of *tadlees* ("deception in narration") wherein he would drop the names of weak narrators from the chain. In particular, when he used the term *qaala* ("he said"), his narrations are considered very weak. Such is the case with this particular narration quoted above. Hence, there is no question that this particular narration is weak. Ibn Ishaaq has a different narration with the chain: "Ibn Ishaaq said: Utbah ibn Muslim narrated to me saying: on the authority of Naafi ibn Jubair ibn Mutim on the authority of ibn Abbaas who said..." This chain is *sahih* as all of the narrators are trustworthy and the chain is unbroken. In this narration, which also goes through Naafi ibn Jubair, it states that the Angel Jibreel led the Prophet (peace be upon him) in the prayers, but there is no explicit mention of the event occurring immediately after the Night of the Ascencion, nor is there any mention of the Prophet (peace be upon him) performing the prayers in congregation. The fact that the Angel led the Prophet (peace be upon him) in the prayers,

The Prophet (peace be upon him) would pray in congregation with some of his Companions on some occasions but not most of the time. He prayed with Alee in *Daar al-Arqam* and with the Mother of the Believers, Khadeejah, and that was after Jibreel (peace be upon him) led him (peace be upon him) in prayer.

Prayer in congregation was not stressed at that time. [It was stressed] in Madeenah, where it became a symbol from the symbols outwardly manifesting Islam. Al-Bukhaaree reports from ibn Umar that "when the Muslims came to Madeenah, they would gather together and calculate the time of prayer and no one would call them. Once they came together and discussed this. Some of them said, 'We should have a bell like the Christians.' Others said, 'We should have a horn like the Jews.' Umar suggested, 'Why don't we have one person call the others to prayer?' The Messenger of Allah (peace be upon him) said, 'Stand Bilaal and make the call to prayer.'"[1]

Abu Daawood recorded in his *Sunan* from Abu Umayr bin Anas from an uncle of his of the Ansaar, "The Prophet (peace be upon him) was concerned as to how to gather the people for prayer. It was suggested, 'Hoist a flag at the time of prayer; when the people see it they will inform one another.' However this suggestion did not appeal to the Prophet (peace be upon him). The use of the horn was then suggested—and Ziyaad said, 'a horn of the Jews'—but this suggestion also did not appeal to him as he said, 'This is a matter for the Jews.'

---

demarcating the timings of the prayers, is confirmed in numerous authentic hadith. However, in this book, Shaikh al-Sadlaan is attempting to prove that a congregational prayer took place immediately after the prayers were made obligatory. The only evidence for that is the narration discussed abvoe from the *Musannaf,* but that narration is definitely either weak or very weak. Hence, the author has not proven his point. And Allah knows best. For the texts of the above reports or information about the particular narrators discussed in this footnote, see Abdul Razzaaq ibn Hammaam, *al-Musannaf* (Beirut: al-Maktab al-Islaami, 1983), vol. 1, pp. 454-455; ibn Hishaam, *al-Seerah al-Nabawwiyah* (Al-Zarqa, Jordan: Maktabah al-Manaar, 1988), vol. 1, p. 311; Yoosuf al-Mizi, *Tahdheeb al-Kamaal fi Asmaa al-Rijaal* (Beirut: Muassasah al-Risaalah, 1992), vol. 29, pp. 272-276 (for Naafi ibn Jubair), vol. 19, pp. 323-324 (for Utbah ibn Muslim); Ahmad ibn Hajr, *Tahdheeb al-Tahdheeb* (Beirut: Muassasah al-Risaalah, 1996), vol. 2, pp. 616-618 (for ibn Juraij); Misfir al-Dumaini, *al-Tadlees fi al-Hadeeth* (published by its author, 1992), pp. 383-386 (for ibn Juraij).—JZ]

[1] *Saheeh al-Bukhaaree* [Eng. Trans. 1/334 no. 578].

Then the bell of the Christians was mentioned and he said, 'This is a matter of the Christians.' Abdullaah bin Zayd returned anxiously because of the concern of the Messenger of Allah (peace be upon him) and he was then taught the call to prayer in a dream. He informed the Messenger of Allah (peace be upon him) about it, saying, 'O Messenger of Allah, I was in a state between sleep and wakefulness when a person came to me and taught me the call to prayer. Umar bin al-Khattaab has also seen the same dream before me but he kept it hidden for twenty days.' The Prophet (peace be upon him) said to Umar, 'What prevented you from informing me?' He replied, 'Abdullaah bin Zayd has already informed you and so I was shy to say it.' Then the Messenger of Allah (peace be upon him) said to Bilaal, 'O Bilaal stand and do what Abdullaah bin Zayd tells you to do. Bilaal then called the prayer.'" Abu Bishr reported from Abu Umayr: The Ansaar thought that had Abdullaah bin Zayd not been ill on that day, the Messenger of Allah (peace be upon him) would have ordered him to make the call to prayer.[1] Al-Haafidh ibn Hajr said, "The hadeeth has a *saheeh* chain."[2]

From what has preceded it becomes clear that:

There was no call to prayer during the Meccan period and during the beginning of the Madeenan period. During this period, the Muslims would just estimate the time for prayer and gather for it.

The *adhaan* with the legislated wording became established after the dream of Abdullaah bin Zayd.[3]

This is how the *adhaan* came to be established for the five daily prayers: by the voice of a man and not via the means of a flag, bell, horn or fire. Instead, it is the words of man, glorifying Allah, resounding to the farthest reaches of the land and distinguishing the Muslims from all others and in accord with the uniqueness of the rest of the religion. Indeed, the people of Islam do not follow the others with respect to their dress, manners or appearance. In fact, this is true with respect to all aspects of their lives.

The Muslim should respond when he hears the call to prayer, whatever the time of day or night it may be. He must

---

[1] Abu Daawood [Eng. Trans. 1/126 no. 498].
[2] *Fath* (2/81).
[3] *al-Adhaan* (p. 9) of al-Qusee.

respond to the call of Allah no matter what affair or [non-valid] excuse he may have in front of him. Abu Hurayrah reported that the Messenger of Allah (peace be upon him) said,

لَوْ يَعْلَمُ النَّاسُ مَا فِي النِّدَاءِ وَالصَّفِّ الأَوَّلِ ثُمَّ لَمْ يَجِدُوا إلاَّ

أَنْ يَسْتَهِمُوا عَلَيْهِ لاسْتَهَمُوا وَلَوْ يَعْلَمُونَ مَا فِي التَّهْجِيرِ

لاسْتَبَقُوا إلَيْهِ وَلَوْ يَعْلَمُونَ مَا فِي الْعَتَمَةِ وَالصُّبْحِ لأَتَوْهُمَا وَلَوْ

حَبْوًا

"If the people knew the reward that came with the call to prayer and the first row and found no other way to get that except by drawing lots, they would draw lots. If they knew the reward that came with going to the prayer early, they would race for it. If they knew the reward for *Ishaa* and *Fajr* Prayers, they would come to offer them even if they had to crawl."[1]

Encouragement to Perform the Prayer in Congregation

Indeed, congregational prayer in its outward form and its reality is a perfect expression of unity and togetherness. This is because everyone bowing or prostrating is facing one *Qiblah* and calling only to one God. Every Muslim, wherever he may be in the world, faces one House, the first House that was appointed as a place of worship for mankind, the foundations of which were raised by Ibraaheem and Ismaa`eel. It will remain as the *Qiblah* of the Muslims until Allah inherits the earth and everyone on it and mankind will stand on the Day of Judgment before the Lord of the Universe.

Praying in congregation is a means of raising the ranks and increasing one's good deeds. It is twenty-seven times better than the prayer prayed individually. Abdullaah bin Umar narrated that the Messenger of Allah (peace be upon him) said,

---

[1] *Saheeh al-Bukhaaree.*

صَلَاةُ الرَّجُلِ فِي الْجَمَاعَةِ تَزِيدُ عَلَى صَلَاتِهِ وَحْدَهُ سَبْعًا وَعِشْرِينَ

"The prayer of a person in congregation is twenty-seven times better than the prayer of the person individually."[1]

Ibn Hajr presents a beneficial discussion concerning the reasons behind this increase in reward. He wrote, "By his responding to the caller to prayer, having the intention to join the congregation, coming early to the mosque at the beginning of the time for prayer, walking to the mosque with tranquillity, entering the mosque while supplicating, waiting for the congregational prayer, the Angels invoking prayers upon those praying and seeking forgiveness for them, Satan being forced away through their gathering for prayer, practicing the proper recital of the Qur'aan and learning the pillars of Islam and secondary issues, and being secure from hypocrisy..." He lists twenty-five aspects, hence actualizing the number mentioned.[2]

When the people follow one Imaam in prayer, they stand in rows behind him such that all of their worldly differences disappear and each one of them forgets his material standing. The poor stand next to the rich, the leaders next to the subjects, the black next to the white, and the Arab next to the non-Arab. With respect to this they become the same, standing side by side prostrating to Allah and worshipping Him Alone, supplicating to Him for guidance and direction. No head is above another's and there is no distinction between their faces. They gather together five times a day seeking to come close to Allah, with their hearts clean and their souls purified. They get closer to Allah not through wealth, property or social standing but, instead, by acts of obedience and by acknowledging their servitude to Him. All of them seek His guidance, saying,

إِيَّاكَ نَعْبُدُ وَإِيَّاكَ نَسْتَعِينُ

"It is only You we worship and it is only Your Aid we seek" [al-Faatihah (1):5].

---

[1] *Saheeh Muslim* [Eng. Trans. 1/315 no. 1365].
[2] *Fath al-Baaree* (2/133 under no.'s 645, 646, 647).

Indeed, Islam strongly urges that this great sign of Islam be an occasion of gathering for the Muslims such that they can meet and help each other to fulfil it. As the number of the Muslims increases, the greater is the blessing from Allah. Muslim reports from Abu Hurayrah that the Messenger of Allah (peace be upon him) said,

صَلَاةُ الرَّجُلِ فِي الْجَمَاعَةِ تُضَعَّفُ عَلَى صَلَاتِهِ فِي بَيْتِهِ وَفِي سُوقِهِ خَمْسًا وَعِشْرِينَ ضِعْفًا وَذَلِكَ أَنَّهُ إِذَا تَوَضَّأَ فَأَحْسَنَ الْوُضُوءَ ثُمَّ خَرَجَ إِلَى الْمَسْجِدِ لَا يُخْرِجُهُ إِلَّا الصَّلَاةُ لَمْ يَخْطُ خَطْوَةً إِلَّا رُفِعَتْ لَهُ بِهَا دَرَجَةٌ وَحُطَّ عَنْهُ بِهَا خَطِيئَةٌ فَإِذَا صَلَّى لَمْ تَزَلِ الْمَلَائِكَةُ تُصَلِّي عَلَيْهِ مَا دَامَ فِي مُصَلَّاهُ اللَّهُمَّ صَلِّ عَلَيْهِ اللَّهُمَّ ارْحَمْهُ اللَّهُمَّ اغْفِرْ لَهُ اللَّهُمَّ تُبْ عَلَيْهِ مَا لَمْ يُؤْذِ فِيهِ مَا لَمْ يُحْدِثْ فِيهِ

"The prayer of a person in congregation is twenty odd levels better than the prayer of a person prayed in his house or in the market. This is because when one of you performs *wudu`* in an excellent manner and then goes to the mosque desiring only the prayer, he will not walk a step except that he will be raised a rank and a sin will be expiated until he enters the mosque. When he enters the mosque, he is considered to be in a state of prayer so long as it remains his sole purpose. The Angels invoke prayers upon him for as long as he remains seated in his place of worship, saying, 'O Allah have mercy on him, O Allah forgive him, O Allah turn towards him' so long as he does not harm anyone else or break his *wudu`*"[1]

Muslim also reports from Uthmaan that he heard the Messenger of Allah (peace be upon him) saying,

---

[1] *Saheeh Muslim* [Eng. Trans. 1/322 no. 1394].

مَنْ تَوَضَّأً لِلصَّلَاةِ فَأَسْبَغَ الْوُضُوءَ ثُمَّ مَشَى إِلَى الصَّلَاةِ
الْمَكْتُوبَةِ فَصَلَّاهَا مَعَ النَّاسِ أَوْ مَعَ الْجَمَاعَةِ أَوْ فِي الْمَسْجِدِ
غَفَرَ اللَّهُ لَهُ ذُنُوبَهُ

"Whoever performs *wudu`* for prayer in an excellent way and then walks to pray the obligatory prayer, praying it with the people or with the congregation or in the mosque, Allah will forgive him his sins."[1]

Ibn Mas`ud said, "Whoever wishes to meet Allah tomorrow as a Muslim should guard these prayers when he is called to them. Allah, the Exalted, has legislated for your Messenger (peace be upon him) the *sunan* of guidance and these prayers are certainly from the *sunan* of guidance. If you were to pray in your homes as this person who stay behind the congregation and prayed in his home, then you would have abandoned the *sunnah* of your Prophet (peace be upon him) and become misguided. There is not a single person who purifies himself in an excellent manner and then goes to the mosque except that for every step he will be raised a rank and a sin will be expiated. Indeed I have looked at us and witnessed the time when not a single person missed the congregational prayer except that a hypocrite whose hypocrisy was known. Indeed, a person would come to the prayer being aided by two people (due to being ill) until they guided him to the row." In another narration, "Indeed, I have looked at us and witnessed the time when not a single person missed the (congregational) prayer except a hypocrite whose hypocrisy was well known or a sick person. Even then, if a sick person could be helped by two people to come to the prayer he would come." He also said, "Indeed, the Messenger of Allah (peace be upon him) taught us the *sunan* of guidance and from these *sunan* is the prayer in congregation in the mosque in which the *adhaan* is given."[2]

Abu ad-Dardaa` heard the Messenger of Allah (peace be upon him) say,

---

[1] *Saheeh Muslim* [Eng. Trans. 1/151 no. 447].
[2] *Saheeh Muslim* [Eng. Trans. 1/317 no.'s 1375, 1376].

مَا مِنْ ثَلاثَةٍ فِي قَرْيَةٍ وَلَا بَدْوٍ لا تُقَامُ فِيهِمْ الصَّلاةُ إلاَّ قَدْ
اسْتَحْوَذَ عَلَيْهِمْ الشَّيْطَانُ فَعَلَيْكُمْ بِالْجَمَاعَةِ فَإِنَّمَا يَأْكُلُ الذِّئْبُ
الْقَاصِيَةَ

"There are no three men in a village or in the desert who do not establish the congregational prayer except that Shaytaan has gained mastery over them. So upon you is the congregational prayer for the wolf only eats the sheep that strays from the flock."[1]

Intimidation Concerning Missing the Congregational Prayer

By reason of the prayer enjoying such a great position in Islam and the congregational prayer possessing such a lofty status and numerous benefits, Islam has shown a strong sign of rejection for the one who is lax with respect to it. It has threatened those who are lax in performing it or consider it inconsequential and has warned them of fearful punishments. Indeed, it has considered their prayer that is prayed at home as not being a prayer at all.

Ibn Abbaas said that the Messenger of Allah (peace be upon him) said,

مَنْ سَمِعَ الْمُنَادِيَ فَلَمْ يَمْنَعْهُ مِنْ اتِّبَاعِهِ عُذْرٌ قَالُوا وَمَا الْعُذْرُ
قَالَ خَوْفٌ أَوْ مَرَضٌ لَمْ تُقْبَلْ مِنْهُ الصَّلاةُ الَّتِي صَلَّى

"Whoever hears the caller to prayer and has no excuse that can prevent him from responding to it..." The Companions asked, "What constitutes a valid excuse, O Messenger of Allah?" He

---

[1] *Sunan Abu Daawood* [Eng. Trans. 1/144 no. 547] and *Sunan an-Nasaa`ee* (2/106-107) with a *hasan* chain.

replied, "Fear or sickness, otherwise the prayer that he prayed (outside of the congregation) is not accepted."[1]

Ibn Abbaas also reported that the Messenger of Allah (peace be upon him) said,

$$ مَنْ سَمِعَ النِّدَاءَ فَلَمْ يَأْتِهِ فَلَا صَلَاةَ لَهُ إِلاَّ مِنْ عُذْرٍ $$

"Whoever hears the call to prayer and does not come to it then there is no prayer for him unless he has a valid excuse."[2]

Abu ad-Dardaa` reported that he heard the Messenger of Allah (peace be upon him) saying,

$$ مَا مِنْ ثَلَاثَةٍ فِي قَرْيَةٍ وَلَا بَدْوٍ لَا تُقَامُ فِيهِمُ الصَّلَاةُ إِلاَّ قَدْ اسْتَحْوَذَ عَلَيْهِمُ الشَّيْطَانُ فَعَلَيْكُمْ بِالْجَمَاعَةِ $$

"There are no three people in a village or desert among whom the prayer is not established except that Shaytaan has gained mastery over them. So upon you is the congregation." Recorded by al-Haakim.[3]

Ibn Abbaas was asked about a person who fasts the day and prays the night but he does not attend the *Jumu`ah* [the Friday Prayer] or congregational prayer. He replied, "Such a person is in the Fire."[4]

---

[1] Abu Daawood [Eng. Trans. 1/145 no. 551]. Its chain contains Abu Junaab Yahyaa bin Abu Hayya who has been declared weak due to his frequent *tadlees*. However, the hadeeth has evidence that support it being reported by ibn Maajah (no. 793), ad-Daaruqutnee, and al-Haakim. Hence, the authenticity of the hadeeth is raised to a level whereby it can be depended upon. [Although al-Nawawi called this hadith *sahih*, it seems that it is a weak hadith. See al-Albani, *Irwa*, vol. 2, p. 336; Muhammad ibn Ismail al-Sanani, *Subul al-Salaam*, (Cairo: Maktabah al-Jamhuriyah al-Arabiya, 1977) vol. 2, p. 34; Muhammad al-Adheemabadi, *Aun al-Mabood Sharh Sunan Abi Dawud* (Cairo: Maktaba ibn Taimiya, 1987), vol. 2, p. 256.—JZ]
[2] Reported by ibn Maajah (no. 793), ad-Daaruqutnee (1/420), ibn Hibbaan (no. 2064), and al-Haakim (1/245) with a *saheeh* chain.
[3] Reported by al-Haakim (1/245).
[4] Reported by at-Tirmidhee (no. 218). Shaykh Ahmad Shaakir, may Allah have mercy upon him, said in his notes to at-Tirmidhee, "The chain to this is *saheeh*. This narration, even if it be a statement of ibn Abbaas, has the ruling of being from the Prophet (peace be upon him) because the likes of this cannot come to be known through opinion and neither is it from those narrations reported from

Abu Hurayrah reported that the Messenger of Allah (peace be upon him) said,

إِنَّ أَثْقَلَ صَلاةٍ عَلَى الْمُنَافِقِينَ صَلاةُ الْعِشَاءِ وَصَلاةُ الْفَجْرِ وَلَوْ
يَعْلَمُونَ مَا فِيهِمَا لأَتَوْهُمَا وَلَوْ حَبْوًا وَلَقَدْ هَمَمْتُ أَنْ آمُرَ
بِالصَّلاةِ فَتُقَامَ ثُمَّ آمُرَ رَجُلاً فَيُصَلِّيَ بِالنَّاسِ ثُمَّ أَنْطَلِقَ مَعِي
بِرِجَالٍ مَعَهُمْ حُزَمٌ مِنْ حَطَبٍ إِلَى قَوْمٍ لا يَشْهَدُونَ الصَّلاةَ
فَأُحَرِّقَ عَلَيْهِمْ بُيُوتَهُمْ بِالنَّارِ

"The hardest prayer upon the hypocrites is the prayer of *Ishaa* and *Fajr*. If they knew the reward that these prayers contained they would come to them even if they had to crawl. Indeed, I considered to order the *Mu`adhdhin* to call the *iqaamah* and then order a man to lead the prayer. Then I would go with some people, each carrying torches, to the people who have not attended the prayer (in congregation) and burn down their houses."[1]

Ibn Hubairah, may Allah the Exalted have mercy on him, said, "They [the scholars] have unanimously agreed that the congregational prayer is legislated and that it is obligatory to manifest it among the people. If the inhabitants of a land prevent it from being carried out, they must be fought until they desist."[2]

---

the People of the Book. It is not possible that ibn Abbaas could be certain that such a person be in the Fire unless he had a narration from the Messenger of Allah (peace be upon him) concerning this, inshaa`Allah."

[1] Reported by al-Bukhaaree [Eng. Trans. 1/355 no. 626] and Muslim [Eng. Trans. 1/316 no. 1370] and the wording is Muslim's.

[2] *al-Ifsaah `an Ma`anee as-Sihaah* (1/142).

The Different Levels of Excellence and Reward for the Congregational Prayer

The excellence and reward for the congregational prayer differs due to a number of reasons, including:

(1) The superiority of the place as compared to other places and the distance (of the person) from the mosque.

(2) Performing it in a mosque as opposed to another place.

(3) Performing all of the prayer in congregation vis-a-vis only some of it.

(4) The perfection of the prayer and preserving its mannerisms, the level of *khushoo`* in it, the number of people attending it and the excellence of the Imaam leading it.

(5) The different prayers—those that have greater excellence have a greater reward for them.

In order to complete the benefit that one attains in understanding this subject, I quote here the opinions of the people of knowledge concerning this. The scholars fall into two opinions concerning this.

The First Opinion: The congregational prayers are all equal with regards to excellence and reward. No congregation can be said to be better than another. This is the opinion of some of the Maalikee scholars and the well-known opinion of Imaam Maalik and the apparent conclusion of his school.[1]

The Second Opinion: The congregational prayers differ with regards to their excellence and reward. This is the opinion of the Shaafi`ees and the majority of scholars.[2]

The Proofs for the First Opinion

Abdullaah bin Umar narrated that the Messenger of Allah (peace be upon him) said,

صَلَاةُ الْجَمَاعَةِ أَفْضَلُ مِنْ صَلَاةِ الْفَذِّ بِسَبْعٍ وَعِشْرِينَ دَرَجَةً

---

[1] Refer to: *Jawaahir al-Ikleel* (1/76) and *al-`Uddah Haashiyah Ihkaam al-Ahkaam Sharh `Umdah al-Ahkaam* (2/107-108).

[2] Refer to *al-Majmoo` Sharh al-Muhadhdhab* (4/94) and *al-Mughnee* (3/9).

"The congregational prayer is twenty-seven times better than the prayer of a person prayed individually." Recorded by al-Bukhaaree.[1]

Abu Sa`eed al-Khudree heard the Prophet (peace be upon him) saying,

صَلاةُ الْجَمَاعَةِ تَفْضُلُ صَلاةَ الْفَذِّ بِخَمْسٍ وَعِشْرِينَ دَرَجَةً

"The congregational prayer is twenty-five times better than the prayer of a person prayed individually."[2]

"This hadeeth is used to prove that the excellence of congregational prayers is the same regardless of whether there is a large or small number of attendees. This is because the hadeeth proves the excellence of congregation and there is no room for analogy in matters of reward and excellence. Therefore, when the hadeeth proves a specific excellence and it is not allowed to make analogy, this specific excellence includes the large and small congregation because the word 'congregation' in the hadeeth refers to both. This opinion is strengthened by what is reported from Ibraaheem an-Nakha`ee with a *saheeh* chain that he said, 'When a person prays with another, they are a *jamaa`ah* and will have their reward multiplied twenty five times.'"[3]

"It is safe to assume that this reward will definitely be attained."[4]

The Proofs for the Second Opinion

The proponents of the second opinion use as a proof what the compilers of the *Sunan*, ibn Khuzaimah and others have recorded from Ubayy bin Ka`b that the Messenger of Allah (peace be upon him) said,

---

[1] Reported by al-Bukhaaree [Eng. Trans. 1/353 no. 621].
[2] Reported by al-Bukhaaree [Eng. Trans. 1/353 no. 621].
[3] *Fath al-Baaree* (2/136).
[4] *al-`Uddah* (2/107-108) of as-Sana`aanee.

صَلاةَ الرَّجُلِ مَعَ الرَّجُلِ أَزْكَى مِنْ صَلاتِهِ وَحْدَهُ وَصَلاتُهُ مَعَ
الرَّجُلَيْنِ أَزْكَى مِنْ صَلاتِهِ مَعَ الرَّجُلِ وَمَا كَثُرَ فَهُوَ أَحَبُّ إِلَى
اللّهِ تَعَالَى

"The prayer of a person with a person is better than the prayer of a person prayed individually. The prayer of a person prayed with two people is better than the prayer of a person prayed with one. The larger the number, the more beloved this prayer is to Allah, the Exalted"[1]

This hadeeth has strong supporting evidence in the hadeeth of Qubbaath bin Ashyam that follows shortly. This hadeeth clearly proves that as the number of the congregation increases, this congregation is more excellent and more beloved to Allah, the Exalted.

They also use as evidence the hadith in *Sunan Abi Dawood* from Abu Sa`eed al-Khudree who reported that the Messenger of Allah (peace be upon him) said,

الصَّلاةُ فِي جَمَاعَةٍ تَعْدِلُ خَمْسًا وَعِشْرِينَ صَلاةً فَإِذَا صَلاَّهَا
فِي فَلاةٍ فَأَتَمَّ رُكُوعَهَا وَسُجُودَهَا بَلَغَتْ خَمْسِينَ صَلاةً

"Congregational prayer is equivalent to twenty-five prayers. When it is prayed in an open desert and its *ruku`* and *sujood* is perfected then it reaches the equivalent of fifty prayers."[2]

The evidence proving that the reward of congregational prayer can differ from prayer to prayer is a lot and well known. I shall mention some more of it shortly, *inshaa`Allah*.

---

[1] *Sunan Abu Daawood* [Eng. Trans. 1/145 no. 554], *Sunan an-Nasaa`ee* (2/104-105) and ibn Khuzaymah (no. 1477) who declared it to be *saheeh*.
[2] Abu Daawood [Eng. Trans. 1/147 no. 560].

Discussion of the Evidence of the First Opinion

The Shaafi`ee scholars and the majority refute the evidence adduced by some of the Maalikee scholars by saying that the reward of the prayer of a person with a person is multiplied twenty-five times and it is safe to say that at least this much will be attained. But this fact does not negate the fact that greater reward is possible, especially when there exists a text that explicitly states this, such as the hadith, "The prayer of a person with a person is better than the prayer of a person prayed individually. The prayer of a person prayed with two people is better than..."[1]

The Strongest Opinion

The opinion that is supported by the evidence and reconciles the authentic narrations concerning this is the second opinion: the excellence of one congregation can differ from another congregation. The proofs for this opinion are many, including:

The previously mentioned hadeeth of Abu Sa`eed al-Khudree reports that the Messenger of Allah (peace be upon him) said,

$$الصَّلاةُ فِي جَمَاعَةٍ تَعْدِلُ خَمْسًا وَعِشْرِينَ صَلاةً فَإِذَا صَلاَّهَا
فِي فَلاةٍ فَأَتَمَّ رُكُوعَهَا وَسُجُودَهَا بَلَغَتْ خَمْسِينَ صَلاةً$$

"Congregational prayer is equivalent to twenty-five prayers. When it is prayed in an open desert and its *ruku`* and *sujood* is perfected, it reaches the equivalent of fifty prayers."[2]

Ash-Shawkaanee said,

> The hadeeth proves the excellence of prayer in a desert when the *ruku`* and *sujood* are perfected and that it is equivalent to fifty prayers in congregation. Based on this, the

---

[1] *Fath* (2/126-138).
[2] Abu Daawood [Eng. Trans. 1/147 no. 560].

prayer prayed in the desert is the equivalent of one thousand two hundred and fifty prayers that are not prayed in congregation. This is considering the case that the prayer prayed in congregation is multiplied twenty-five times. Taking into consideration that the congregational prayer is multiplied twenty-seven times then the prayer prayed in the desert is the equivalent of one thousand three hundred and fifty prayers that are not prayed in congregation. This holds true assuming that the person prays in the desert alone. If he were to pray in congregation then the reward is further multiplied by the excellence attained for praying in congregation and indeed the bounty of Allah is expansive.[1]

And Qubbaath bin Ashyam reported that the Messenger of Allah (peace be upon him) said,

صلاة الرجلين يؤم أحدهم صاحبه أزكى عند الله من صلاة أربعة تترى، و صلاة أربعة أزكى عند الله من صلاة ثمانية تترى، و صلاة ثمانية يؤم أحدهم أزكى عند الله من صلاة مائة تترى

"The prayer of two persons, with one of them leading his companion, is better with Allah than the prayer of four people prayed individually. The prayer of four people [in congregation] is better with Allah than the prayer of eight people prayed individually. The prayer of eight people [in congregation] with one of them leading is better with Allah than the prayer of one hundred people prayed individually." Al-Haafidh al-Mundhiree, may Allah have mercy upon him, said, "Reported by at-Tabaraanee and al-Bazzaar with a chain that has no problem."[2]

---

[1] *Nayl al-Awtaar* (3/147).
[2] *Targheeb wa at-Tarheeb* (1/265).

Muslim reports from Uthmaan bin `Affaan that he heard the Messenger of Allah (peace be upon him) saying,

$$مَنْ صَلَّى الْعِشَاءَ فِي جَمَاعَةٍ فَكَأَنَّمَا قَامَ نِصْفَ اللَّيْلِ وَمَنْ صَلَّى الصُّبْحَ فِي جَمَاعَةٍ فَكَأَنَّمَا صَلَّى اللَّيْلَ كُلَّهُ$$

"Whoever prays *Ishaa* in congregation, it is as if he has prayed half the night. And whoever prays *Fajr* in congregation, it is as if he has prayed the whole night."[1]

"This hadeeth proves that *Fajr* prayed in congregation is better than *Ishaa* prayed in congregation and that its excellence is double that of *Ishaa*."[2]

Abu Daawood reported from Abu Hurayrah that the Messenger of Allah (peace be upon him) said,

$$الأَبْعَدُ فَالأَبْعَدُ مِنْ الْمَسْجِدِ أَعْظَمُ أَجْرًا$$

"The farthest from the mosque has greater reward and than the one next furthers to him."[3]

Summary

The reward of the congregational prayer differs from congregation to congregation based upon differences in the congregation, performance of prayer, the prayer itself, the difference of place and the condition of the Imaam.

All of this holds with the exception of the three Holy Mosques—the Inviolable Mosque in Mecca, the Mosque of the Prophet (peace be upon him) and al-Aqsaa—for there occurs a text that proves that the excellence of the prayer in these places is more excellent than the prayer in other mosques, on top of the reward of the prayer in and of itself. Abu al-Dardaa` reported that the Prophet (peace be upon him) said,

---

[1] Muslim [Eng. Trans. 1/317 no. 1379].
[2] *Saheeh ibn Khuzaymah* (2/365 no. 1473).
[3] Abu Daawood [Eng. Trans. 1/146 no. 556].

الصلاة في المسجد الحرام بمائة ألف صلاة، والصلاة في

مسجدي بألف صلاة، والصلاة في بيت المقدس بخمسمائة

صلاة

"The prayer in the Inviolable Mosque (of Mecca) is equivalent to one hundred thousand prayers, the prayer in my Mosque is equivalent to a thousand prayers and the prayer in Bayt al-Maqdis [in Jerusalem] is equivalent to five hundred prayers."[1]

The Fruits of the Difference of Opinion

Al-Haafidh ibn Hajr said,

As an outcome of this difference of opinion those who hold that the reward and excellence differs recommend that one repeat the congregational prayer unrestrictedly in order to attain the larger congregation. This is not recommended by the proponents of the other opinion. From this group there are some who specify the case by saying that it is possible to repeat the congregational prayer only behind one who is more knowledgeable and has greater *waraa'* or in a place which is more excellent than the first. Maalik agreed to this last opinion but he restricted it to the three mosques and the famous opinion reported from him is that he restricted this to Mecca and Madeenah only.[2]

I say: The correct opinion is not to repeat the prayer. However, if one were to pray without the intention of repeating the (same) prayer, desiring thereby to attain the reward, this is sanctioned and it will be counted as an optional prayer for him.

---

[1] *Nayl al-Awtaar* (8/262). [According to al-Albaani and ibn al-Qaisaraani, this hadith is weak. See, for example, Muhammad Naasir al-Deen al-Albaani, *Dhaeef al-Jaami al-Sagheer* (Beirut: al-Maktab al-Islaami, 1988), p. 521.—JZ]

[2] *Fath al-Baaree* (2/137).

This is due to what al-Haakim in *al-Mustadrak* reported from Jaabir bin Yazeed al-Aswad from his father who said, "I prayed with the Messenger of Allah (peace be upon him) at Minaa and when he had said the *tasleem,* he saw two people behind the congregation and he called them and asked, 'What prevented you from praying with the people?' They replied, 'O Messenger of Allah we have already prayed in our homes.' He said,

فلا تفعلا، إذا صلى أحدكم في رحله ثم أدرك الصلاة مع

الإمام فليصلها معه، فإنما له نافلة

'Do not do this again. If one of you has prayed in his home and then comes across the prayer with the Imaam, then pray with him for indeed it will be counted as an optional prayer for him.'"[1]

Manners of Walking to the Congregational Prayer and of Leaving It

It is recommended for the one who leaves his house with the intention of going to the mosque to be in a state of purity and *khushoo*`. This is based the saying of Allah,

إنَّ اللَّهَ يُحِبُّ التَّوَّابِينَ وَيُحِبُّ الْمُتَطَهِّرِينَ

"Indeed Allah loves those who repent and those who purify themselves" [*al-Baqarah* (2):222].

It is detested that he interlace his fingers, as Prophet (peace be upon him) said,

إِذَا تَوَضَّأَ أَحَدُكُمْ فَأَحْسَنَ وُضُوعَهُ ثُمَّ خَرَجَ عَامِدًا إِلَى

الْمَسْجِدِ فَلَا يُشَبِّكَنَّ يَدَيْهِ فَإِنَّهُ فِي صَلَاةٍ

---

[1] Al-Haakim (1/244). This issue is dealt with seperately later.

"When one of you performs *wudu`* in an excellent manner and then leaves with the intention of going to the mosque, let him not interlace his hands because he is in prayer."[1]

It is recommended that one be clean, having a nice smell and wearing nice clothes as Islam enjoins upon its followers that they be pleasing to behold and of good composure. Allah says,

$$ يَابَنِي عَادَمَ خُذُوا زِينَتَكُمْ عِنْدَ كُلِّ مَسْجِدٍ وَكُلُوا وَاشْرَبُوا وَلَا تُسْرِفُوا إِنَّهُ لَا يُحِبُّ الْمُسْرِفِينَ $$

"O Children of Adam! Wear your beautiful apparel at every time and place of prayer. Eat and drink but waste not by excess for Allah does not Love the wasters" [*al-A`raaf* (7):31].

The Messenger of Allah (peace be upon him) used to teach the Muslims to adhere to these matters in all of their affairs such that the Muslims' appearance, clothes and mannerism becomes beautiful and acceptable.

Muslim reports that the Prophet (peace be upon him) said,

$$ لَا يَدْخُلُ الْجَنَّةَ مَنْ كَانَ فِي قَلْبِهِ مِثْقَالُ ذَرَّةٍ مِنْ كِبْرٍ قَالَ رَجُلٌ إِنَّ الرَّجُلَ يُحِبُّ أَنْ يَكُونَ ثَوْبُهُ حَسَنًا وَنَعْلُهُ حَسَنَةً قَالَ إِنَّ اللَّهَ جَمِيلٌ يُحِبُّ الْجَمَالَ الْكِبْرُ بَطَرُ الْحَقِّ وَغَمْطُ النَّاسِ $$

"Anyone who has an atom's weight of arrogance shall not enter Paradise." A person asked, "O Messenger of Allah indeed a person likes that he wear nice clothes and shoes." He replied, "Indeed, Allah is Beautiful and He Loves beauty. Arrogance is to reject the truth and have contempt for people."[2]

Cleaning oneself without going to extravagance and adorning oneself without causing difficulty are from the manners that Islam promotes.

---

[1] Abu Daawood [Eng. Trans. 1/148 no. 562].
[2] *Saheeh Muslim* [Eng. Trans. 1/53 no. 164].

45

From the manners of going to the congregational prayer is that one leaves having cleaned himself of everything that he could be reprimanded for, such as cleaning the mouth and brushing the teeth. Abu Umaamah reports that the Messenger of Allah (peace be upon him) said,

تَسَوَّكُوا فَإِنَّ السِّوَاكَ مَطْهَرَةٌ لِلْفَمِ مَرْضَاةٌ لِلرَّبِّ مَا جَاءَنِي

جِبْرِيلُ إِلاَّ أَوْصَانِي بِالسِّوَاكِ حَتَّى لَقَدْ خَشِيتُ أَنْ يُفْرَضَ

عَلَيَّ وَعَلَى أُمَّتِي وَلَوْلا أَنِّي أَخَافُ أَنْ أَشُقَّ عَلَى أُمَّتِي لَفَرَضْتُهُ

لَهُمْ وَإِنِّي لَأَسْتَاكُ حَتَّى لَقَدْ خَشِيتُ أَنْ أُحْفِيَ مَقَادِمَ فَمِي

"Use the *siwaak* (toothstick) for indeed it purifies the mouth and is pleasing to the Lord. Each time Jibreel has come to me he has enjoined me to employ the *siwaak* to the point that I feared that it would become obligatory upon my nation and me. If I did not fear that it would become difficult for my nation I would have obligated its use upon them. Indeed I employ the *siwaak* to the point that I fear that my front teeth would be uprooted."[1]

Similarly, it is obligatory upon the Muslim to avoid all foul smells. Islam has deterred the one who eats garlic, onion, or leek from going to the mosque due to the smell emitting from this person's mouth, harming his brother Muslims. Jaabir reports from the Messenger of Allah (peace be upon him) that he said,

مَنْ أَكَلَ ثُومًا أَوْ بَصَلاً فَلْيَعْتَزِلْنَا و لِيَعْتَزِلْ مَسْجِدَنَا وَلْيَقْعُدْ فِي

بَيْتِهِ

"Let he who eats garlic or onion remain away from us and our mosque and instead sit in his house."[2] Recorded by al-Bukhari

---

[1] *Sunan ibn Maajah* (no. 288).
[2] Al-Bukhaaree [Eng. Trans. 1/452 no. 814] and Muslim (Eng. Trans. 1/279 no. 1146). Also refer to *Faydh al-Qadeer Sharh al-Jaami` as-Sagheer* (6/84 no. 8515). [Al-Bukhaaree and Muslim also report the hadeeth from Jaabir that the

and Muslim. In fact, the *ahaadeeth* that give this meaning are many.

From the things that resemble garlic and onion with respect to their harming those who pray and the Angels is the smell of cigarette smoke emitting from the mouths and clothes of smokers. So let them be aware of this.

Similarly it is recommended that one avoid all matters that would negate the manners of prayer, such as interlacing the fingers, frequently looking left and right, raising one's voice and walking fast. Rather one should walk to the mosque calmly and in a state of sobriety. This is based on what Muslim reported from Abu Hurayrah that the Prophet (peace be upon him) said,

إِذَا أُقِيمَتْ الصَّلاةُ فَلا تَأْتُوهَا تَسْعَوْنَ وَأْتُوهَا تَمْشُونَ وَعَلَيْكُمْ السَّكِينَةُ فَمَا أَدْرَكْتُمْ فَصَلُّوا وَمَا فَاتَكُمْ فَأَتِمُّوا

"When the *iqaamah* for the prayer has been called, do not come to it hastily. Come to it calmly. That part of the prayer that you catch, pray it and complete what you missed."[1]

From the manners of walking to the mosque is to say the reported supplications concerning those who walk to the mosque, enter and leave the mosque. From these is:

It is recommended for one to say when leaving his house in general that which is reported by Abu Daawood from Anas bin Maalik that the Prophet (peace be upon him) said,

إِذَا خَرَجَ الرَّجُلُ مِنْ بَيْتِهِ فَقَالَ بِسْمِ اللَّهِ تَوَكَّلْتُ عَلَى اللَّهِ لا حَوْلَ وَلا قُوَّةَ إِلاَّ بِاللَّهِ قَالَ يُقَالُ حِينَئِذٍ هُدِيتَ وَكُفِيتَ

Prophet (peace be upon him) said, "Whoever eats garlic, onion or leek should not come close to our mosque for the Angels are harmed by what harms the Children of Aadam." – Trans.]
[1] *Saheeh Muslim* [Eng. Trans. 1/296 no.1249].

$$\text{وَوُقِيتَ فَتَنَحَّى لَهُ الشَّيَاطِينُ فَيَقُولُ لَهُ شَيْطَانٌ آخَرُ كَيْفَ لَكَ}$$

$$\text{بِرَجُلٍ قَدْ هُدِيَ وَكُفِيَ وَوُقِيَ}$$

"When a person leaves his home and says, 'With the name of Allah, I put my trust in Allah and there is no might or movement except with Allah'[1] It will be said, 'You are guided, sufficed and protected.' The devils will go away from him and one shall say to the other, 'What can you do with a person who has been guided, sufficed and protected?'"[2]

Umm Salamah narrated that the Prophet (peace be upon him) used to say when he left his house,

$$\text{بِسْمِ اللَّهِ تَوَكَّلْتُ عَلَى اللَّهِ اللَّهُمَّ إِنِّي أَعُوذُ بِكَ أَنْ أَضِلَّ أَوْ}$$

$$\text{أُضَلَّ أَوْ أَزِلَّ أَوْ أُزَلَّ أَوْ أَظْلِمَ أَوْ أُظْلَمَ أَوْ أَجْهَلَ أَوْ يُجْهَلَ}$$

$$\text{عَلَيَّ}$$

"With the name of Allah, I put my trust in Allah. O Allah I seek refuge with You lest I stray or be led astray, or I cause injustice or suffer injustice, or I do wrong or have wrong done to me, or I behave foolishly or be treated foolishly.[3]"[4]

Upon reaching the mosque, one should enter with his right foot first and then say the supplication that is narrated from the Prophet (peace be upon him) via his daughter Faatimah: When he used to enter the mosque he used to invoke peace and blessings upon Muhammad and then say,

---

[1] *bismillaahi, tawakkaltu `alaaAllahi laa hawla wa laa quwwata illaa billaahi.*

[2] Abu Daawood [Eng. Trans. 3/1413 no. 5076].

[3] *Bismillaahi tawakkaltu `alaAllahi. Allahumma innee A`udhubika an adilla aw udalla, aw azilla aw uzalla, aw adhlima aw udhlama, aw ajhala aw yujhala alayya.*

[4] *Jaami` at-Tirmidhee* (no. 3423).

48

اللَّهُمَّ اغْفِرْ لِي ذُنُوبِي وَافْتَحْ لِي أَبْوَابَ رَحْمَتِكَ وَإِذَا خَرَجَ
صَلَّى عَلَى مُحَمَّدٍ وَسَلَّمَ ثُمَّ قَالَ اللَّهُمَّ اغْفِرْ لِي ذُنُوبِي وَافْتَحْ
لِي أَبْوَابَ فَضْلِكَ

"O Allah forgive me my sins and open for me the doors of Your Mercy."[1] When he left the mosque he used to invoke peace and blessings upon Muhammad and say, "O Allah forgive me my sins and open for me the doors of Your Bounty.[2]"[3]

Upon reaching the place of sitting in the mosque, one should greet others with the *salaam* in a voice loud enough that those close to him can hear. One should not sit until he has prayed the two *rak`ahs* for greeting the mosque. This is based on the Prophet's saying,

إِذَا دَخَلَ أَحَدُكُمُ الْمَسْجِدَ فَلْيَرْكَعْ رَكْعَتَيْنِ قَبْلَ أَنْ يَجْلِسَ

"When anyone of you enters the mosque, let him pray two *rak`ahs* before sitting."[4]

It is preferred to sit in the first row and on the right side of the row if this does not require crowding. This is based on the Prophet's saying,

إِنَّ اللَّهَ وَمَلَائِكَتَهُ يُصَلُّونَ عَلَى مَيَامِنِ الصُّفُوفِ

"Indeed Allah and His Angels invoke blessings upon those who are on the right side of the rows."[5] In other words, they

---

[1] *Allahumma ighfirlee dhunoobee waftah lee abwaaba rahmatika.*

[2] *Allahumma ighfirlee dhunoobee waftah lee abwaaba fadlika.*

[3] *Musnad Ahmad* (6/283).

[4] *Saheeh Muslim* [Eng. Trans. 1/347 no. 1540].

[5] Abu Daawood [Eng. Trans. 1/175 no. 676] and ibn Maajah (no. 1005). Imaam an-Nawawee said in *Riyaadh as-Saaliheen* (no. 1094), "its chain meets the conditions of Muslim and it contains a narrator whose (state) is differed over." It was declared *hasan* by both Haafidh ibn Hajr and Haafidh al-Mundhiree. [This hadith was declared *hasan* by ibn Hajr and Abdul Qaadir al-Arnaaoot. However, al-Albaani and his student al-Hilaali have declared it weak. Upon close inspection, it seems that the correct wording is that which is found in *Sunan ibn Maajah*:

seek forgiveness for those who are to the right of the Imam in any row.

Imaam al-Ghazaalee, may Allah have mercy upon him, said, "The one who enters the mosque should seek to sit on the right side of the row because it is a place of good fortune and a source of blessings. Indeed Allah, the Exalted, invokes blessings upon those who are on the right side of the rows. One should do this if there is room on the right side; if not, he should not harm those already there nor make the space tight and uncomfortable."[1]

It is also desired that one busy himself with the *dhikr* of Allah, devoting his heart towards this (while waiting for the prayer). It is not desired for anyone to walk over the necks of others nor cause someone to move from his place nor cause someone's place to become tight in the row. Also, one should not spit. He should not crack his fingers or interlace them and he should avoid anything that disturbs the peace and sanctity of the mosque.

"Allah and His Angels invoke blessings upon those who connect the rows." Allah knows best.—JZ]

[1] *Faydb al-Qadeer* of al-Munaawee (2/270 no. 1815).

Whom the Congregational Prayer Is Sanctioned

The congregational prayer has been legislated upon the following categories of people, with some restrictions:

1. **Men.** It is not necessary for the woman to attend the congregational prayer according to the consensus of the scholars.

The congregational prayer is a sunnah with respect to women provided that there is no fear of *fitnah* and they fulfil the manners that Islam requires of them. This issue will be dealt with in detail later.

It is not obligatory upon the one who has not yet reached the age of maturity or those men who have a valid excuse that allows them to miss the congregation. This issue will also be dealt with in detail later.

2. **Free (non-slave).** This is because the servant is busy with serving his master. Therefore, obligating the congregational prayer upon him would be difficult for him and the *Sharee`ah* has stated the principle of removing the harm.

3. **The absence of any excuse** preventing the person from performing the obligatory prayer in congregation or making it difficult for him due to one of the excuses that allow a person not to attend the congregational prayer.

4. **That the prayer being prayed is obligatory.** "As for the *sunan* prayers, it is not obligatory to pray these in congregation. This also applies to the Prayer of the Eclipse and any obligatory prayer that is being made up (*qadaa*). It is not obligatory to make up the missed prayers in congregation if one takes to the opinion that it is obligatory to make up missed prayers."[1] This is because the texts of the Shareeah simply state the making up of the prayer [and do not mention anything about the need for a congregation].

---

[1] *ar-Rawd al-Marba` bi Sharh Zaad al-Mustaqni`* (1/256) with the notes of ibn Qaasim an-Najdee.

The Number Which Constitutes a Congregation

The minimum number that constitutes a congregational prayer is two: the Imaam and another person with him. As the number of attendees increases, this prayer becomes more beloved to Allah. This is based on the Prophet's (peace be upon him) saying,

$$
\text{صَلاةُ الرَّجُلِ مَعَ الرَّجُلِ أَزْكَى مِنْ صَلاتِهِ وَحْدَهُ وَصَلاتُهُ مَعَ}
$$

$$
\text{الرَّجُلَيْنِ أَزْكَى مِنْ صَلاتِهِ مَعَ الرَّجُلِ وَمَا كَثُرَ فَهُوَ أَحَبُّ إِلَى}
$$

$$
\text{اللهِ تَعَالَى}
$$

"The prayer of a person with another person is better than the prayer of a person prayed individually. The prayer of a person prayed with two people is better than the prayer of a person prayed with one. The larger the number, the more beloved it is to Allah the Exalted."[1]

It is possible for one of the two to be a child or a woman. In this case, the prayer is still considered to be congregational. Ibn Abbaas said,

$$
\text{بِتُّ عِنْدَ خَالَتِي فَقَامَ النَّبِيُّ صَلَّى اللَّهُ عَلَيْهِ وَسَلَّمَ يُصَلِّي مِنْ}
$$

$$
\text{اللَّيْلِ فَقُمْتُ أُصَلِّي مَعَهُ فَقُمْتُ عَنْ يَسَارِهِ فَأَخَذَ بِرَأْسِي}
$$

$$
\text{فَأَقَامَنِي عَنْ يَمِينِهِ}
$$

"I spent the night at my aunt's and the Messenger of Allah (peace be upon him) awoke to pray the night prayer. I stood to pray with him, standing on his left side and he took hold of my head and stood me on his right side."[2]

Muslim reports from Anas bin Maalik that the Messenger of Allah (peace be upon him) prayed with him and his mother or aunt. Anas said,

---

[1] *al-Mustadrak* (3/269).
[2] *Saheeh al-Bukhaaree* [Eng. Trans. 1/376 no. 665, 666].

$$\text{فَأَقَامَنِي عَنْ يَمِينِهِ وَأَقَامَ الْمَرْأَةَ خَلْفَنَا}$$

"He made me stand on his right side and made the woman stand behind us."[1]

Al-Wazeer ibn Hubairah said, "They [the scholars] have unanimously agreed that the least number that makes a congregation for an obligatory prayer, other than the prayer of *Jumu`ah* (Friday), is two: an Imaam and a follower standing on his right side."[2]

Ibn Qudaamah, may Allah have mercy upon him, said,

> The congregation is considered to be such with two people and we know of no difference concerning this. Abu Musaa reports that the Prophet (peace be upon him) said,

$$\text{اثْنَانِ فَمَا فَوْقَهُمَا جَمَاعَةٌ}$$

"Two and more constitute a congregation."[3]

The Prophet (peace be upon him) led Hudhayfah on one occasion, ibn Mas`ud on another and ibn Abbaas on another. If a person were to lead his slave or wife, they would have attained the excellence of the congregational prayer. If one were to lead a child, this is permissible for optional prayers because the Prophet (peace be upon him) led ibn Abbaas in an optional prayer while he was a child. If one were to lead a child in the obligatory prayer, then Imaam Ahmad said that this is not counted as a congregational prayer because it is not correct that a child be an Imaam due to his deficient condition and therefore this situation most closely resembles the case of

---

[1] *Saheeh Muslim* [Eng. Trans. 1/321 no. 1390].
[2] *al-Ifsaah `an Ma`aanee as-Sihaah* (1/155).
[3] Ibn Maajah (no. 959). [This hadith has been declared weak by a number of scholars. See, for example, al-Albaani, *Dhaeef al-Jaami*, p. 22.—JZ]

one whose prayer is not valid. Abu al-Hasan al-Aamidee said, "There is another opinion that is voiced concerning this. This being that it is not permissible for the child to be the Imaam but it is permissible for him to be a follower in the obligatory prayer in the same way as this is permissible for one who has reached the age of discernment. This is why the Prophet (peace be upon him) said concerning the man who had missed the congregational prayer, 'Who will give him charity and pray with him?'' This was the opinion declared to be the strongest by the Hanafee and Shaafi`ee scholars. As for the Maalikee scholars, in their view the prayer prayed with only a child, be it obligatory or optional, is not considered a valid congregational prayer.[1]

Summary

The least number that would constitute a congregation is two: an Imaam and an follower, even if he were a child according to the Hanafee scholars. However according to the Hanbalee scholars, the child can only be considered a follower in the optional prayers because the Prophet (peace be upon him) led ibn Abbaas while he was a child in the *Tahajjud* prayer.[2]

I say: The opinion that is closest to the truth is that the Imaamate of a child is valid in obligatory and optional prayers due to the generality of the evidences. From the most clear of these is what al-Bukhaaree reports from `Amr bin Salma that the Prophet (peace be upon him) said to his father,

---

[1] *al-Mughnee* of ibn Qudaamah (2/177-178).
[2] Refer to *al-Badaa`i as-Sanaa`i* (1/156), *al-Majmoo`* (4/93ff), *ash-Sharh as-Sagheer* (1/427ff) of ad-Dardeer and *al-Mughnee* (1/177-178).

وَلْيَؤُمَّكُمْ أَكْثَرُكُمْ قُرْآنَا فَنَظَرُوا فَلَمْ يَكُنْ أَحَدٌ أَكْثَرَ قُرْآنَا مِنِّي

لِمَا كُنْتُ أَتَلَقَّى مِنَ الرُّكْبَانِ فَقَدَّمُونِي بَيْنَ أَيْدِيهِمْ وَأَنَا ابْنُ

سِتٍّ أَوْ سَبْعِ سِنِينَ

'Let one of you lead you who knows the most Qur`aan.' So the people looked and they did not find anyone who knew more Qur`aan than I because I used to learn from the entire traveling group. So they put me forward (to lead them) and at that time I was a child of six or seven years."[1]

So the Companions appointing of `Amr as the Imaam while he was a small child lends proof to the validity of a child who has reached the age of discernment leading the prayer. If this were not permissible, a revelation would have been revealed rejecting this action. Also, there is no distinction to be made between the regulations of optional and obligatory prayers unless there occurs a text that necessitates this. An example of such a distinction is the permissibility of praying optional prayers while riding a beast (whereas this is not allowed for obligatory prayers). Allah knows best.

The Portion of the Prayer that Must Be Caught to be Considered Part of the Congregation

The scholars fall into two opinions concerning this:

The First Opinion

One is considered to have prayed in congregation if one catches a *rak`ah* (with the congregation). This is the opinion of the Maalikee scholars, al-Ghazaalee from the Shaafi`ee scholars, a reported opinion from Imaam Ahmad, the clear sense derived from the words of ibn Abee Musaa, the chosen opinion of Shaykh al-Islam ibn Taymiyyah, Shaykh

---

[1] *Saheeh al-Bukhaaree* [Eng. Trans. 5/413 no. 595].

Muhammad bin Abdul Wahhaab, and Shaykh Abdurrahmaan bin Sa`dee, may Allah have mercy upon them all.[1]

The Proofs for the First Opinion

Abu Hurayrah reported that the Prophet (peace be upon him) said,

مَنْ أَدْرَكَ رَكْعَةً مِنْ الصَّلاة فَقَدْ أَدْرَكَ الصَّلاةَ

"Whoever catches one *rak`ah* has caught the prayer."[2]

Ibn Umar reported that the Messenger of Allah (peace be upon him) said,

مَنْ أَدْرَكَ رَكْعَةً مِنْ صَلاةِ الْجُمُعَةِ أَوْ غَيْرِهَا فَقَدْ أَدْرَكَ الصَّلاةَ

"Whoever catches a *rak`ah* of the *Jumu`ah* (Friday) prayer or any other prayer, he has caught the prayer."[3]

The hadeeth clearly proves that whoever catches a *rak`ah* of the *Jumu`ah* prayer or any other prayer has succeeded in catching the prayer. Congregational prayer comes under the heading of any other prayer and therefore it can be attained by catching one *rak`ah*. Shaykh al-Islam ibn Taymiyyah gave two reasons for this, saying,

---

[1] Refer to *Jawaahir al-Ikleel Sharh Mukhtasar al-Khaleel* (1/76), *al-Wajeez* (p. 55), *al-Insaaf* (2/222), *Majmoo` Fataawaa ibn Taymiyyah* (23/331), *al-Mukhtaaraat al-Jaliyyah fee al-Masaa`il al-Fiqhiyyah* of ibn Sa`dee (2/25) and *Kitaab Aadaab al-Mashee ilaa as-Salaah* (p. 29).

[2] *Saheeh al-Bukhaaree* [Eng. Trans. 1/322 no. 554] and *Saheeh Muslim* [Eng. Trans. 1/298 no. 1260]. [It should be noted that one is considered to have caught the *rak`ah* if he performs the *ruku`* (bow) of that *rak`ah* with the Imaam. If one joins the congregation at any time after the *ruku`* then he is not considered to have caught that *rak`ah*. Abu Daawood reports from Abu Hurayrah that the Messenger of Allah (peace be upon him) said, "If you come to the prayer and we are in prostration, then make the prostration but do not count it as a *rak`ah*. Whoever catches the *ruku`* catches the prayer." – Trans.]

[3] Ibn Maajah (no.1110), an-Nasaa`ee (3/112), ibn Khuzaymah (3/173), and al-Haakim (1/291) who declared it *saheeh* upon considering three of its routes and adh-Dhahabee agreed.

First, the Legislator has made no regulations of the prayer dependent upon the length of the *takbeer*, neither with regards to catching the prayer in its time or attaining the congregational prayer.[1] Hence it is a void description in the eyes of the Legislator, indeed the Legislator has only made regulations dependent upon whether one attains a *rak'ah* of the prayer or not. Second, anything which is less than one *rak'ah* is not considered to be anything in the prayer and therefore a person is not considered to have caught anything (if he catches less than a *rak'ah*, meaning anything past the *ruku'*). Therefore, he has not prayed anything that can be taken into consideration alongside the Imaam and hence all of his prayer (that he now prays after the *tasleem* of the Imaam) is to be considered an individual prayer.[2]

The Second Opinion

One is considered to have prayed in congregation if one says the opening *takbeer* before the Imaam says the *salaam*. This is the opinion of the Shaafi'ee and Hanafee scholars and the reported opinion that is famous from Ahmad and it is the chosen opinion of the majority of his followers.[3]

These scholars depended upon the hadeeth reported from Abu Hurayrah that the Prophet (peace be upon him) said,

إِذَا أُقِيمَتِ الصَّلَاةُ فَلَا تَأْتُوهَا تَسْعَوْنَ وَأْتُوهَا تَمْشُونَ وَعَلَيْكُمُ السَّكِينَةُ فَمَا أَدْرَكْتُمْ فَصَلُّوا وَمَا فَاتَكُمْ فَأَتِمُّوا

---

[1] [Meaning that if one were to say the opening *takbeer* just before the time for that prayer had expired, or said it just before the Imaam said the *salaam* then he is not considered to have caught the prayer in either of the two cases – Trans.]

[2] *Majmoo' Fataawaa* (23/332-333).

[3] Refer to: *Haashiyah ibn Aabideen* (2/59), *al-Majmoo'* (4/184), and *al-Insaaf* (2/221).

"When the *iqaamah* has been called for prayer then do not come to it running, rather come to it walking calmly. Pray that part of the prayer which you catch and complete what you missed."[1]

Therefore, the one who catches the Imaam prostrating or sitting in the last *tashahhud* can be said to have caught the prayer and he makes up what he missed. Hence, the one who says his opening *takbeer* before the Imaam says the *salaam* is considered to have caught the congregation.

Ibn Qudaamah gave two reasons for this. First, whoever catches a portion of the prayer with the Imaam is similar to his having caught a *rak`ah* of the prayer. Second, if one catches a portion of the prayer with the Imaam and says the opening *takbeer,* he must have the intention of being a follower and therefore it is desired that he attain the reward of the congregation.[2]

The Strongest Opinion

After considering the evidence of the two opinions and the reasons given by each of their proponents, it becomes clear that the first opinion is the strongest opinion. This is because it is supported by an authentic hadeeth on the actual issue at hand and therefore "the evidences relating to the actual issue take precedence over the evidences from which one can imply a correlation to the issue" as established in Islamic legal theory.[3]

---

[1] *Saheeh Muslim* [Eng. Trans. 1/296 no. 1249].
[2] *al-Mughnee* (2/177-178).
[3] Refer to *Athar al-Ikhtilaaf fee al-Qawaa`id al-Usuliyyah fee Ikhtilaaf al-Fuquhaa'* by Mustafaa Sa`eed al-Khann (pg. 146).

The Place for Performing the Congregational Prayer and the Virtue of Maintaining the Mosques and Walking to Them For Prayer

The congregational prayer is either performed in a mosque or outside of a mosque.

Maintaining the Mosques and Walking to Them for Prayer

The mosques are the houses of Allah, the Mighty and Magnificent. In them, He is worshipped and His Exalted name mentioned. They are the signposts of guidance and marks of the religion. Allah has ennobled them and exalted them by mentioning them alongside His Name, saying,

وَأَنَّ الْمَسَاجِدَ لِلَّهِ فَلا تَدْعُوا مَعَ اللَّهِ أَحَدًا

"And indeed the mosques are for Allah, so do not supplicate to any other alongside Allah" [*al-Jinn* (72):18].

The mosques have been built for the purpose of prayer, performing the *dhikr* of Allah, the Mighty and Magnificent, reciting the Qur`aan, seeking to draw close to Him and humbling oneself before Him hoping for His reward.

Indeed, maintaining the mosques is one of the greatest means of getting closer to Allah. Maintaining them is done through building them, cleaning them, furnishing them, providing lights for them and other such things. Similarly, maintaining them is done through performing *i`tikaaf* (seclusion for the purpose of worship) in them and praying in them, frequently visiting them to be present in the congregational prayer and to learn beneficial knowledge, and to recite, learn and teach the Qur`aan. The sunnah has encouraged one to maintain the mosques and clarified the great reward that lies in store for the one who does this.

Al-Bukhaaree and Muslim record from Uthmaan bin `Affaan that he heard the Messenger of Allah (peace be upon him) say,

مَنْ بَنَى مَسْجِدًا يَبْتَغِي بِهِ وَجْهَ اللَّهِ بَنَى اللَّهُ لَهُ بَيْتًا فِي الْجَنَّةِ

"Whoever builds a mosque desiring thereby the Face of Allah, Allah will build a house in Paradise for him."[1] This means that he does so sincerely for Allah alone, seeking His pleasure without showing off or seeking the praise of people or the fulfillment of some personal objective.

Just as their occurs encouragement for maintaining the mosques, there also occurs encouragement for cleaning them and preparing them for prayer. Imaam Muslim recorded from Abu Hurayrah that

أَنَّ امْرَأَةً سَوْدَاءَ كَانَتْ تَقُمُّ الْمَسْجِدَ أَوْ شَابًّا فَفَقَدَهَا رَسُولُ
اللَّهِ صَلَّى اللَّهُ عَلَيْهِ وَسَلَّمَ فَسَأَلَ عَنْهَا أَوْ عَنْهُ فَقَالُوا مَاتَ قَالَ
أَفَلا كُنْتُمْ آذَنْتُمُونِي قَالَ فَكَأَنَّهُمْ صَغَّرُوا أَمْرَهَا أَوْ أَمْرَهُ فَقَالَ
دُلُّونِي عَلَى قَبْرِه فَدَلُّوهُ فَصَلَّى عَلَيْهَا ثُمَّ قَالَ إِنَّ هَذِهِ الْقُبُورَ
مَمْلُوءَةٌ ظُلْمَةً عَلَى أَهْلِهَا وَإِنَّ اللَّهَ عَزَّ وَجَلَّ يُنَوِّرُهَا لَهُمْ
بِصَلاتِي عَلَيْهِمْ

"A black woman, or a youth, used to sweep the mosque. The Messenger of Allah (peace be upon him) missed her or him on one occasion and asked about her or him. The people said, '[She or] he has died.' The Prophet said, 'Why did you not inform me?' It turned out that the people thought little of her, or his, affair. He said, 'Lead me to her grave.' They led him to

---

[1] *Saheeh al-Bukhaaree* [Eng. Trans. 1/263 no. 441] and *Saheeh Muslim* [Eng. Trans. 1/269 no. 1084].

the grave and he said the prayer over her and then commented, 'Indeed these graves are full of darkness for their dwellers and indeed Allah, the Mighty and Magnificent, illuminates the graves for their inhabitants due to my prayer over them."[1]

There are many explicit and authentic texts that occur mentioning the excellence of walking to the mosques in order to pray, perform *dhikr* or recite the Noble Qur'aan. Indeed, the one who visits the mosque is under the care of Allah and His Mercy for as long as he observes the manners of sitting and his heart is attentive to Allah, the Magnificent and Exalted.

The texts also prove that the prayer of a person in congregation is twenty-five or twenty-seven times better than the prayer he prays individually at home or in the market.

The texts also prove that for whoever walks to the mosque in darkness, Allah completes and perfects his light for him on the Day of Judgement.

The texts also prove that for whoever goes back and forth from the mosque (for the prayers), Allah prepares a feast for him in Paradise for each of his journeys.[2] This is a great excellence that none would miss out on save one who is negligent or one who is lazy and does not care to attain the good.

So, my dear brother in Islam, here are some of the *ahaadeeth* that prove what I have stated so that you may be upon sure knowledge and guidance to attain this great reward and that you may encourage your brother Muslims to enact this great pillar in the mosques in congregation so that they may attain the reward of Allah in this life and the Hereafter.

Abu Hurayrah reported that the Prophet (peace be upon him) said,

صَلاةُ الرَّجُلِ فِي جَمَاعَةٍ تَزِيدُ عَلَى صَلاتِهِ فِي بَيْتِهِ وَصَلاتِهِ فِي سُوقِهِ بِضْعًا وَعِشْرِينَ دَرَجَةً وَذَلِكَ أَنَّ أَحَدَهُمْ إِذَا تَوَضَّأَ

---

[1] *Saheeh Muslim* [Eng. Trans. 2/453 no. 2088].

[2] [Abu Hurayrah reported that the Messenger of Allah (peace be upon him) said, "If anyone goes back and forth to the mosque (to attend the prayers), Allah will prepare for him a feast in Paradise as often as he goes back and forth." Reported by al-Bukhaaree and Muslim. – Trans.]

فَأَحْسَنَ الْوُضُوءَ ثُمَّ أَتَى الْمَسْجِدَ لا يَنْهَزُهُ إِلاَّ الصَّلاةُ لا يُرِيدُ
إِلاَّ الصَّلاةَ فَلَمْ يَخْطُ خَطْوَةً إِلاَّ رُفِعَ لَهُ بِهَا دَرَجَةٌ وَحُطَّ عَنْهُ
بِهَا خَطِيئَةٌ حَتَّى يَدْخُلَ الْمَسْجِدَ

"The prayer of a person in congregation is twenty odd levels
better than the prayer of a person prayed in his house or in the
market. This is because when one of you performs *wudu`* in an
excellent manner and then goes to the mosque desiring only
the prayer, he will not walk a footstep except that he will be
raised a rank and a sin will be expiated until he enters the
mosque…"[1]

Abu Hurayrah also reported that the Messenger of
Allah (peace be upon him) said,

أَلا أَدُلُّكُمْ عَلَى مَا يَمْحُو اللَّهُ بِهِ الْخَطَايَا وَيَرْفَعُ بِهِ الدَّرَجَاتِ
قَالُوا بَلَى يَا رَسُولَ اللَّهِ قَالَ إِسْبَاغُ الْوُضُوءِ عَلَى الْمَكَارِهِ
وَكَثْرَةُ الْخُطَا إِلَى الْمَسَاجِدِ وَانْتِظَارُ الصَّلاةِ بَعْدَ الصَّلاةِ
فَذَلِكُمُ الرِّبَاطُ فَذَلِكُمُ الرِّبَاطُ

"Shall I not direct you to that by which Allah will efface sins
and raise the ranks?" They replied, "Of course, O Messenger
of Allah!" He said, "Performing the *wudu`* in an excellent
manner despite it being difficult, taking many steps towards
the mosques and waiting for the next prayer after having
prayed the current prayer. That is mindfulness! That is
mindfulness!"[2]

Allah said,

---

[1] *Saheeh al-Bukhaaree* [Eng, Trans. 1/352 no. 620] and *Saheeh Muslim* [Eng,
Trans. 1/322 no. 1394].
[2] *Saheeh Muslim* [Eng. Trans. 1/157 no. 485].

فِي بُيُوتٍ أَذِنَ اللَّهُ أَنْ تُرْفَعَ وَيُذْكَرَ فِيهَا اسْمُهُ يُسَبِّحُ لَهُ فِيهَا بِالْغُدُوِّ

وَالْآصَالِ رِجَالٌ لَا تُلْهِيهِمْ تِجَارَةٌ وَلَا بَيْعٌ عَنْ ذِكْرِ اللَّهِ وَإِقَامِ

الصَّلَاةِ وَإِيتَاءِ الزَّكَاةِ يَخَافُونَ يَوْمًا تَتَقَلَّبُ فِيهِ الْقُلُوبُ وَالْأَبْصَارُ

لِيَجْزِيَهُمُ اللَّهُ أَحْسَنَ مَا عَمِلُوا وَيَزِيدَهُمْ مِنْ فَضْلِهِ وَاللَّهُ يَرْزُقُ مَنْ

يَشَاءُ بِغَيْرِ حِسَابٍ

"(Lit is such a Light) in houses which Allah has allowed to be raised such that His *dhikr* (remembrance) is performed in them. In them He is glorified in the mornings and evenings by men whom neither trade nor sale can divert from the *dhikr* of Allah, nor from establishing the prayer or paying *zakaat*. They fear the Day when the hearts and eyes will be turned about—that Allah may reward them according to the best of their deeds and add even for them out of His Grace. Indeed Allah provides for whoever He Wills without measure" [*an-Nur* (24):36-38].

Congregational Prayer in Other Than a Mosque

The scholars have differed about the ruling concerning praying in congregation in a place other than the mosque. There are three opinions on this question.

The First Opinion

It is permissible to pray in congregation in a place other than the mosque. This is the opinion of Maalik, ash-Shaafi`ee, an opinion reported from Imaam Ahmad, and the chosen opinion of the Hanafee school.

Ibn al-Qaasim said, "I asked Maalik about a man who prays the obligatory prayer with his wife at home to which he replied, 'There is no problem with that.'"[1]

Imaam ash-Shaafi`ee, may Allah have mercy upon him, said, "Every congregation that a man prays in, be it in his

---

[1] *al-Mudawwana al-Kubraa* (1/86).

home or in a mosque, small or large, and be it a small or large congregation, would be valid for him. The larger the mosque, such that the congregation is larger, is more beloved to me."[1]

Ar-Raafi`ee, from the Shaafi`ee scholars said, "Congregational prayer prayed at home is better than praying individually in the mosque."

Ibn Qudaamah said, "It is permissible to pray in congregation at home or in the desert."[2]

These scholars depended upon the following ahaadeeth:

Jaabir reported that the Messenger of Allah (peace be upon him) said,

أُعْطِيتُ خَمْسًا ... وَجُعِلَتْ لِي الأَرْضُ مَسْجِدًا وَطَهُورًا
فَأَيُّمَا رَجُلٍ مِنْ أُمَّتِي أَدْرَكَتْهُ الصَّلاةُ فَلْيُصَلِّ

"I have been given five things... The earth has been made as a mosque and has been made pure and purifying for me. So whoever from my nation comes across the time for prayer, let him pray."[3]

Anas said,

كَانَ رَسُولُ اللهِ أَحْسَنَ النَّاسِ خُلُقًا فَرُبَّمَا تَحْضُرُ الصَّلاةَ وَهُوَ
فِي بَيْتِنَا فَيَأْمُرُ بِالبِسَاطِ الَّذِي تَحْتَهُ فَيُكْنَسُ ثُمَّ يُنْضَحُ ثُمَّ يَؤُمُّ
رَسُولُ اللهِ وَنَقُومُ خَلْفَهُ فَيُصَلِّي بِنَا

"The Messenger of Allah (peace be upon him) used to have the best manners from among the people. Sometimes he would be in our house when the time for prayer came. He would call for a mat to pray on, he would sweep it clean and then sprinkle water on it (to soften it). Then the Messenger of Allah (peace

---

[1] *al-Umm* (1/136).
[2] *al-Mughnee* (3/8).
[3] *Saheeh al-Bukhaaree* [Eng. Trans. 1/199 no. 331].

be upon him) would lead the prayer and we would stand behind him and pray in congregation."[1]

Aa`ishah said,

صلى رسول الله صلى الله عليه وسلم في بيته وهو شاك

فصلى جالسا وصلى وراءه قوم قياما فأشار إليهم أن اجلسوا

"The Messenger of Allah (peace be upon him) prayed in his house sitting due to pain and a group of people prayed behind him standing, so he indicated to them to sit."[2]

They also depend upon other *ahaadeeth* that space does not allow us to mention.

The Second Opinion

It is not permissible for a man to pray in congregation except in a mosque.

This is a reported opinion of Imaam Ahmad and it was the opinion that ibn al-Qayyim declared to be the strongest in his *Kitaab as-Salaah*. He said, "For whoever investigates the sunnah as it deserves to be done, it will become clear to him that praying in congregation in the mosque is *fard `ayn*. This is so unless one has a valid excuse that allows him to miss the *Jumu`ah* and congregational prayers. Abandoning attending the mosque without a valid excuse is like abandoning the essence of congregation without a valid excuse and in this way the various evidences are reconciled."[3]

He, may Allah have mercy upon him, also said, "That which we take to be our *deen* is that it is not permissible for anyone to miss the congregation in the mosque unless he has a valid excuse and Allah knows best."[4]

Some of the scholars declared the prayer prayed at home in congregation is not valid. Abu al-Barakaat from the Hanbalee scholars said, "Whoever misses (the congregational

---

[1] *Sunan al-Kubraa* (3/66) of an-Nasaa`ee.
[2] *Saheeh al-Bukhaaree* [Eng. Trans. 1/372 no. 656].
[3] *Kitaab as-Salaah* (p. 461).
[4] Ibid.

prayer in the mosque) and prays in congregation in his home, then his prayer is not valid unless he has a valid excuse." This is building upon his premise that the one who leaves the congregation has performed something forbidden (and that the prohibition of something necessitates its invalidity).[1]

In the commentary to *Fath al-Qadeer*, ibn al-Hummaam said, "Al-Halwaanee was asked about one who gathered his family together sometimes to pray—does he attain the reward of congregational prayer? He replied, 'No, if he does not have a valid excuse (for missing the prayer in the mosque), this is a reprehensible innovation.'"[2]

These scholars depended upon the *ahaadeeth* that prove that congregational prayer is obligatory and that it is *fard `ayn* [some of which are mentioned in the following chapter].

Furthermore the Shaafi`ee scholars[3] differed about whether the *fard kifaayah* to establish congregational prayer in the mosque (once the time for prayer arrives) is lifted if the congregational prayer is prayed outside of the mosque. On this point, they have two opinions: One, establishing a congregational prayer in a place other than the mosque for the obligatory prayers is not sufficient in lifting the *fard kifaayah* of praying in congregation in the mosque. Two, it is acceptable if the place in which it is being done is famous and commonly attended such as a marketplace.

Ibn Daqeeq al-Eid, may Allah have mercy upon him, said, "The first opinion is more correct in my view. This is because the foundation of the legislation concerning this occurred with regards the congregations in the mosques and it is not permissible to deviate from that."[4]

The Third Opinion

The third opinion differentiates between one who has heard the call to prayer and the one who has not.

---

[1] *al-Insaaf* (2/123, 214) by al-Mardaawee.
[2] *Sharh Fath al-Qadeer* (1/345) by ibn al-Hummaam al-Hanafee.
[3] [The opinion of the generality of the Shaafi`ee scholars is that it is *fard kifaayah* to pray in the mosque in congregation. – Trans.]
[4] *al-`Uddah `alaa Ihkaam al-Ahkaam* (2/114).

This is the opinion of ibn Hazm adh-Dhaahiree, may Allah have mercy upon him. He said, "The obligatory prayer of a person is not valid if he hears the *adhaan* unless he prays in the mosque with the Imaam. If he deliberately leaves this without a valid excuse, his prayer (prayed outside of the mosque) is rendered null and void. If he does not hear the *adhaan,* it is obligatory upon him to pray in congregation (in a place other than the mosque) even it be with one other person. If he does not do this, his prayer is null and void unless he cannot find someone else to pray with. If a person has a valid excuse that allows him to miss the congregation, his prayer is valid."[1]

Ibn Taymiyyah said, "If one prays in congregation in his house, is the obligation of attending the congregation in the mosque lifted? There is a difference concerning this and it is desired that a person not leave off attending the mosque unless he has a valid excuse."[2]

At this juncture, it would be good to close this discussion with the words of ibn al-Qayyim, may Allah have mercy upon him,

> For whoever investigates the sunnah as it deserves to be done, it will become clear to him that praying in the mosque is *fard `ayn.* This applies unless one has a  valid excuse that allows him to miss the *Jumu`ah* and congregational prayers. Abandoning attending the mosque without a valid excuse is like abandoning the essence of congregation without a valid excuse and in this way the various evidences are reconciled.... When the Messenger of Allah (peace be upon him) died and the people of Mecca learned of his death, Suhail bin `Amr addressed them, Attaab bin Usayd was one of his governors in Mecca who had gone into hiding out of fear of the people. So Suhayl reinstated him and the people of Mecca became firm in Islam. Then after this Attaab

---

[1] *al-Muhallaa Sharh al-Mujallaa* (4/265).
[2] *Mukhtasar Fataawaa al-Misriyyah* (p. 52) by ibn Taymiyyah.

bin Usayd addressed the people and said, 'By Allah! O people of Mecca, if it reaches me that anyone of you misses the prayer in the mosque I will strike his neck.' The Companions of the Messenger of Allah (peace be upon him) thanked him for this and he gained prominence in their eyes. Therefore that which we take to be our *deen* is that it is not permissible for anyone to miss the congregation in the mosque unless he has a valid excuse and Allah knows best.[1]

Addendum: Now that we have established that it is not permissible to leave off the congregational prayer in the mosque, it becomes necessary to point out three things:

If someone misses the congregational prayer in the mosque and is unable to find anyone to pray with him in the mosque, it is desired that he return home and pray in congregation with his family.

If he is on a journey or on a trip and has his family with him, it is desired that he pray with his family in congregation.

If he missed the congregational prayer in a mosque that is close by, it is desired that he go to another mosque as long as this does not cause him undue difficulty and he is sure that he will catch the prayer.

The Ruling of a Congregation for the Obligatory Prayers

The scholars have differed concerning the ruling of congregational prayer, falling into four opinions:

The First Opinion

Congregational prayer is *fard kifaayah*. Ibn Hubairah attributed this opinion to ash-Shaafi`ee and Abu Haneefah.[2] Al-Haafidh ibn Hajr said, "The clear sense of the words of ash-Shaafi`ee is that it is *fard kifaayah*. This was the opinion of the

---

[1] *Kitaab as-Salaah* (p. 461).
[2] *al-Ifsaab* (1/142).

majority of the early Shaafi`ee scholars and it is the opinion of many Hanafee and Maalikee scholars."[1]

The meaning of *fard kifaayah* is that if a sufficient number of people establish it, the sin of not praying in congregation is lifted from the rest of the people. If a sufficient number of people do not fulfil the obligation or no one fulfils the obligation, everyone is sinful. [It is *fard kifaayah*] because the congregational prayer is a manifest sign from the signs of Islam.

An-Nawawee said in *Raudh al-Taalibeen*, "A congregation is *fard `ayn* for the *Jumu`ah* prayer. As for the other obligatory prayers, there are a number of opinions. The most correct is that it is *fard kifaayah*. A second opinion is that it is sunnah. The third opinion is that it is *fard `ayn*. This last opinion was voiced by ibn al-Mundhir and ibn Khuzaymah from our companions (the Shaafi`ees). The opinion of ash-Shaafi`ee, may Allah have mercy upon him is, 'We say it is *fard kifaayah* and if the people of a land prevent it from being established, the Imaam must fight them until they establish it such that this sign becomes manifest among them.'"[2]

These scholars depended upon the following *ahaadeeth*:

Abu ad-Dardaa` narrated that the Messenger of Allah (peace be upon him) said,

$$\text{مَا مِنْ ثَلَاثَةٍ فِي قَرْيَةٍ وَلَا بَدْوٍ لَا تُقَامُ فِيهِمُ الصَّلَاةُ إِلاَّ قَدِ}$$

$$\text{اسْتَحْوَذَ عَلَيْهِمُ الشَّيْطَانُ فَعَلَيْكَ بِالْجَمَاعَةِ فَإِنَّمَا يَأْكُلُ الذِّئْبُ}$$

$$\text{الْقَاصِيَةَ}$$

"There are no three men in a village or in the desert who do not establish the congregational prayer except that Shaytaan has gained mastery over them. So upon you is the congregation for the wolf only eats the sheep that strays from the flock."[3]

---

[1] *al-Fath* (2/26 Kitaab al-Adhaan, Baab Wujoob Salaah al-Jamaa`ah)
[2] *Rawdah at-Taalibeen* (1/339).
[3] *Sunan Abu Daawood* [Eng. Trans. 1/144 no. 547], an-Nasaa`ee (2/106-107), al-Haakim (1/211) with a *hasan* chain.

Maalik bin Huwayrith stated, "We came to the Messenger of Allah (peace be upon him) while we were all youth of nearly equal age and stayed with him for twenty nights. The Messenger of Allah (peace be upon him) was extremely merciful and kind and thought that we missed our families, so he asked us about them and we told him. He said,

$$ارْجِعُوا إِلَى أَهْلِيكُمْ فَأَقِيمُوا فِيهِمْ وَعَلِّمُوهُمْ وَمُرُوهُمْ فَإِذَا حَضَرَتْ الصَّلَاةُ فَلْيُؤَذِّنْ لَكُمْ أَحَدُكُمْ وَلْيَؤُمَّكُمْ أَكْبَرُكُمْ$$

'Return to your families and stay among them. Teach them (the religion) and enjoin them (to righteousness). When the time for prayer comes, let one of you call the *adhaan* and then let the eldest of you lead the prayer.'"[1]

Ibn Umar narrated that the Messenger of Allah (peace be upon him) said,

$$صَلَاةُ الْجَمَاعَةِ أَفْضَلُ مِنْ صَلَاةِ الْفَذِّ بِسَبْعٍ وَعِشْرِينَ دَرَجَةً$$

"The congregational prayer is twenty seven-times better than the prayer prayed alone."[2]

Al-Khattaabee said, "The majority of the Shaafi'ee scholars are of the opinion that congregational prayer is *fard kifaayah* and not *fard 'ayn* and they depended upon the hadeeth,

$$صَلَاةُ الْجَمَاعَةِ أَفْضَلُ مِنْ صَلَاةِ الْفَذِّ بِسَبْعٍ وَعِشْرِينَ دَرَجَةً$$

'The congregational prayer is twenty-seven times better than the prayer prayed alone.'"[3]

---

[1] *Saheeh Muslim* [Eng. Trans. 1/327 no. 1423].
[2] *Saheeh Muslim* [Eng. Trans. 1/315 no. 1366].
[3] *Ma'aalim as-Sunan* (1/160).

The Second Opinion

The congregational prayer is *Sunnah Mu`akkadah* (a stressed Sunnah). This is the chosen opinion of the Hanafee and Maalikee schools. Ash-Shawkaanee, may Allah have mercy on him, said, "The most just opinion and the one that is closest to the truth is that the congregational prayer is *Sunnah Mu`akkadah*. None who is able would leave off attending it unless he be void of any desire to attain good. As for the opinion that it is *fard `ayn* or a condition for the prayer, such is not the case."[1]

Ibn Abdul Barr attributed this opinion to the majority of the Jurists of Iraaq, Shaam and the Hijaaz.[2]

Al-Kharkee, from the Hanafee scholars, said, "Congregational prayer is a sunnah. It is not sanctioned for anyone to miss attending it unless he has a valid excuse. This is the understanding of *waajib* (obligatory) in the eyes of the general masses, that is, *waajib* and *sunnah mu`akkadah* are the same."[3]

Khaleel said in his *Mukhtasar* of the Maalikee school of fiqh, "Congregational prayer, with the exception of *Jumu`ah*, is *Sunnah Mu`akkadah*."[4]

Ibn Juzayy said, "Congregational prayer is *Sunnah Mu`akkadah* for the obligatory prayers."[5]

Ad-Dardeer said, "Congregational prayer, meaning a prayer in congregation being led by an Imaam, for the obligatory prayers, even if it be for missed prayers or a prayer that is *fard kifaayah* such as the funeral prayer, is *Sunnah Mu`akkadah* with the exception of *Jumu`ah*."[6]

These scholars depended upon the following *ahaadeeth*:

Ibn Umar narrated that the Messenger of Allah (peace be upon him) said,

.

---

[1] *Nayl al-Awtaar* (3/146).
[2] *At-Tamheed limaa fee al-Muwatta min al-Ma`aanee wal Asaaneed* (6/318).
[3] *Badaa`i as-Sanaa`i* (1/155) of al-Kasaanee.
[4] *Jawaahir al-Ikleel* (1/76).
[5] *Qawaaneen al-Ahkaam ash-Shar`iyyah* (p. 83).
[6] *Sharh as-Sagheer* (1/244).

صَلَاةُ الْجَمَاعَةِ أَفْضَلُ مِنْ صَلَاةِ الْفَذِّ بِسَبْعٍ وَعِشْرِينَ دَرَجَةً

"The congregational prayer is twenty-seven times better than the prayer prayed alone." As-Sana`aanee said after mentioning this hadeeth, "This hadeeth contains evidence that prayer in congregation is not obligatory."[1]

Abu Musaa al-Ash`aree narrated that the Prophet (peace be upon him) said,

إِنَّ أَعْظَمَ النَّاسِ أَجْرًا فِي الصَّلاةِ أَبْعَدُهُمْ إِلَيْهَا مَمْشًى فَأَبْعَدُهُمْ وَالَّذِي يَنْتَظِرُ الصَّلاةَ حَتَّى يُصَلِّيَهَا مَعَ الإِمَامِ أَعْظَمُ أَجْرًا مِنَ الَّذِي يُصَلِّيهَا ثُمَّ يَنَامُ

"The person who has the greatest reward for prayer is the one who has to walk the farthest distance (to the mosque) and then the next furthest after him. The one who waits for the prayer such that he can pray it with the Imaam in congregation has a greater reward than the one who prays it and then sleeps."[2]

From the evidence that they also depend upon is that the Messenger (peace be upon him) used to order the delegations that came to him with prayer, but he did not order them to perform it in a congregation.

This last point was mentioned by ash-Shawkaanee who said, "It is not permissible to delay explaining the issue at a time when it needs to be explained and clarified. Therefore, these evidences [showing non-obligation] necessitate that the evidences that indicate obligation be explained in their light, as has preceded."[3]

---

[1] *Subul as-Salaam* (2/40). [This is because the Messenger (peace be upon him) has compared two situations and declared that there is reward for both. If not attending the congregation was forbidden then the Messenger (peace be upon him) would not have made such a comparison or declared there to be a reward for praying alone – Trans]

[2] *Saheeh Muslim* [Eng. Trans. 1/323 no. 1401] and refer to *Fath al-Baaree* (2/278).

[3] *Nayl al-Awtaar* (3/146).

The Third Opinion

Congregational prayer is a condition for the prayer. Prayer is not valid if not prayed in congregation. It is *Fard `Ayn*.

This was the opinion of a group from the people of knowledge, including Shaykh al-Islam ibn Taymiyyah in one of the two opinions reported from him, his student ibn al-Qayyim, ibn Aqeel and ibn Abee Musaa. It is the opinion of the Dhaahiree scholars, some of the Scholars of Hadeeth, Abu al-Hasan at-Tameemee al-Hanbalee, one of the opinions reported from Imaam Ahmad, Abu al-Barakaat from the Hanbalee scholars and Taaj ad-Deen as-Subkee related it as an opinion of ibn Khuzaymah.[1]

These scholars depended upon the following proofs:

Ibn Abbaas narrated that the Messenger of Allah (peace be upon him) said,

$$ مَنْ سَمِعَ النِّدَاءَ فَلَمْ يَأْتِهِ فَلا صَلاةَ لَهُ إِلاَّ مِنْ عُذْرٍ $$

"Whoever hears the call and does not come to the prayer, then there is no prayer for him unless he has a valid excuse."[2]

Al-Bukhaaree recorded from Abu Hurayrah that the Messenger of Allah (peace be upon him) said,

$$ وَالَّذِي نَفْسِي بِيَدِهِ لَقَدْ هَمَمْتُ أَنْ آمُرَ بِحَطَبٍ فَيُحْطَبَ ثُمَّ آمُرَ بِالصَّلاةِ فَيُؤَذَّنَ لَهَا ثُمَّ آمُرَ رَجُلاً فَيَؤُمَّ النَّاسَ ثُمَّ أُخَالِفَ إِلَى رِجَالٍ فَأُحَرِّقَ عَلَيْهِمْ بُيُوتَهُمْ وَالَّذِي نَفْسِي بِيَدِهِ لَوْ يَعْلَمُ $$

---

[1] Refer to *Kitaab as-Salaah* (p. 460ff) by ibn al-Qayyim, *Majmoo` Fataawaa ibn Taymiyyah* (23/333), *al-Muhallaa* (4/265), *al-Majmoo`* (4/77) and *Tabaqaat ash-Shaafi`iyyah* (3/199) by as-Subkee.

[2] Reported by ibn Maajah (no. 793), ad-Daaruqutnee (1/420), ibn Hibbaan (no. 2064), al-Haakim (1/245) and its chain is *saheeh*.

أَحَدُهُمْ أَنَّهُ يَجِدُ عَرْقًا سَمِينًا أَوْ مِرْمَاتَيْنِ حَسَنَتَيْنِ لَشَهِدَ الْعِشَاءَ

"By the One in Whose hand is my soul, I considered ordering a stick be lit on fire and then order the *adhaan* to be announced and then command a person to lead the prayer and myself go to the houses of those who did not attend (the congregational prayer) and burn them down. By the One in Whose hand is my soul, if one of them knew that he was to gain a bone heavy with meat or meat between two rib bones, he would have definitely attended the *Ishaa* Prayer."[1]

Muslim recorded from Abu Hurayrah that a blind man came to the Prophet (peace be upon him) saying, "O Messenger of Allah, I have no one to guide me to the mosque." He therefore asked the Messenger of Allah (peace be upon him) to excuse him from the congregation and allow him to pray in his house. The Messenger of Allah (peace be upon him) granted him permission. When the blind man had turned away, he called him back and asked,

هَلْ تَسْمَعُ النِّدَاءَ بِالصَّلَاةِ قَالَ نَعَمْ قَالَ فَأَجِبْ

"Do you hear the call to prayer?" He replied, "Yes." He said, "Then respond to it."[2]

They also depend upon the aforementioned saying of ibn Mas'ud concerning preserving the five daily prayers [in congregation] and that they are from the *Sunan* of guidance.

They also refer to what Al-Bayhaqee recorded from ibn Abbaas: The Messenger of Allah (peace be upon him) said,

مَنْ سَمِعَ الْمُنَادِي فَلَمْ يَأْتِ فَلَا صَلَاةَ لَهُ إِلاَّ مِنْ عُذْرٍ

---

[1] *Saheeh al-Bukhaaree* [Eng. Trans. 9/250 no. 330], *Saheeh Muslim* [Eng. Trans. 1/315 nos. 1369-1371].
[2] *Saheeh Muslim* [Eng. Trans. 1/316 no. 1374].

74

"Whoever hears the caller to prayer and does not come (to the congregation) then there is no prayer for him unless he has a valid excuse."[1]

The Fourth Opinion

Congregational prayer is *Fard `Ayn* but it is not a condition of the prayer [such that the prayer would be invalid if not prayed in congregation]. This opinion is reported from ibn Mas`ud and Abu Musaa from the Companions. This was also the opinion of `Ataa bin Abee Rabaah, al-Awaza`ee, Abu Thawr, ibn Khuzaymah and ibn Hibbaan from the Shaafi`ee scholars. It is the opinion of most of the Hanafee scholars, and it is the chosen opinion of the Hanbalee School and the opinion adhered to by most of their scholars.[2]

`Ataa, may Allah have mercy upon him, said, "The obligatory duty, which is necessary to enact and concerning which it is not permissible to do anything else, is that when one hears the *adhaan,* he goes and attends the (congregational) prayer."[3]

"This is what is textually reported from Ahmad and others from the Imaams and Scholars of Hadeeth."[4]

---

[1] *As-Sunan al-Kubraa* (3/174).

[2] *al-Musannaf* (1/245) of Abdur-Razzaaq as-Sana`aanee. [It should be noted that sometimes there occurs a discrepancy between the analysis of various scholars as to what exactly is the chosen opinion or majority opinion of any particular *madh-hab*. One of the reasons for this occurring is simply that scholar presenting the opinion of that *madh-hab* in his time. Hence it is possible that a scholar who lived at the time of the students of Abu Haneefah (for example) presents an opinion of the *madh-hab* at that time and a scholar who lived centuries later presents a totally different opinion as being the stance of that *madh-hab*. This is why the contemporary Hanafee scholar, Shu`ayb al-Arna`ut writes in the the introduction to his notes on *Sharh as-Sunnah* (1/6 fn. 1), "It is possible that the reader will find a discrepency between what the author (al-Baghawee) presents as the opinions of the Imaams and that which one would find in books of the later scholars. The reason for this is that the author, may Allah have mercy upon him, quotes from the books of the early scholars who took great care in quoting and recording the opinions of the Imaams... It is also possible that the Imaam in question has voiced more than one opinion concerning the issue at hand." – Trans]

[3] *Mukhtasar Fataawaa al-Misriyyah* (p. 50).

[4] *al-Musannaf* (1/497 no. 1917) of Abdur-Razzaaq.

Aa`ishah said, "Whoever hears the call to prayer and does not respond does not desire the good and the good does not desire him."[1]

Ibn Qudaamah said, "Congregational prayer is obligatory upon men for the five obligatory prayers but it is not a condition."[2]

Based on this opinion, if a person were to leave attending the congregational prayer without a valid excuse, he commits a sin but his prayer is valid.

Allah, the Exalted said,

وَإِذَا كُنْتَ فِيهِمْ فَأَقَمْتَ لَهُمُ الصَّلَاةَ فَلْتَقُمْ طَائِفَةٌ مِنْهُمْ مَعَكَ وَلْيَأْخُذُوا أَسْلِحَتَهُمْ فَإِذَا سَجَدُوا فَلْيَكُونُوا مِنْ وَرَائِكُمْ وَلْتَأْتِ طَائِفَةٌ أُخْرَى لَمْ يُصَلُّوا فَلْيُصَلُّوا مَعَكَ وَلْيَأْخُذُوا حِذْرَهُمْ وَأَسْلِحَتَهُمْ وَدَّ الَّذِينَ كَفَرُوا لَوْ تَغْفُلُونَ عَنْ أَسْلِحَتِكُمْ وَأَمْتِعَتِكُمْ فَيَمِيلُونَ عَلَيْكُمْ مَيْلَةً وَاحِدَةً

"When you (O Messenger) are with them and stand to lead them in prayer, then let one party of them stand (in prayer) with you, taking their weapons with them. When they finish their prostrations, let them take their position in the rear and let the other party come that has not yet prayed and let them pray with you, taking all precautions and bearing arms. The unbelievers wish that you were negligent of your weapons and baggage so that they can assault you in a single rush" [*an-Nisaa* (4):102].

This verse embodies clear evidence that congregational prayer is obligatory and that it is not permissible to leave it unless one has a genuine excuse, such as fear or illness.

Furthermore, Allah, the Exalted, said,

وَأَقِيمُوا الصَّلَاةَ وَآتُوا الزَّكَاةَ وَارْكَعُوا مَعَ الرَّاكِعِينَ

"And establish the prayer and give the *zakaah* and bow along with those who are bowing" [*al-Baqarah* (2): 43]. This verse

---

[1] *al-Muqni`* (1/193).
[2] Ibid.

comes in the form of a command and the command necessitates obligation.[1]

Allah, the Exalted, also said,

فِي بُيُوتٍ أَذِنَ اللَّهُ أَنْ تُرْفَعَ وَيُذْكَرَ فِيهَا اسْمُهُ يُسَبِّحُ لَهُ فِيهَا بِالْغُدُوِّ وَالْآصَالِ رِجَالٌ لَا تُلْهِيهِمْ تِجَارَةٌ وَلَا بَيْعٌ عَنْ ذِكْرِ اللَّهِ وَإِقَامِ الصَّلَاةِ وَإِيتَاءِ الزَّكَاةِ يَخَافُونَ يَوْمًا تَتَقَلَّبُ فِيهِ الْقُلُوبُ وَالْأَبْصَارُ لِيَجْزِيَهُمُ اللَّهُ أَحْسَنَ مَا عَمِلُوا وَيَزِيدَهُمْ مِنْ فَضْلِهِ وَاللَّهُ يَرْزُقُ مَنْ يَشَاءُ بِغَيْرِ حِسَابٍ

"(Lit is such a Light) in houses which Allah has allowed to be raised such that His *dhikr* (remembrance) is performed in them. In them, He is glorified in the mornings and evenings by men whom neither trade nor sale can divert from the *dhikr* of Allah, nor from establishing the prayer or paying *zakaat*. They fear the Day when the hearts and eyes will be turned about—that Allah may reward them according to the best of their deeds and add even for them out of His Grace. Indeed, Allah provides for whomever He Wills without measure" [*an-Nur* (24):36-38].

Allah, the Exalted, also says,

قُلْ أَمَرَ رَبِّي بِالْقِسْطِ وَأَقِيمُوا وُجُوهَكُمْ عِنْدَ كُلِّ مَسْجِدٍ

"Say: My Lord has commanded justice and that you should face Him only in every mosque" [*al-A`raaf* (7): 29]. Again, command dictates obligation.

And Allah, the Exalted, says,

يَوْمَ يُكْشَفُ عَنْ سَاقٍ وَيُدْعَوْنَ إِلَى السُّجُودِ فَلَا يَسْتَطِيعُونَ خَاشِعَةً أَبْصَارُهُمْ تَرْهَقُهُمْ ذِلَّةٌ وَقَدْ كَانُوا يُدْعَوْنَ إِلَى السُّجُودِ وَهُمْ سَالِمُونَ

"The Day when the Shin shall be laid bare and they shall be called to prostrate (to Allah) but they (the hypocrites) shall not

---

[1] *al-Mukhtasar fee Usool al-Fiqh `alaa Madh-hab al-Imaam Ahmad bin Hanbal* (p. 98) by ibn al-Lahhaam.

be able to do so. Their eyes will be cast down and ignominy will cover them. They used to be called to prostrate while they were healthy (but did not respond)" [*al-Qalam* (68):42-43]. Ibn al-Qayyim said,

> This verse is used as proof because Allah, far is He from imperfection, punishes them on the Day of Judgement by making it impossible for them to prostrate due to their having refused to respond to the caller in this world. When this becomes established, know that the way to answer the caller is to go to the mosque and join the congregation, not to pray alone in one's house. This is how the Prophet (peace be upon him) explained the meaning of "response"… More than one of the Salaf said concerning Allah's words, "They used to be called to prostrate while they were healthy (but did not respond)," that it refers to the saying of the *Mu`adhdhin*, "Come to prayer, come to success." The meaning of "*hayya*" is to respond and turn your attention towards the prayer. Therefore, this statement explicitly expresses that to answer this call means to attend the congregation and that the one who missed the congregation did not respond to the call."[1]

There is also evidence from the sunnah. Abu Hurayrah reported that the Messenger of Allah (peace be upon him) said,

وَالَّذِي نَفْسِي بِيَدِهِ لَقَدْ هَمَمْتُ أَنْ آمُرَ بِحَطَبٍ فَيُحْطَبَ ثُمَّ
آمُرَ بِالصَّلَاةِ فَيُؤَذَّنَ لَهَا ثُمَّ آمُرَ رَجُلاً فَيَؤُمَّ النَّاسَ ثُمَّ أُخَالِفَ
إِلَى رِجَالٍ فَأُحَرِّقَ عَلَيْهِمْ بُيُوتَهُمْ وَالَّذِي نَفْسِي بِيَدِهِ لَوْ يَعْلَمُ

---

[1] *Kitaab as-Salaah* (pp. 460-475) by ibn al-Qayyim.

أَحَدُهُمْ أَنَّهُ يَجِدُ عَرْقًا سَمِينًا أَوْ مِرْمَاتَيْنِ حَسَنَتَيْنِ لَشَهِدَ الْعِشَاءَ

"By the One in Whose hand is my soul, I considered ordering a stick be lit and then order the *adhaan* to be announced and then command a person to lead the prayer and myself go to the houses of those who did not attend (the congregational prayer) and burn them down. By the One in Whose is my soul, if one of them knew that he was to gain a bone heavy with meat or meat between two rib bones, he would have definitely attended the *Ishaa* Prayer."[1]

Al-Haafidh ibn Hajr, may Allah have mercy upon him, said, "The clear sense of this hadeeth proves that attending the congregational prayer is *fard `ayn* because, if it were a sunnah, the one who abandoned praying in congregation would not be threatened with having his house burnt down. It is also not possible that this threat be actualized in the case of one who has left a *fard kifaayah,* as there occurs the case of fighting those who collectively leave a *fard kifaayah* (until they re-establish it). This is because the thing that led to the threat of killing (those who left off the congregational prayer) is more specific then the thing that led to fighting because fighting is only legislated when everyone leaves the *fard kifaayah*."[2]

Ibn Daqeeq al-Eid, may Allah have mercy upon him, said, "Those who say that congregational prayer is obligatory upon every (male) individual depend upon this hadeeth. If it is said that it is *fard kifaayah,* then the obligation was fulfilled by the Messenger of Allah (peace be upon him) and those who attended the congregation with him (so there would no need for the threat). If it is said that it is a sunnah, then a person who leaves a sunnah is not killed and therefore it becomes clear that it is *fard `ayn*."[3]

Muslim reports from Abu Hurayrah that a blind man came to the Prophet (peace be upon him) saying, "O Messenger of Allah I have no one to guide me to the mosque."

---

[1] *Saheeh al-Bukhaaree* [Eng. Trans. 9/250 no. 330], *Saheeh Muslim* [Eng. Trans. 1/315 nos. 1369-1371].
[2] *Fath al-Baaree* (2/125).
[3] *Ihkaam al-Ahkaam* (1/164).

He therefore asked the Messenger of Allah (peace be upon him) to excuse him from the congregation and allow him to pray in his house. The Messenger of Allah (peace be upon him) granted him permission. When the blind man had turned away he called him back and asked,

هَلْ تَسْمَعُ النِّدَاءَ بِالصَّلاةِ قَالَ نَعَمْ قَالَ فَأَجِبْ

"Do you hear the call to prayer?" He replied, "Yes." He said, "Then respond to it."[1]

Therefore, the Messenger of Allah (peace be upon him) did not give leave to this blind man to miss the congregational prayer despite his being blind and having no one to guide him. This despite his living far away from the mosque and their being a valley between him and the mosque and despite Madeenah being a place fraught with danger and predatory animals. Despite all these factors, the Messenger of Allah (peace be upon him) did not excuse him from attending the congregational prayer, instead he asked, *"Do you hear the call to prayer?"* When the blind man replied in the affirmative, he said, *"Then respond to it."* In another narration, it states, *"Then I do not find any excuse for you."* Hence, this hadeeth is explicit that congregational prayer is obligatory. Now if a blind man is not excused from attending it then how about the one who can see?

Ibn Qudaamah, may Allah have mercy on him, said, "If he did not excuse the blind man who had no guide, then those other than him have even less of an excuse for not attending."[2]

Ibn al-Mundhir, may Allah have mercy upon him, said, "Mentioning the necessity for the blind to attend the congregational prayer, even if they live far away, proves that doing so is obligatory and not recommended. So when he said to ibn Umm Maktum, the blind man, 'Then I do not find any excuse for you,' for sure the one who can see has even less of an excuse."[3]

---

[1] *Saheeh Muslim* [Eng. Trans. 1/316 no. 1374].
[2] *al-Mughnee* (2/130).
[3] *Kitaab as-Salaah* (p. 461) by ibn al-Qayyim.

Al-Khattaabee said, "This hadeeth constitutes evidence that it is obligatory to attend the congregational prayer for were it to be a mere recommendation, it would have been more deserving for those who were in a similar situation to ibn Umm Maktum to leave off attending it."[1]

Al-Haakim recorded that Madaan ibn Abi Talhah al-Yamari was asked by Abu ad-Dardaa`, "Where do you live?" He replied that he lived in a village outside of Hims. Abu ad-Dardaa` then told him that the Messenger of Allah (peace be upon him) said,

مَا مِنْ ثَلاثَةٍ فِي قَرْيَةٍ وَلا بَدْوٍ لا تُقَامُ فِيهِمُ الصَّلاةُ إلاَّ قَدِ اسْتَحْوَذَ عَلَيْهِمُ الشَّيْطَانُ فَعَلَيْكَ بِالْجَمَاعَةِ فَإِنَّمَا يَأْكُلُ الذِّئْبُ الْقَاصِيَةَ

"There are no three men in a village or in the desert who do not establish the congregational prayer except that Shaytaan has gained mastery over them. So upon you is the congregation for the wolf only eats the sheep that strays from the flock."[2]

Ibn al-Qayyim, may Allah have mercy upon him, said,

> This hadeeth proves that Shaytaan has gained mastery over them due to their leaving the congregation, whose signs are the *adhaan* and the establishment of the prayer. If the congregational prayer was recommended such that a person has a choice over attending or not attending it, then why would Shaytaan have gained mastery over one who leaves it and its signs?

> All of the previously mentioned Qur`aanic verses and *ahaadeeth* prove that congregational prayer is obligatory and that it is not permissible to leave it unless one has a

---

[1] *Ma`aalim as-Sunan* (1/160-162).
[2] *Sunan Abu Daawood* [Eng. Trans. 1/144 no. 547], *an-Nasaa`ee* (2/106-107), *al-Haakim* (1/211) with a *hasan* chain.

valid excuse, such as fear or illness. This is the opinion of the majority of the scholars from among the Companions and the Followers. It is the clear opinion of the Hanbalee school of thought and it was an opinion voiced by ash-Shaafi`ee. Al-Muzanee, may Allah have mercy on him, reports from al-Shafi'ee that he said, "As for the congregational prayer, I find no leeway in leaving it unless one has a valid excuse."

From all that has been mentioned thus far it becomes clear that the four Imaams, may Allah have mercy upon them, regarded attending congregational prayer to be obligatory and that the one who leaves it without a valid excuse is sinful, even though they used different expressions to state this conclusion. This opinion is borne testimony to by the Words of Allah and the Sunnah of His Messenger (peace be upon him) and there is no room for voicing one's opinion when Allah and His Messenger (peace be upon him) have spoken.[1]

The Strongest Opinion

We have mentioned the opinions about the congregational prayer, which are four opinions: (1) It is a *fardh kifaayah*. (2) It is a stressed sunnah. (3) It is a condition for the soundness of the prayer. (4) It is a *fardh ain*. We have also mentioned who holds what opinion of the early and later scholars.

After all that has preceded, it becomes clear that the strongest opinion is the fourth opinion. This being that praying in congregation is *fard `ayn*—meaning that it is obligatory upon each individual. This is due to the strength of the

---

[1] *Kitaab as-Salaah* (p. 461) by ibn al-Qayyim.

evidences supporting this opinion and the clarity of the texts from the Qur'aan and Sunnah. Allah Knows best.

The Ruling of a Congregational for the Optional Prayers

Aside from the obligatory prayers, the prayers are divided into three types:

The *Sunan* prayers: These include the set prayers prayed after the obligatory prayers as well as the *Witr* and *Tahajjud* prayers.

The *Mustahabbaat* (recommended): Any prayer for whose excellence there occurs a text but there is nothing narrated that would indicate that one should be constant in performing them.

At-Tatawwu`aat (optional): Any other prayer prayed for which no specific text occurs but the servant is free to perform.

These three types are called *nawaafil* or *tatawwu`*.

The Meaning of *Nawaafil* in the Language

Nawaafil is the plural of *naafilah*. *An-nafal* and *an-naafila* mean additional. *At-tanafful* means to perform something optional.

The Meaning of *Nawaafil* in the *Sharee`ah*

"[*Nawaafil* is] a term referring to what has been legislated over and above that which is obligatory. It is also called *mandub* (recommended), *mustahabb* (recommended) and *at-tatawwu`* (optional)."[1]

It is also called "*sunnah, al-muraghghab feehee* (that which is desired), and *al-hasan* (good)."[2]

"*Nawaafil* is so called because it is additional to what Allah, the Exalted, has obligated."[3]

---

[1] *At-Ta`reefaat* (p. 315) by Shareef al-Jarjaanee.
[2] *al-Qaamoos al-Fiqhee Lughatan wa Istillaahan* (p. 358) of Sa`dee Abu Jaib.
[3] *Mughnee al-Muhtaaj* (1/219) by Sharbeenee al-Khateeb.

The Position of the *Nawaafil* Among the Other Prayers

The levels of the *Nawaafil* differ in accordance to the excellence mentioned in the *ahaadeeth* and narrations concerning any particular prayer.

The Types of *Nawaafil* Prayers with Respect to Praying Them in Congregation

The different *madh-hab*s have their own conventions for categorizing the *nawaafil* prayers but this is not the place to mention them, for all we are concerned with here is to understand the ruling of praying them in congregation.

With respect to praying *nawaafil* in congregation, the *nawaafil* fall into two categories:

The Type That is Sanctioned to be Performed With a Congregation:

Salaatul Kusoof (The Prayer of the Solar Eclipse)

It is legislated to pray this in congregation by agreement of the Jurists. As for the lunar eclipse, Maalik and Abu Haneefah said that it is not to be prayed in congregation. It is to be prayed individually. Ash-Shaafi`ee and Ahmad said that the Sunnah with regards the lunar eclipse is that it be prayed in congregation like the solar eclipse. As for other natural events, such as earthquakes, lightening storms, and darkness during the day, according to Abu Haneefah, Maalik and ash-Shaafi`ee there is no legislation requiring one to pray on these occasions. It is reported from Ahmad that one prays in congregation for each of these natural events and it is reported from Alee that he prayed during an earthquake.[1]

---

[1] Refer to *Rahmah al-Ummah fee Ikhtilaaf al-A`immah* (pp. 65-66) by Abu Abdullaah Muhmmad bin Abdurrahman ad-Dimishqee ash-Shaafi`ee.

Salaatul Istisqaa (The Prayer for Seeking Rain)

According to the Maalikee[1], Shaafi`ee[2], and Hanbalee[3] scholars and the two students of Abu Haneefah (Abu Yoosuf and Muhammad), it is sanctioned to pray this prayer with a congregation. Abu Haneefah said, "There is no (congregational) prayer sanctioned for this. Instead the Imaam is to go out and supplicate. If the people were to pray individually, it is permissible."[4]

Salaatul Eidayn (The Two Eid Prayers)

This is sanctioned in congregation by agreement of the scholars. It is also permissible for a person to pray it alone but he does not deliver a *khutbah*. There is no known difference of opinion concerning this.[5]

Salaatut Taraaweeh (The Night Prayer during Ramadaan)

It is sanctioned to pray this with a congregation and I have devoted a separate chapter to discuss this.

The *Nawaafil* That Are Prayed Individually:

These are the specifically mentioned Sunan prayers, such as those prayed with the obligatory prayers and any other *nawaafil* prayer that is prayed during the day or night. It is permissible to pray these in congregation according to the Shaafi`ee[6] and Hanbalee[7] scholars. It is disliked to do so in the opinion of the Hanafee scholars if the intent behind this is to make it habitual.[8]

---

[1] *Jawaahir al-Ikleel* (1/74-76).
[2] *al-Majmoo`* (3/501-509).
[3] *Kashf al-Qinaa`* (1/414) and *Nayl al-Maarib* (1/204).
[4] *al-Ifsaah `an Ma`aanee as-Sihaah* (1/178).
[5] Refer to *al-Majmoo`* (5/22) by an-Nawawee and *al-Muhallaa* (5/128 no. 544).
[6] *al-Majmoo`* (3/501, 510, 528).
[7] *al-Mughnee* (2/567).
[8] *al-Mawsoo`ah al-Fiqhhiyyah* (12/154-155).

According to the Maalikee scholars, praying the *witr* prayer in congregation is a Sunnah and to pray the Sunnahs of Fajr in congregation is not the best course of action. As for the remaining (optional) prayers, it is permissible to pray them in congregation with the condition that the congregation not be large or the place not be famous. If this is the case then it is disliked to pray them in congregation for fear of showing off[1] and for fear of making the ignorant think that what is being prayed is an obligatory prayer.[2]

It is established from the Prophet (peace be upon him) that he did both matters and his predominant course in praying the optional prayers was to pray them individually.[3]

Muslim reports from Anas bin Maalik that his grandmother, Mulaika, invited the Messenger of Allah (peace be upon him) to a dinner that she had prepared. He partook of it and then said,

قُومُوا فَأُصَلِّيَ لَكُمْ قَالَ أَنَسُ بْنُ مَالِكٍ فَقُمْتُ إِلَى حَصِيرٍ لَنَا قَدْ اسْوَدَّ مِنْ طُولِ مَا لُبِسَ فَنَضَحْتُهُ بِمَاءٍ فَقَامَ عَلَيْهِ رَسُولُ اللَّهِ صَلَّى اللَّهُ عَلَيْهِ وَسَلَّمَ وَصَفَفْتُ أَنَا وَالْيَتِيمُ وَرَاءَهُ وَالْعَجُوزُ مِنْ وَرَائِنَا فَصَلَّى لَنَا رَسُولُ اللَّهِ صَلَّى اللَّهُ عَلَيْهِ وَسَلَّمَ رَكْعَتَيْنِ ثُمَّ انْصَرَفَ

"Stand so that I may pray with you." Anas bin Maalik said, "So I stood up on a mat which had turned black on account of its long use. I sprinkled water on top of it and the Messenger of Allah (peace be upon him) stood on it and an orphan and I formed a row behind him and the old woman stood behind us. The Messenger of Allah (peace be upon him) prayed two *rak`ahs* with us and then left."[4]

---

[1] *Ash-Sharh as-Sagheer* (1/414) by ad-Dardeer.
[2] *Fath al-Baaree.*
[3] *al-Mughnee* (2/567).
[4] *Saheeh Muslim* [Eng. Trans. 1/320 no. 1387].

An-Nawawee said, "His saying, 'Stand so that I may pray with you' contains the permissibility of praying *nawaafil* in congregation."[1]

Bukhaaree reports from Itbaan bin Maalik al-Ansaaree who said,

كُنْتُ أُصَلِّي لِقَوْمِي بِبَنِي سَالِمٍ وَكَانَ يَحُولُ بَيْنِي وَبَيْنَهُمْ وَادٍ إِذَا جَاءَتْ الأَمْطَارُ فَيَشُقُّ عَلَيَّ اجْتِيَازُهُ قِبَلَ مَسْجِدِهِمْ فَجِئْتُ رَسُولَ اللَّهِ صَلَّى اللَّهُ عَلَيْهِ وَسَلَّمَ فَقُلْتُ لَهُ إِنِّي أَنْكَرْتُ بَصَرِي وَإِنَّ الْوَادِيَ الَّذِي بَيْنِي وَبَيْنَ قَوْمِي يَسِيلُ إِذَا جَاءَتْ الأَمْطَارُ فَيَشُقُّ عَلَيَّ اجْتِيَازُهُ فَوَدِدْتُ أَنَّكَ تَأْتِي فَتُصَلِّي مِنْ بَيْتِي مَكَانًا أَتَّخِذُهُ مُصَلًّى فَقَالَ رَسُولُ اللَّهِ صَلَّى اللَّهُ عَلَيْهِ وَسَلَّمَ سَأَفْعَلُ فَغَدَا عَلَيَّ رَسُولُ اللَّهِ صَلَّى اللَّهُ عَلَيْهِ وَسَلَّمَ وَأَبُو بَكْرٍ رَضِيَ اللَّهُ عَنْهُ بَعْدَ مَا اشْتَدَّ النَّهَارُ فَاسْتَأْذَنَ رَسُولُ اللَّهِ صَلَّى اللَّهُ عَلَيْهِ وَسَلَّمَ فَأَذِنْتُ لَهُ فَلَمْ يَجْلِسْ حَتَّى قَالَ أَيْنَ تُحِبُّ أَنْ أُصَلِّيَ مِنْ بَيْتِكَ فَأَشَرْتُ لَهُ إِلَى الْمَكَانِ الَّذِي أُحِبُّ أَنْ أُصَلِّيَ فِيهِ فَقَامَ رَسُولُ اللَّهِ صَلَّى اللَّهُ عَلَيْهِ وَسَلَّمَ فَكَبَّرَ وَصَفَفْنَا وَرَاءَهُ فَصَلَّى رَكْعَتَيْنِ ثُمَّ سَلَّمَ وَسَلَّمْنَا

"I used to lead my people, Bani Saalim, in prayer and there was a valley between me and that tribe. Whenever it rained, it became difficult for me to traverse the valley in order to reach their mosque. So I went to the Messenger of Allah (peace be upon him) and said, 'I have weak eyesight and the valley between my people and me flows when it rains and therefore it

---

[1] *Irshaad as-Saaree bi Sharh Saheeh al-Bukhaaree* in the margin of which is *Sharh Saheeh Muslim* (3/347).

becomes difficult for me to cross it. I wish that you could come to my house and pray at a place so that I can take that place as a *musalla* [designated place for prayer].' The Messenger of Allah (peace be upon him) said, 'I will do so.' The next morning the Messenger of Allah (peace be upon him) and Abu Bakr came to my house after the sun had risen high. I gave him permission to enter my house but he did not sit until he asked, 'Where would you like me to pray in your house?' I pointed to a place that I wished to pray in. The Messenger of Allah (peace be upon him) stood there and said the *takbeer* and we aligned in a row behind him. He prayed two *rak`ahs* and then he said the *salaam* and so did we..."[1]

His (peace be upon him) praying *nawaafil* in congregation is authentically reported from ibn Abbaas, Hudhayfah and Aa`ishah (RAA) as reported by al-Bukhaaree and others.[2]

Even though, the best course is to pray *nawaafil* individually, except for those previously mentioned *nawaafil* that are sanctioned to be prayed in congregation. Ibn Hazm adh-Dhaahiree was of the opinion that it is recommended to pray all *nawaafil* prayers in congregation.[3]

I say: The correct opinion is that it is permissible to pray the *nawaafil* in congregation regardless of whether they are the set sunnahs (prayed with the obligatory prayers) or the recommended sunnahs or any optional prayer. However, this only holds true for the condition that this is not taken as a habitual action and that it does not become famous and commonly employed and that there be a reason for it, such as the owner of a place requesting it or it happening by chance such as the host and guest deciding to pray *Witr* in congregation. There is also the condition that it does not lead to innovation or enacting a matter that has not been legislated.

---

[1] *Saheeh al-Bukhaaree* [Eng. Trans. 2/154 no. 279].
[2] Refer to *al-Muntaqaa min Akhbaar al-Mustafaa* (1/554 no.'s 1265-1267).
[3] *al-Muhallaa Sharh al-Mujallaa* (4/61-65), *Tarh at-Tathreeb fee Sharh at-Taqreeb* (3/99).

Qiyaam Ramadaan [1] or Salaatut Taraaweeh in Congregation

From the *nawaafil* prayers that are to be prayed in congregation is *Salaatut Taraaweeh* during Ramadaan. Before I delve into the ruling of this prayer and the manner of performing it, it would be good to first clarify a number of matters.

The Reason Behind Its Being Called *Salaatut Taraaweeh*

The author of *al-Mubdi`* (1/17) said, "It was called so because the people used to sit after every four *rak`ahs* to rest. It is also said that it is derived from *al-maraawiha* which means the repetition of an action."

The Ruling of *Salaatut Taraaweeh*

Salaatut Taraaweeh is a recommended sunnah that is established from the Prophet (peace be upon him), both his saying and action.

As for his sayings, al-Bukhaaree reports from Abu Hurayrah that he heard the Messenger of Allah (peace be upon him) saying concerning Ramadaan,

مَنْ قَامَهُ إِيمَانًا وَاحْتِسَابًا غُفِرَ لَهُ مَا تَقَدَّمَ مِنْ ذَنْبِهِ

"Whoever prays during it out of faith and hoping for reward then all of his previous [minor] sins will be forgiven."[2]

---

[1] Al-Kirmaanee said, "They have agreed that the meaning of *Qiyaam Ramadaan* is *Salaatut Taraaweeh*." Refer to *Nayl al-Awtaar* (3/57).

[2] *Saheeh al-Bukhaaree* [Eng. Trans. 3/126 no. 226].

As for his actions, the Prophet (peace be upon him) prayed it in congregation with the people for two nights. Al-Bukhaaree reports from Aa'ishah that

أَنَّ رَسُولَ اللَّهِ صَلَّى اللَّهُ عَلَيْهِ وَسَلَّمَ صَلَّى ذَاتَ لَيْلَةٍ فِي
الْمَسْجِدِ فَصَلَّى بِصَلَاتِهِ نَاسٌ ثُمَّ صَلَّى مِنَ الْقَابِلَةِ فَكَثُرَ النَّاسُ
ثُمَّ اجْتَمَعُوا مِنَ اللَّيْلَةِ الثَّالِثَةِ فَلَمْ يَخْرُجْ إِلَيْهِمْ رَسُولُ اللَّهِ صَلَّى
اللَّهُ عَلَيْهِ وَسَلَّمَ فَلَمَّا أَصْبَحَ قَالَ قَدْ رَأَيْتُ الَّذِي صَنَعْتُمْ وَلَمْ
يَمْنَعْنِي مِنَ الْخُرُوجِ إِلَيْكُمْ إِلَّا أَنِّي خَشِيتُ أَنْ تُفْرَضَ عَلَيْكُمْ
وَذَلِكَ فِي رَمَضَانَ

"The Messenger of Allah (peace be upon him) prayed in the mosque one night and some people prayed with him. The next night, the Prophet (peace be upon him) prayed in the mosque again and even more people prayed with him. On the third night, the people gathered together waiting but the Messenger of Allah (peace be upon him) did not come out to pray with them. The next day he said, 'Indeed I saw what you did and nothing prevented me from coming to pray with you except that I feared that it would become obligatory upon you.' And that was in Ramadaan."[1]

An-Nawawee said, "They [the scholars] have agreed that *Salaatut Taraaweeh* is a recommended sunnah."[2]

At-Tahaawee reports in his *Sharh* from al-Hasan ibn Ziyaad al-Luluai al-Hanafi that Abu Haneefah said, "*Taraaweeh* is for both men and women. This is what the later people inherited from the Salaf. A group of the *Rawaafidah* said that it was a sunnah for men and not for women. Another group said that it is not a sunnah at all, neither for men or for women and that it was innovated by Umar bin al-Khattaab. According to *Ahlus Sunnah wal Jamaa'ah*, it is the Sunnah of

---

[1] *Saheeh al-Bukhaaree* [Eng. Trans. 2/128 no. 229], *Saheeh Muslim* [Eng. Trans. 1/367 no. 1666] and *Abu Daawood* [Eng. Trans. 1/359 no. 1368].
[2] *Sharh Saheeh Muslim* (6/39).

the Messenger of Allah (peace be upon him) for he prayed it (in congregation) for some nights and then explained the reason behind his not persisting in praying it in congregation—this being his fear that it become obligatory upon them. Then the *Khulaafaa ar-Raashideen* persisted in performing it after him and the people were gathered during the time of Umar bin al-Khattaab to this day."[1]

How Should *Taraaweeh* be Performed?

The Jurists have differed as to how *Salaatut Taraaweeh* should be performed. There are five opinions.

The First Opinion: It is recommended to perform it in the mosque. This is the opinion of some of the Companions and the Followers, from among them: Umar bin al-Khattaab, Alee bin Abee Taalib, Abdullaah bin Mas'ud and others.[2]

This is the chosen opinion of the Hanbalee[3] scholars, textually reported from some of the Shaafi'ee[4] scholars and some Hanafee scholars.[5]

The Second Opinion: It is legislated as a communal act to pray it in congregation such that if the people of a mosque were all not to pray it, they would be sinful. The one who does not pray it in congregation has left the best course. This is the chosen opinion of the Hanafee school.[6]

The Third Opinion: It is best to pray it in one's home, individually. This is the opinion of some of the Companions and the Followers, including Abdullaah bin Umar, 'Urwah, Sa'eed bin Jubair, Saalim, al-Qaasim, and Naafi'. It is the opinion of ash-Shaafi'ee and the majority of his companions, Abu Haneefah, Ahmad and some of the Maalikee scholars.[7]

The Fourth Opinion: It is recommended to pray it individually in one's house with the conditions that, first, the mosque does not become neglected, second, one is eager and

---

[1] *Anees al-Fuqahaa* (p. 107).
[2] *Al-Mughnee* (2/605).
[3] Ibid.
[4] *al-Majmoo'* (3/525).
[5] *al-Mughnee* (2/605).
[6] *al-Inaayah Sharh al-Hidaayah* (2/586).
[7] *al-Majmoo'* (3/525).

energetic in praying it at home and, third, that he be distant from the Two Holy Mosques. If any one of these conditions is missing, it is best to pray in the mosque. This is the chosen opinion of the Maalikee school[1] and an opinion of the Shaafi'ee school.[2]

The Fifth Opinion: To pray it in congregation is a *bid'ah*. This is the opinion of the *Itrah* (the children of Faatimah and the Prophet's (peace be upon him) wives).[3]

The Strongest Opinion

Upon investigating the above opinions, it becomes clear that the fifth opinion is totally invalid, having no proof to support it. As for the remaining four opinions, they are close to each other in the sense that they agree that it is sanctioned to pray *Taraaweeh* in congregation despite their differing as to what ruling this congregation takes. The opinion that is closest to the action of the Prophet (peace be upon him) and the *Khaleefah ar-Raashid* Umar bin al-Khattaab and those who came after him is to pray it in congregation in the mosque. Based on this opinion, praying *Taraaweeh* in congregation in the mosque is a recommended sunnah for both men and women. This is due to three reasons:

The Prophet's (peace be upon him) endorsing congregational prayer for *Taraaweeh*.

The Prophet's praying it in congregation.

His explaining its excellence.

What follows is an explanation to the above three reasons.

The Prophet's Endorsing of the Congregation

This is based on the hadeeth of Tha'laba bin Abee Maalik al-Qardhee who said,

---

[1] Refer to *Nayl al-Awtaar* (3/59) and *al-Mudawwana al-Kubraa* (1/222).
[2] *al-Majmoo'* (3/525).
[3] *Nayl al-Awtaar* (3/59). The word *Itrah* refers to the children of Faatimah and the Prophet's (peace be upon him) wives. For the difinition of *al-Itrah* see *Mu'jam Lugha al-Fuqahaa'* (p. 304). [In the above context, it is used to refer to the leaders of the Shiah who are descended from Faatimah.]

خَرَجَ رَسُولُ اللهِ ذَاتَ لَيْلَةٍ فِي رَمَضَانَ فَرَأَى ناساً فِي ناحِيَةٍ
الْمَسْجِدِ يُصَلُّونَ فَقَالَ ما يَصْنَعُ هَؤُلاءِ، قالَ قائِلٌ ناسٌ لَيْسَ
مَعَهُمْ قُرْآنٍ وأُبَيُّ بن كَعْبٍ يَقْرَأُ وَهُمْ مَعَهُ يُصَلُّونَ بِصَلاتِهِ،
فَقالَ قَدْ أَحْسَنُوا أَوْ قَدْ أَصابُوا وَلَمْ يكره ذلِكَ لَهُمْ

"The Messenger of Allah (peace be upon him) went out to the mosque one night during Ramadaan and saw some people praying in congregation in a part of the mosque. He asked, 'What are they doing?' A person replied, 'O Messenger of Allah, these people do not know any of the Qur`aan so Ubayy bin Ka`b recites and they pray with him.' He said, 'They have done well' or 'They are correct,' and he did not dislike their action."[1]

His Establishing It Himself

There are many *ahaadeeth* concerning this, including the previously mentioned hadeeth of Aa`ishah concerning his praying in congregation for two nights.

Ahmad reports from Anas who said,

كَانَ النَّبِيُّ صَلَّى اللَّهُ عَلَيْهِ وَسَلَّمَ يُصَلِّي فِي رَمَضَانَ فَجِئْتُ
فَقُمْتُ خَلْفَهُ قَالَ وَجَاءَ رَجُلٌ فَقَامَ إِلَى جَنْبِي ثُمَّ جَاءَ آخَرُ
حَتَّى كُنَّا رَهْطاً فَلَمَّا أَحَسَّ رَسُولُ اللَّهِ صَلَّى اللَّهُ عَلَيْهِ وَسَلَّمَ
أَنَّا خَلْفَهُ تَجَوَّزَ فِي الصَّلَاةِ ثُمَّ قَامَ فَدَخَلَ مَنْزِلَهُ فَصَلَّى صَلَاةً
لَمْ يُصَلِّهَا عِنْدَنَا قَالَ فَلَمَّا أَصْبَحْنَا قَالَ قُلْنَا يَا رَسُولَ اللَّهِ

---

[1] *Sunan al-Kubraa* (2/495) and al-Bayhaqee said that it was *mursal saheeh*.

$$\text{أَفَطِنْتَ بِنَا اللَّيْلَةَ قَالَ نَعَمْ فَذَاكَ الَّذِي حَمَلَنِي عَلَى الَّذِي}$$

$$\text{صَنَعْتُ}$$

The Messenger of Allah (peace be upon him) prayed in Ramadaan and I came and stood behind him. Then another person came and then another until we were a group. When the Messenger of Allah (peace be upon him) realized we were behind him, he shortened his prayer, stood and entered his house. When he went into his house, he prayed a prayer that he had not prayed with us. The next day we asked, 'O Messenger of Allah did you see us last night?' He replied, 'Yes and that was what led me to do what I did.'"[1]

Al-Haakim reports in *al-Mustadrak* from an-Nu`maan bin Basheer who said,

$$\text{قُمْنَا مَعَ رَسُولِ اللَّهِ صَلَّى اللَّهُ عَلَيْهِ وَسَلَّمَ فِي شَهْرِ رَمَضَانَ}$$

$$\text{لَيْلَةَ ثَلَاثٍ وَعِشْرِينَ إِلَى ثُلُثِ اللَّيْلِ الْأَوَّلِ ثُمَّ قُمْنَا مَعَهُ لَيْلَةَ}$$

$$\text{خَمْسٍ وَعِشْرِينَ إِلَى نِصْفِ اللَّيْلِ ثُمَّ قُمْنَا مَعَهُ لَيْلَةَ سَبْعٍ}$$

$$\text{وَعِشْرِينَ حَتَّى ظَنَنَّا أَنْ لَا نُدْرِكَ الْفَلَاحَ وَكَانُوا يُسَمُّونَهُ}$$

$$\text{السُّحُورَ}$$

"We stood in prayer with the Messenger of Allah (peace be upon him) on the night of the twenty-third of Ramadaan until the first third of the night. Then we stood in prayer with him on the twenty-fifth night until half the night had passed. Then we stood with him on the twenty-seventh night until we thought that we would miss the *falaah*. We used to call the *sahoor* (the pre-dawn meal), *falaah*."[2]

Al-Haakim said, "This hadeeth contains clear evidence that praying *Taraaweeh* in congregation in the mosque is

---

[1] *Musnad Ahmad* (3/99, 212, 291).
[2] *al-Mustadrak* (1/440), al-Haakim declared it *saheeh*.

sanctioned. Alee bin Abee Taalib encouraged Umar bin al-Khattaab to establish this sunnah until he did so."

His Explaining Its Excellence

Abu Dharr reported that

صُمْنَا مَعَ رَسُولِ اللَّهِ صَلَّى اللَّهُ عَلَيْهِ وَسَلَّمَ فَلَمْ يُصَلِّ بِنَا فِي السَّادِسَةِ وَقَامَ بِنَا فِي الْخَامِسَةِ حَتَّى ذَهَبَ شَطْرُ اللَّيْلِ فَقُلْنَا لَهُ يَا رَسُولَ اللَّهِ لَوْ نَفَّلْتَنَا بَقِيَّةَ لَيْلَتِنَا هَذِهِ فَقَالَ إِنَّهُ مَنْ قَامَ مَعَ الإِمَامِ حَتَّى يَنْصَرِفَ كُتِبَ لَهُ قِيَامُ لَيْلَةٍ ثُمَّ لَمْ يُصَلِّ بِنَا حَتَّى بَقِيَ ثَلاثٌ مِنْ الشَّهْرِ وَصَلَّى بِنَا فِي الثَّالِثَةِ وَدَعَا أَهْلَهُ وَنِسَاءَهُ فَقَامَ بِنَا حَتَّى تَخَوَّفْنَا الْفَلاحَ قُلْتُ لَهُ وَمَا الْفَلاحُ قَالَ السُّحُورُ

"We fasted but the Messenger of Allah (peace be upon him) did not pray with us on the twenty-fourth but prayed with us on the twenty-fifth until half of the night had passed. We asked, 'O Messenger of Allah what if you were to pray this optional prayer with us for the rest of the night?' He replied, 'Whoever prays with the Imaam until he leaves, it is as if he has prayed the whole night.' Then he did not pray with us until three days of the month remained, praying with us on the twenty-seventh, calling his family and wives, till we feared that we would miss the *falaah* (success)." I asked, 'What is *falaah*?' He replied, '*As-sahoor*.'[1]

Imaam ibn al-Arabee, may Allah have mercy upon him, said,

> Praying the night (in congregation) is a sunnah from the *sunan* of Islam. It was done by the Prophet (peace be upon him) and then he left it for fear that it would become obligatory upon

---

[1] At-Tirmidhee (4/28 with *Aaridah al-Ahwadhee*) and he said that it was *hasan saheeh*.

his nation. This was because at his time laws were being revealed and the obligations would be increased and decreased. When Umar was appointed as *khaleefah*, he renewed this sunnah and ordered that it be prayed in congregation as was done by the Prophet (peace be upon him) since the reason for which the Prophet (peace be upon him) left the congregation was no longer present. This can be seen in his [the Prophet's] saying,

$$\text{فَلَمْ يَمْنَعْنِي مِنْ الْخُرُوجِ إِلَيْكُمْ إِلاَّ أَنِّي خَشِيتُ أَنْ يُفْرَضَ عَلَيْكُمْ}$$

"Nothing prevented me from coming out and praying with you except that I feared that it would become obligatory upon you."[1]

The Reason the Prophet (peace be upon him) Did Not Continue to Perform the Prayer in Congregation

From the previous words of ibn Arabee, it becomes clear that the Prophet (peace be upon him) did not pray in congregation for the remainder of the month fearing that the night prayer during Ramadaan would become obligatory upon his nation, such that they would be unable to perform it, as occurs in the previously mentioned hadeeth of Aa'ishah. This fear was no longer present after his passing away due to Allah having completed and perfected the *Sharee'ah*. Or this was due to the fact that whatever he continuously did with the people in congregation used to become obligatory as mentioned. Aa'ishah said,

---

[1] Ibid.

إِنْ كَانَ رَسُولُ اللَّهِ صَلَّى اللَّهُ عَلَيْهِ وَسَلَّمَ لَيَدَعُ الْعَمَلَ وَهُوَ

يُحِبُّ أَنْ يَعْمَلَ بِهِ خَشْيَةَ أَنْ يَعْمَلَ بِهِ النَّاسُ فَيُفْرَضَ عَلَيْهِمْ

"The Prophet (peace be upon him) used to leave an action that
he loved to perform for fear that it might become obligatory
upon his nation."[1]

It is also possible that the reason be as al-Qaadee Abu
Bakr al-Baaqilaanee, may Allah have mercy upon him,
explained,

A possible reason behind this is that Allah
revealed to him that persisting in this prayer in
congregation would have made doing so
obligatory. Either obligatory simply because
Allah wished it, if one takes to the opinion that
the actions of Allah do not have to have a
wisdom behind them, or because He knew that
certain affairs and situations would arise
among the Muslims that would be better for
them than the obligation of this prayer upon
them. It is also possible that he feared that
someone of his nation after him would make it
obligatory upon the people if he continuously
performed it. All of these possibilities
disappeared after the death of the Messenger
of Allah (peace be upon him). So, if this were
the case, when the reason that prevented him
from praying in congregation disappeared, the
permissibility of praying the night prayer in
Ramadaan in congregation becomes
established. This hadeeth constitutes the basis
for permitting the praying of optional prayers
in Ramadaan in congregation.

---

[1] *Saheeh Muslim* [Eng. Trans. 1/348 no. 1548].

Performing *Salaatut Taraaweeh* Improperly

Some Imaams in various Muslim lands, may Allah guide them, have become accustomed to quickening the *Taraaweeh* prayer such that they leave off some of the pillars and recommended acts of the prayer. [For example, they are] not being calm and still in *ruku`* and *sujood* and they recite very fast, such that they merge letters and words into each other, praying twenty three *rak`ahs* in about twenty minutes. This is from the greatest ploys of Shaytaan for the believers. He makes the action of the actor void to the point that his prayer seems closer to being mere play then being an action of worship. It is a duty upon the one who is praying to establish the prayer—obligatory or optional—in the sanctioned manner both outwardly and inwardly: Outwardly by reciting the Qur`aan, standing, bowing and prostrating; inwardly by having *khushoo`*, presence of the heart, being calm and tranquil, sincere, and contemplating upon the meaning of the Qur`aan.

Innovations and Evil Actions Done During *Taraaweeh* Prayer

From the evil actions and innovations that are widespread in many of the Muslim lands is the saying of some of them when commencing *Salaatut Taraaweeh*, "All those who are present invoke *salaah* upon the chosen Prophet", or their announcing, "*Salaatul Qiyaam*, may Allah reward you." Similarly the practice of *tahleel* and *takbeer* between every two *taraaweehs* and invoking *salaah* upon the Prophet[1] and doing all of this in a loud voice, thereby causing commotion in the Houses of Allah, are all innovations and misguidance that is necessary for one to avoid.

The saying of some of the Imaams when there remains three *rak`ahs* of *Taraaweeh*, "*Witr* may Allah reward you" is an innovation. Similarly the saying of some of them in a loud voice, "Glory be to the Unique (*Waahid*), the One (*Ahad*), The Self-Sufficient (*as-Samad*)" and then praying a *rak`ah* of *witr*

---

[1] [It should be noted that there is nothing wrong with many of the matters mentioned above in and of themselves, however what is objected to is the institutionalisation of these matters. Allah knows best - Trans.]

is also an innovation. It is necessary to steer clear of these types of acts.

Reciting the Qur'aan With a Musical Voice and To Be Enraptured by It

The meaning of this is that the one elongates the letters and goes to extremes in pronouncing the *madd* [elongated vowel sounds] and lengthens the vowel points such that they begin to sound like additional letters.

Imaam Maalik said, "Recitation with a musical voice does not appeal to me. I do not like the Qur'aan to be recited in this way during Ramadaan or any other time because it resembles singing and causes one to laugh at the Qur'aan. It also causes one to say that 'I am a better reciter than such and such.' It has reached me that the slave-girls are taught to recite the Qur'aan in the same way that they are taught singing."

Abu Dharr said that he heard the Messenger of Allah (peace be upon him) fearing that his nation would take the Qur'aan as a tool for music and they would have leading them not the most learned of them but the one who would satisfy their (desires).

By this reading, they do not intend to understand the Quran's meanings, such as its commands and prohibitions, promises and threats, exhortation or deterrents, its parables or other such things for which the Qur'aan was revealed. Instead, all they wish is to gain pleasure and delight and hear melody and song, such as they gain from listening to actual songs. Allah, the Mighty and Magnificent, censured the Quraysh by saying,

$$ \text{وَمَا كَانَ صَلَاتُهُمْ عِنْدَ الْبَيْتِ إِلَّا مُكَاءً وَتَصْدِيَةً} $$

"Their prayer at the House was nothing but whistling and clapping their hands" [*al-Anfaal* (8):35].

Indeed, the Qur'aan has been revealed so that its verses be contemplated and understood. Allah said,

$$ \text{كِتَابٌ أَنْزَلْنَاهُ إِلَيْكَ مُبَارَكٌ لِيَدَّبَّرُوا عَايَاتِهِ} $$

"A Book which We have revealed, full of blessings that you may ponder over its verses" [*Saad* (38):29].

This fact alone prevents one from reading the Qur'aan in a musical voice that resembles singers because this is the opposite of *khushoo'* and fear.

Mimicking the Voices of and Blindly Following Some Reciters

Some people in this time have started to blindly follow some reciters and have expended great efforts in doing so, such that the sole intention of the person becomes to beautify his voice and attract and charm the people. Such a person organizes the loudspeakers such that his voice reverberates and echoes around the mosque in further attempts to charm the people. On top of this, the people seek out and come only to these mosques in which this is done and end up abandoning their own local mosque and praying with their neighbors and their locality.

Artificial Crying and Excessive Displays of Humility When the Qur'aan Is Recited

It is truly strange that it has become common in some mosques that the Imaam cries (artificially) and those behind him do so, such that it has come about that some of the followers start crying just upon hearing the voice of the Imaam even if they do not understand what he has said. All of this is merely Satan playing with the humans.

Going from Mosque to Mosque During Ramadaan

If the Muslims were to consider what they are missing by going from mosque to mosque, then any one of the following points would be sufficient in preventing them from doing so:

(1) Some people go to a mosque that is far away and lose a great deal of time in doing so. If they, instead, were to use this time in going to the mosque close to them in order to sit in the first row and wait for the prayer to start, the reward for doing this would be many times that which they sought in going to the far away mosque.

(2) Some of them are forced to go in cars via busy roads (in order to go to other mosques) and it is possible that something might occur, such as an accident, that would cause them to miss or be late for the prayer.

(3) By doing this, the people miss out on meeting with their neighbors and the congregation of their mosque.

(4) The gathering in the mosques could lead to an aspect of showing off and showing preference to the Imaam of that mosque, such that it enter his heart that all these people are coming to his mosque because of him. *Inna lillaaahi wa inna ilayhi raaji`oon.*

(5) [It demonstrates] a lack of concern for fulfilling the rights of the Imaam, the *Mu`adhdhin* and the congregation of one's local mosque.

Ibn al-Qayyim, may Allah have mercy upon him, said, while mentioning the evidences that prove that what leads to something prohibited in turn becomes prohibited even if in and of itself the act is permissible, "The fifty-fourth evidence: The Lawgiver has prohibited that a person disregard the mosque that is close to him and instead go to others. Baqiyyah bin al-Majaashi` bin Amr bin Ubaidullaah reports from Naafi` from ibn Umar that the Prophet (peace be upon him) said,

$$ \text{لِيُصَلِّ أَحَدُكُمْ فِي الْمَسْجِدِ الَّذِي يَلِيهِ وَلَا يَتَخَطَّاهُ إِلَى غَيْرِه} $$

'Let one of you pray in the mosque that is close to him and not disregard it and go to another.'"[1]

Ibn al-Qayyim continues in *Ilaam* by saying, "The reason behind this is that doing so is a cause for abandonment of the mosque that is close to him and abandoning the Imaam. As for the case where the Imaam does not perform the prayer correctly or he is accused of innovation or openly shows disobedience, there is no harm in going to another mosque."[2]

---

[1] *I`laam al-Muwaqqi`een* (3/160) and this is the wording of the hadeeth contained therein. In *Faydh al-Qadeer* (5/392 no. 7707) of al-Munaawee, the wording is, "Let the person pray in the mosque that is close to him and not go from mosque to mosque." Refer to Muhammad Naasir al-Deen al-Albaani, *Silsilat al-Ahaadeeth al-Saheebab*, no. 2200. – Trans]

[2] *I`laam al-Muwaqqi`een `an Rabbil `Aalameen* (3/160).

Ibn al-Qayyim also wrote in *Badaai al-Fawaaid*, "On the authority of Muhammad bin Bahr who said, 'I saw Abu Abdullaah—meaning Ahmad bin Hanbal—in the month of Ramadaan while Fadl bin Ziyaad al-Qattaan came and prayed *Taraaweeh* with Abu Abdullaah and he used to have a beautiful recitation. So the scholars and some people in the area gathered together until the mosque was full. Abu Abdullaah left and went up one floor of the mosque, looked at the gathering and said, 'What is this? You leave your mosques and go to another?' He prayed with them for some nights and then stopped doing so due to his dislike of what had happened.' Meaning the vacating of the other mosques and that it is upon the one neighboring a mosque to pray in his mosque."[1]

I say: The reason for all of this happening is people being distant from correct knowledge, lack of understanding of the religion, blind following that is devoid of any thought and lack of concern as to what the Salaf of this nation and their Imaams were upon. Furthermore, the prohibition of going from mosque to mosque is textually stated in the hadeeth and has been voiced by many scholars, from the earliest of them Imaam Ahmad bin Hanbal, may Allah have mercy upon him. It is not known from any of the people of knowledge that they were of the opinion that it was virtuous to go from mosque to mosque and to find an Imaam that has a beautiful recitation. The very least that can be said is that such going from mosque to mosque is permissible but it goes against what has been stated here and such a practice has not been narrated from any of the early scholars. This is not even to mention the fact that praying behind an Imaam with a beautiful voice is not a goal of the Shareeah; it is something that occurs secondarily. And Allah knows best.

Al-Haafidh ibn Katheer said, rejecting what some people did in putting others to trial through their voices and the neglect of looking to the true purposes of the *Sharee`ah*, "The purpose here is to point out that the legislated objective is to beautify one's voice in a way that would inculcate contemplating the Qur'aan, understanding it, having *khushoo`*, submission, humility and obedience. As for these newly

---

[1] *Badaa`i al-Fawaa`id* (4/149).

invented musical tones consisting of scales and entertaining rules, the Qur'aan is free of them and is far greater and deserves far more respect than to recite it in accordance to this way."[1]

"I advise every Muslim who recites the Book of Allah, the Exalted, especially the Imaams of the mosques, to refrain from mimicking and blind following when it comes to reciting the Book of the Lord of the Universe. The Speech of Allah is too great and deserves far too much respect for the reciter to bring about something that is not sought by the *Sharee'ah,* by beautifying his voice over and above his natural ability through this mimicking and blind following, rather than beautifying his voice according to his natural ability. He should refrain from blind following as much as is possible for Allah, the Exalted said about His Prophet (peace be upon him),

وَمَا أَنَا مِنَ الْمُتَكَلِّفِينَ

'Nor am I one of those who pretend' [*Saad* (38):86].

Let the servant exert himself in having presence of heart and a good intention and let him recite the Qur'aan in a nice voice without going to extremes. Let him avoid going to these extremes involving musical tones and reciting obscurely. It is desired for the one to whom Allah has given authority to choose the most knowledgeable and pious Imaam, the one who has sound belief and is secure from the disease of doubts and following desires and give precedence to a naturally beautiful voice rather than an artificial one.

Al-Haafidh ibn Hajr, may Allah have mercy upon him said, 'As for beautifying one's voice and giving the person with a nice voice precedence, there is no difference concerning this.'[2]"[3]

---

[1] *Fadaa'il al-Qur'aan* (pp. 125-126).
[2] *Fath al-Baaree* (9/72).
[3] *Bida'ul Qurraa al-Qadeemah wal Mu'aasirah* (pp. 55-56) by Shaykh Bakr Abu Zayd.

Saying the Supplication for Completing the Qur`aan Within the Prayer

Some of the Imaams go to great lengths in doing this, they write supplications with specific musical notes, going to extremes in crying and changing their voice to one that was different from the one they used in their recitation of the Qur`aan, for example—a Book which if it had been revealed on a mountain one would have seen the mountain humble itself and cleave asunder for fear of Allah. Furthermore, supplicating for finishing the Qur`aan within the prayer is not supported from authentic *ahaadeeth* nor was it done by the Rightly Guided *Khaleefs*. Those who do this do so based upon the action of the Salaf of saying this supplication upon completing the Qur`aan outside of the prayer and based upon the general texts pertaining to supplication.

The likes of such texts are not sufficient to prove the validity of saying these supplications within the prayer, not to mention being used as the support of these supplications that these Imaams go to extremes in composing. They make the supplications very long and boring. They compose rhyming, extravagant supplications. If only they said a succinct supplication within the prayer when they finish the Qur`aan and they depended upon the action of the Salaf outside of the prayer, this would be much easier upon the people. However, it is best not to say this supplication within the prayer and instead to adhere to what the Salaf of this nation were upon and those who followed them in good. Peace and blessings be upon Muhammad and his Companions.

Waiting for a Congregational Prayer Is Better Than Praying Individually at the Onset of the Time For That Prayer

The Muslims are unanimously agreed that the five daily prayers are set according to the well known times that have been generally mentioned in the Qur'aan and specified in detail by the Sunnah. The Jurists are agreed that the best time to pray the prayer is at the beginning of the time for each prayer. However, some of them recommended that the individual delay the prayer in hopes of attaining the congregational prayer, in order for him to gain its excellence.[1]

Al-Bukhaaree reports from Muhammad bin Amr bin al-Hasan bin Alee that, "The pilgrims went to Madeenah and we asked Jaabir bin Abdullaah about the times of the prayers and he replied,

كَانَ يُصَلِّي الظُّهْرَ بِالْهَاجِرَةِ وَالْعَصْرَ وَالشَّمْسُ حَيَّةٌ وَالْمَغْرِبَ إِذَا وَجَبَتْ وَالْعِشَاءَ إِذَا كَثُرَ النَّاسُ عَجَّلَ وَإِذَا قَلُّوا أَخَّرَ وَالصُّبْحَ بِغَلَسٍ

'The Prophet (peace be upon him) used to pray *Dhuhur* at midday, *Asr* when the sun was still hot, *Maghrib* (after the sun had set) as it has been obligated. *Ishaa* was offered early if a lot of people had gathered but late if only a few had gathered. *Fajr* was offered when it was still dark and the dawn was about to break.'"[2]

---

[1] Refer to *Qawaaneen al-Fiqhhiyyah* (p. 43) by ibn al-Juzzayy al-Maalikee and *ash-Sharh as-Sagheer* (1/127) by ad-Dardeer.
[2] *Saheeh al-Bukhaaree* [Eng. Trans. 1/315 no. 540].

Ibn Daqeeq al-Eid, may Allah have mercy upon him, said, "When a person is presented with two options, one of them being to pray individually at the beginning of the time and the other being to delay praying so that he may pray with the congregation, which is better? The most correct opinion in my view is that delaying until one prays in congregation is better and the hadeeth mentioned here proves this due to his saying,

وَإِذَا رَآهُمْ أَبْطَوْا أَخَّرَ

'And when he saw them slow in coming he delayed.' Therefore he delayed praying in congregation despite having ability to pray early. [The congregation is more important] also because of the severe threat of leaving the congregational prayer and the encouragement towards performing it being clearly stated in the authentic *ahaadeeth*. The virtue of praying the prayer early is mentioned in the texts in order to encourage performing it but there is no threat mentioned if one were to delay it as there is mentioned for missing the congregational prayer. All that has been mentioned is proof for waiting for the congregational prayer rather than praying individually at the earlier time."[1]

"Meaning that praying in congregation, even if it be at the end of the time for that prayer, is better than praying it individually at the beginning of its time."[2] This does not contradict what al-Bukhaaree and Muslim report with regards the excellence of praying at the beginning of its time, it being among the best of deeds and it being beloved to Allah.

The Texts That Occur with Respect to This Issue

Ibn Mas'ud said,

---

[1] *Ihkaam al-Ahkaam* (1/134) byf ibn Daqeeq al-Eid.
[2] *al-Uddah* (2/32-33) by as-Sana'aanee and *al-Mabsoot* (1/148) by as-Sarkhasee al-Hanafee.

سَأَلْتُ النَّبِيَّ صَلَّى اللَّهُ عَلَيْهِ وَسَلَّمَ أَيُّ الْعَمَلِ أَحَبُّ إِلَى اللَّهِ
قَالَ الصَّلَاةُ عَلَى وَقْتِهَا قَالَ ثُمَّ أَيٌّ قَالَ ثُمَّ بِرُّ الْوَالِدَيْنِ قَالَ ثُمَّ
أَيٌّ قَالَ الْجِهَادُ فِي سَبِيلِ اللَّهِ قَالَ حَدَّثَنِي بِهِنَّ وَلَوْ اسْتَزَدْتُهُ
لَزَادَنِي

"I asked the Prophet (peace be upon him), 'Which action is most beloved to Allah?' He replied, 'Performing the prayer at its time (`alaa waqtihaa).' I asked, 'Then which one?' He replied, 'Good treatment to parents.' I asked, 'Then which one?' He replied, 'Jihaad in the Way of Allah.' The Messenger of Allah told me these and if I had asked further he would have replied further."[1]

There is nothing in this hadeeth that would make one understand that praying at the beginning of the time is better than praying at the end and there is nothing in this hadeeth that would dictate the need of praying at the beginning or end of the time. This is because his saying "at its time" means praying at any time that falls within its time.[2] Similarly, the recommendation for delaying for the purpose of praying in congregation is not contradicted by his saying, "Prayer at its time *(li waqtihaa)"* for there is no strong indication here mentioning the beginning period of the prayer.[3]

Al-Haakim, ibn Khuzaimah and others record the hadith of ibn Mas`ud in which the Prophet (peace be upon him) was asked, "What action is best?" and he replied,

الصَّلَاةُ لِأَوَّلِ وَقْتِهَا

"Prayer at the beginning of its time."[4] But this hadeeth is from the report of Alee bin Abu Hafsah al-Midaanee about whom ad-Daaruqutnee said, "I do not think that he preserved this properly because he grew old and his memory failed

---

[1] *Saheeh al-Bukhaaree* [Eng. Trans. 4/35 no. 41].
[2] *al-Uddah Haashiyah al-Ihkaam al-Ahkaam* (2/134).
[3] *Ihkaam al-Ahkaam* (1/134-136).
[4] al-Haakim (1/188) and ibn Khuzaymah (1/169 no. 327).

him."[1] In *al-Majmoo Sharh al-Muhadhab*, an-Nawawee said that this narration was weak.[2]

Abu Daawood, at-Tirmidhee and al-Haakim, who said it was *saheeh*, report from the hadeeth of Umm Farwah that the Prophet (peace be upon him) said,

$$ أَفْضَلُ الأَعْمَالِ الصَّلاةُ لِأَوَّلِ وَقْتِهَا $$

"The best of actions is the prayer prayed at the beginning of its time." The chain to this hadeeth contains an unknown narrator.[3]

Therefore, these *ahaadeeth* do not lend evidence to it being better to pray individually at the beginning of the time for prayer rather than delaying for the purpose of praying in congregation. Such was also concluded by an-Nawawee.[4]

What is Exempted From the Virtue of the Beginning Time

The following cases are exempted from the general rule of trying to pray a prayer early in its time: The one who needs to go to the toilet, when the food has been served and one craves it, the one who has performed *tayammum* and is certain that he will come across water later, the one who is ill and is not capable of standing at the beginning period but he is sure that he will be able to stand later on, the one who is alone and knows that the congregation will be held later on and so on.

The above opinion is further supported by what al-Bukhaaree recorded from Abu Musaa al-Ash'aree that the Prophet (peace be upon him) said,

---

[1] *al-Uddah* (2/10).

[2] *al-Majmoo' Sharh al-Muhadhdhab* (3/53). [It is true that al-Nawawi and others have declared this hadith weak. At the same time, others, such as al-Albaani and Abdul Qaadir al-Arnaaoot, have raised it to the level of *hasan*. Allah knows best. See, for exampe, Muhammad Naasir al-Deen al-Albaani, *Saheeh al-Targheeb wa al-Tarbeeb* (Riyadh: Maktabah al-Maarif, 1988), vol. 1, p. 231.]

[3] *at-Ta'leeq al-Mughnee 'alaa Sunan ad-Daaruqutnee* (1/247).

[4] *al-Majmoo'* (3/60-61). [The point here is that these ahaadeeth do not prove that praying the prayer early takes precedence over praying it in a congregation. However, the general recommendation to pray at the beginning of the time remains. – Trans.]

أَعْظَمُ النَّاسِ أَجْرًا فِي الصَّلاةِ أَبْعَدُهُمْ مَمْشًى وَالَّذِي يَنْتَظِرُ
الصَّلاةَ حَتَّى يُصَلِّيَهَا مَعَ الإِمَامِ – زاد مسلم: فِي جَمَاعَةٍ –
أَعْظَمُ أَجْرًا مِنْ الَّذِي يُصَلِّي ثُمَّ يَنَامُ

"The people with the greatest reward are those who have the farthest to walk [to the mosque] and the one who waits for the prayer until he prays it with the Imaam"—Muslim adds in his report "in congregation," [al-Bukhaaree continues,]—"he has greater reward than the one who prays and then goes to sleep."[1]

---

[1] *Saheeh al-Bukhaaree* [Eng. Trans. 1/353 no. 623].

The Time When the People Stand for the Congregational Prayer

There are three issues linked to this:
The time that the followers stand for congregational prayer;
The sanctioned time gap between the *adhaan* and *iqaamah;*
The errors that some people who pray fall into with regards to this.

The Time When the Followers Stand for Congregational Prayer

The Jurists fall into four opinions as to when it is recommended for the followers to stand for prayer. I shall summarize them here:

The First Opinion: The Hanafee scholars are of the opinion that the followers stand when the statement "*hayya alaa al-falaah* (rush to success)" is said in the *iqaamah* after the Imaam has stood.

The Second Opinion: "The Maalikee scholars are of the opinion that this is based upon the ability of the people. They can stand during the *iqaamah,* or at its beginning or at its end due to their being nothing textually reported concerning this save what is reported from Abu Qataadah that the Messenger of Allah (peace be upon him) said,

إِذَا أُقِيمَتْ الصَّلاَةُ فَلا تَقُومُوا حَتَّى تَرَوْنِي

'When the *iqaamah* for prayer has been said do not stand until you see me.'"[1]

---

[1] *Saheeh ibn Khuzaymah* (3/14). [Actually, this hadith is recorded by al-Bukhari, among others, as the author shall point out shortly. It is not clear why, in the author's footnote here, only ibn Khuzaymah is mentioned.—JZ]

Ibn Rushd al-Maalikee said, "If this hadeeth is authentic,[1] then it obligates acting by it. If not, then this issue remains as it is, meaning that the person is free to stand when he wishes."[2]

The Third Opinion: The Shaafi`ee scholars are of the opinion that everyone stands when the one calling the *iqaamah* has finished and the Imaam is present in the mosque with the congregation.[3]

The Fourth Opinion: The Hanbalee scholars are of the opinion that it is preferred to stand when the *Mu`adhdhin* says, "*qad qaamatis salaah*" (the prayer has been established). The use of the term *Mu`adhdhin* herein referring to the one saying the *iqaamah* is in accordance to the terminology that they use.[4]

The Strongest Opinion

I say that the strongest opinion is the fourth opinion, as the most appropriate time to stand is in response to the statement, "*qad qaamatis Salaah*" (the prayer has been established). If one takes the opinion of the Shaafi`ees, their reasoning is that standing is a pillar of the prayer and the first pillar to be enacted to commence the prayer [hence, there is no need to stand until one starts the prayer, that is, after the *iqaamah* has been completed].

The Allowed Gap Between the *Adhaan* and the *Iqaamah*

The Jurists have made it clear that it is recommended to pray (two *rak`ahs*) or sit between the *adhaan* and *iqaamah* or wait some time to allow the congregation to gather while keeping in mind the recommended time to pray. *Maghrib* prayer is an exception to the above. This is due to what is reported from the Messenger of Allah (peace be upon him), that he said to Bilaal,

---

[1] I say: It is authentic for it has been reported by al-Bukhaaree [Eng. Trans. 1/348 no. 610].
[2] *Bidaayatul Mujtahid wa Nihaayatul Muqtasid* (1/145).
[3] *al-Majmoo`* (3/237).
[4] *al-Insaaf* (2/38-29).

اجْعَلْ بَيْنَ أَذَانِكَ وَإِقَامَتِكَ نَفَسًا حَتَّى يَقْضِيَ الْمُتَوَضِّئُ

حَاجَتَهُ فِي مَهَلٍ وَحَتَّى يَفْرُغَ الآكِلُ مِنْ طَعَامِهِ فِي مَهَلٍ

"Make a gap between your saying the *adhaan* and the *iqaamah* such that the one making *wudu`* has time to relieve himself with ease and the one who is eating can finish eating with ease."[1] ...

Errors That Must Be Pointed Out

I have noticed in some of the mosques and on the part of some of the worshippers certain mistakes that I would like to note such that they may be avoided. These include the following:

Sometimes, some of those who pray stand before the *iqaamah* has started, or they stand as soon as it has started, and some delay standing until the Imaam has started the prayer and some of them hurry the Imaam by making him direct the *Mu`adhdhin* to start saying the *iqaamah* if the Imaam is in the mosque.

Some of them look left and right so that they can see when the Imaam enters and as soon as they see him, they stand, even before the *iqaamah* has commenced. Sometimes they stand and put the *Mu`adhdhin* into a difficult situation by making him give the *iqaamah* even before the regular or appointed Imaam has entered the mosque.

I have witnessed in some Muslim lands the *Mu`adhdhin* calling the *adhaan* outside the mosque while all the congregation was inside the mosque standing and waiting for the prayer. As soon as the *Mu`adhdhin* finished the *adhaan*, they immediately made someone else inside the mosque say the *iqaamah*.

---

[1] Reported by at-Tirmidhee (no. 195). Its chain is weak and al-Haafidh declared the hadeeth weak in *Fath* (2/106). He also explained that the hadeeth has supporting evidence but they are extremely weak and therefore the hadeeth cannot be raised to a level whereby it can be depended upon. Al-Haythamee mentions it in *Majma` az-Zawaa`id* (2/4) and declares it defective due to having a broken chain.

All of these are errors to be avoided and it is upon the followers to know the opinions of the Jurists that have preceded so that they know when they should stand for the prayer.

Repeating the Congregational Prayer in the Same Mosque

Repeating the congregational prayer in the same mosque falls into one of six cases:

Case One: The prayer is repeated in a mosque in which there is no appointed Imaam. In this situation, repetition is permissible.

Case Two: The prayer is repeated in a mosque in which there is an appointed Imaam but the mosque is too small for the congregation. This is also permissible.

Case Three: The prayer is repeated, being led by an Imaam who is not the appointed Imaam, after the appointed Imaam has led his congregation. The scholars fall into three opinions concerning this:
The First Opinion: This is unrestrictedly disallowed. Therefore, it is not permissible to repeat the prayer in congregation in a mosque that has an appointed Imaam and is not along a general roadway. This is so the people will not avoid attending the congregational prayer of the appointed Imaam. This is the opinion of a number of the People of Knowledge, among them: Sufyaan ath-Thawree, ibn al-Mubaarak and ash-Shaafi`ee. It is the Hanafee position and the position textually reported from Imaam Maalik; it is the position reported from a group of the Salaf and from Imaam Ahmad. [1]
The Second Opinion: If each congregational prayer is completely independent and separate from the other, then this is unrestrictedly permissible. The evidence for this lies in the hadeeth of Abu Sa`eed:

---

[1] Refer to *al-Mabsoot* (5/135) by as-Sarkhasee (al-Hanafee), *al-Mudawwanah al-Kubraa* (1/89), and *al-Furoo`* (1/583) by ibn Muflih.

أَنَّ رَجُلاً دَخَلَ الْمَسْجِدَ وَقَدْ صَلَّى رَسُولُ اللَّهِ صَلَّى اللَّهُ عَلَيْهِ
وَسَلَّمَ بِأَصْحَابِهِ فَقَالَ رَسُولُ اللَّهِ صَلَّى اللَّهُ عَلَيْهِ وَسَلَّمَ مَنْ
يَتَصَدَّقُ عَلَى هَذَا فَيُصَلِّيَ مَعَهُ فَقَامَ رَجُلٌ مِنْ الْقَوْمِ فَصَلَّى مَعَهُ

"A man entered the mosque and the Messenger of Allah (peace
be upon him) had just finished praying with his Companions,
so the Messenger of Allah (peace be upon him) said, 'Who
will give charity to this person and pray with him?' A man
stood up and prayed with him."[1]

 This is the opinion of more than one of the People of
Knowledge from the Companions of the Prophet (peace be
upon him) and the Followers. They say, "There is no harm in a
group of people praying in congregation in a mosque in which
a congregation has already been held." This is the opinion of
Ahmad, Ishaaq[2] and some of the Shaafi`ee scholars; it is the
chosen opinion of the Dhaahiree school of thought.[3]

 The Third Opinion: This opinion distinguishes
between different cases by saying: It is not disliked to repeat
the congregational prayer led by an Imaam who has not been
appointed after the appointed Imaam has finished leading his
congregation except in the three Mosques—Mecca, Madeenah
and al-Aqsa. It is disliked to repeat the congregational prayer
in these mosques in order to inculcate the desire to join and
increase the congregation.[4]

 The Correct Opinion: The correct opinion is the
second opinion that unrestrictedly allows repetition without
taking into consideration what mosque it is. This conclusion is
based on the generality of the Prophet's (peace be upon him)
saying to the one who missed the congregation, "Who will
give charity to this person and pray with him?" It is clear that
this occurred in his mosque and, furthermore, the meaning of
the hadeeth dictates this unrestricted permission because the

[1] Abu Daawood [Eng. Trans. 1/151 no. 574], at-Tirmidhee (2/21 - *Aaridah al-Ahwadhee*), Ahmad (3/5, 64, 85, 5/254, 269).
[2] Refer to *al-Muntaqaa min Akhbaar al-Mustafaa* by Majd ad-Deen Abu Barakaat ibn Taymiyyah (1/614 no. 1395).
[3] *al-Muhallab* (4/236) by ibn Hazm.
[4] *al-Insaaf* (2/219-220).

excellence and reward of the congregation is achieved in his mosque as in all other mosques. Allah knows best.

Case Four: The congregational prayer is repeated in the same mosque at the same time. This is disliked due to the confusion and turmoil it will cause.

Case Five: The congregational prayer is repeated in a mosque that has been built in a market or a place which many people go by [such as a motorway]. In this case it is not disliked to repeat the congregational prayer because a mosque of that nature is not considered to have a set congregation due to the multitude of people that pass by it. Therefore, the forbidden aspect related to another congregation does not exist there—this being the congregation neglecting to pray behind an appointed Imaam.[1]

Case Six: The same Imaam prays the same prayer twice, leading two different congregations. This is forbidden, even if he were to intend the second time to pray a missed prayer and the first time to pray the obligatory. The Imaams are agreed that this is a despicable innovation.[2]

---

[1] Refer to *Iqaamah al-Hujjah alaa al-Musallee Jamaa'atan qabla al-Imaam ar-Raatib* (p. 33) by Jamaal ad-Deen al-Qaasimee, *Haashiyah ibn Aabideen* (1/553) and *al-Insaaf* (2/219-220).
[2] *al-Fiqh al-Islamee wa Adillatuhu* (2/163-166) by Wahbah az-Zuhaylee.

Repeating a Prayer in Congregation

The Linguistic Meaning of *al-I`aadah*

Al-I`aadah means to return something to its original state or to perform something a second time.

The Sharee`ah Meaning of *al-I`aadah*

According to the Shaafi`ees, it means: What is done (again) within the time of performance due to a deficiency found the first time.

According to the Hanafees, as ibn Aabideen said, it means: Performing the likes of the obligation in the time of that obligation due to a deficiency found in it (when performed the first time) that, however, did not invalidate the action.

According to the Hanbalees it means: To perform something a second time.

According to the Maalikees it means: To perform the act of worship in its time after having already performed it, due to leaving out a portion, such as a pillar, or due to a deficiency in completion and perfection, such as the one who prays alone (and not in congregation).

The Best Definition: Performing the likes of the obligation again in the time of that obligation due to a valid excuse.[1]

---

[1] *al-Mawsoo`ah al-Fiqhhiyyah al-Kuwaytiyyah* (5/177f).

The Reason for Repeating a Congregational Prayer

It is possible to repeat the prayer due to something opposing the *Sharee`ah* that has occurred in the prayer or due to the realization of an overriding benefit.

The Different Scenarios for Repeating the Congregational Prayer

(1) The one who has already prayed finds a congregation and then repeats the prayer. There are two possible cases: (a) He has previously prayed alone, then he finds a congregation and prays the same prayer again. (b) He has previously prayed in congregation, finds another congregation and prays the same prayer again.

(2) The follower repeats the prayer because he had stood in the wrong place with respect to the row.

(3) Someone repeating the prayer due to having prayed behind a sinning Imaam, either with respect to his actions or his beliefs.

(4) The reciter of the Qur`aan repeating the prayer due to his having prayed behind an illiterate Imaam (who cannot recite correctly).

(5) Someone repeating the prayer because he prayed an obligatory prayer behind one who has prayed an optional prayer.

What follows is a detailed analysis of these different cases.

1. The Person Who Has Prayed Alone Finding a Congregation and Praying Again

It is possible to miss the congregational prayer due to many reasons, such that the person is left having to pray alone, or it is possible that a person has prayed in congregation and then finds another congregation praying the same prayer. In these cases, is it legitimate for him to repeat the prayer or not?

We say there are two possible cases:

a) A Person Prays Alone and Then Finds a Congregation

It is recommended for such a person to repeat the prayer with the congregation. There is no difference of opinion over this. The proof for this lies with the command of the Prophet (peace be upon him) to pray in congregation even for the one who has already prayed. Jaabir bin Yazeed al-Aswad reports from his father that he said,

شَهِدْتُ مَعَ النَّبِيِّ صَلَّى اللَّهُ عَلَيْهِ وَسَلَّمَ حَجَّتَهُ فَصَلَّيْتُ مَعَهُ

صَلاةَ الصُّبْحِ فِي مَسْجِدِ الْخَيْفِ وَأَنَا غُلامٌ شَابٌّ فَلَمَّا قَضَى

صَلاتَهُ وَانْحَرَفَ إِذَا هُوَ بِرَجُلَيْنِ لَمْ يُصَلِّيَا مَعَهُ فَقَالَ عَلَيَّ

بِهِمَا فَجِيءَ بِهِمَا تُرْعَدُ فَرَائِصُهُمَا فَقَالَ مَا مَنَعَكُمَا أَنْ تُصَلِّيَا

مَعَنَا فَقَالا يَا رَسُولَ اللَّهِ إِنَّا كُنَّا قَدْ صَلَّيْنَا فِي رِحَالِنَا قَالَ لا

تَفْعَلا إِذَا صَلَّيْتُمَا فِي رِحَالِكُمَا ثُمَّ أَتَيْتُمَا مَسْجِدَ جَمَاعَةٍ

فَصَلِّيَا مَعَهُمْ فَإِنَّهَا لَكُمَا نَافِلَةٌ

"I accompanied the Prophet (peace be upon him) on his Hajj and I prayed *Fajr* with him in the Mosque of Khayf. At that time I was a young man. When he had finished the prayer, he saw two people who had not prayed with him. He said, 'Bring them to me.' So they were summoned and came apprehensively. He asked them, 'What prevented you from praying with us?' They replied, 'O Messenger of Allah we have already prayed in our houses.' He said, 'Do not do this again. If you have prayed in your houses and then come to a congregation in a mosque, pray with them, for it will be counted as an optional prayer for you.'"[1]

However, the Jurists have differed as to which of the prayers can be repeated, dividing into a number of opinions:

---

[1] *Sunan at-Tirmidhee* (2/18 - *Aaridah al-Ahwadhee*), *Sunan Abu Daawood* (Eng. Trans. 1/151 no. 575) and *Mustadrak al-Haakim* (1/244).

First Opinion: Any prayer can be repeated. This is the chosen opinion of the Shaafi`ee school and a reported opinion from the Hanbalee and Maalikee schools.

Second Opinion: Every prayer can be repeated except for *Maghrib*. This is the chosen opinion of the Maalikee and Hanbalee schools and a reported position of the Shaafi`ee school.

Third Opinion: The *Dhuhur* and *Ishaa* prayers can be repeated but not the others. This is the chosen opinion of the Hanafee school.[1]

The Proofs for the First Opinion: It is established from the Prophet (peace be upon him) that he said to Abu Dharr, when he informed him of the rulers who will delay the prayers beyond their times,

صَلِّ الصَّلاةَ لِوَقْتِهَا فَإِنْ أَدْرَكَتْكَ الصَّلاةُ مَعَهُمْ فَصَلِّ وَلَا تَقُلْ
إِنِّي قَدْ صَلَّيْتُ فَلَا أُصَلِّي

"Pray the prayer in its time. If you then happen to come across the prayer with them, pray and do not say, 'I have already prayed and so I will not pray again.'"[2]

They also use the following previously mentioned hadeeth as evidence:

إِذَا صَلَّيْتُمَا فِي رِحَالِكُمَا ثُمَّ أَتَيْتُمَا مَسْجِدَ جَمَاعَةٍ فَصَلِّيَا
مَعَهُمْ فَإِنَّهَا لَكُمَا نَافِلَةٌ

"If you have prayed in your houses and then come to a congregation in a mosque, pray with them, for it will be counted as an optional prayer for you."

There is also the saying of the Prophet (peace be upon him) to Yazeed bin Aamir al-Ansaaree,

---

[1] Refer to *al-Kaafee* (1/218) by ibn Abdul Barr, *al-Majmoo`* (3/223), *al-Mughnee* (2/11) and *al-Mabsoot* (1/152).
[2] *Saheeh Muslim* [Eng. Trans. 1/313 no. 1357].

فَمَا مَنَعَكَ أَنْ تَدْخُلَ مَعَ النَّاسِ فِي صَلَاتِهِمْ قَالَ إِنِّي كُنْتُ قَدْ
صَلَّيْتُ فِي مَنْزِلِي وَأَنَا أَحْسَبُ أَنْ قَدْ صَلَّيْتُمْ فَقَالَ إِذَا جِئْتَ
إِلَى الصَّلَاةِ فَوَجَدْتَ النَّاسَ فَصَلِّ مَعَهُمْ وَإِنْ كُنْتَ قَدْ صَلَّيْتَ
تَكُنْ لَكَ نَافِلَةً وَهَذِهِ مَكْتُوبَةٌ

"What prevented you from praying with the people?" He replied, "I have prayed in my house believing that you had already prayed." So he said, "When you come for prayer and find the people praying, pray with them, even if you have already prayed. It will count as an optional prayer for you and this will be counted as the obligatory prayer."[1]

They also quote the hadeeth in which Abu Mahjan bin Abu Majan ad-Du'lee was sitting with the Prophet (peace be upon him) and the *adhaan* was called. The Messenger of Allah (peace be upon him) stood and prayed and then returned to find Mahjan still sitting in his place. The Messenger of Allah (peace be upon him) said,

مَا مَنَعَكَ أَنْ تُصَلِّيَ مَعَ النَّاسِ أَلَسْتَ بِرَجُلٍ مُسْلِمٍ فَقَالَ بَلَى يَا
رَسُولَ اللَّهِ وَلَكِنِّي قَدْ صَلَّيْتُ فِي أَهْلِي فَقَالَ لَهُ رَسُولُ اللَّهِ
صَلَّى اللَّهُ عَلَيْهِ وَسَلَّمَ إِذَا جِئْتَ فَصَلِّ مَعَ النَّاسِ وَإِنْ كُنْتَ قَدْ
صَلَّيْتَ

"What prevented you from praying with the people? Are you not a Muslim?" He replied, "Of course, O Messenger of Allah, but I have already prayed with my family." He said, "When

---

[1] *Sunan Abu Daawood* [Eng. Trans 1/152 no. 577]. [Meaning that the second prayer will be the optional one and the first will be counted as the obligatory as mentioned in *Awn al-Ma`bood* – Trans] [Most scholars, including al-Nawawi and al-Albaani, consider this particular narration from Abu Dawood to be weak.—JZ]

you come (to the mosque), pray with the people even if you have already prayed."[1]

The general sense of these *ahaadeeth* prove the legitimacy of repeating a prayer by the one who has already prayed and they do not differentiate between one prayer and another. Hence they prove the permissibility of repeating all of the prayers for the one who first prayed them individually.

The Proofs for the Second Opinion: The proponents of the second opinion also base their view on the previous *ahaadeeth* to prove that all of the prayers can be repeated, but they make *Maghrib* an exception. They argue that if it were to be repeated, the number of *rak`ahs* would end up being even. The *Maghrib* prayer has only been legislated with three *rak`ahs* in order to make the total number of *rak`ahs* (of obligatory prayer) prayed during the day and night both odd. Also, repeating the *Maghrib* prayer would mean that one has prayed three *rak`ahs* of optional prayer and this has no basis in the *Sharee`ah*. Therefore the Maghrib prayer is not to be repeated.[2]

The Proofs for the Third Opinion: The proponents of this view also rely on the previously mentioned proofs but they make *Fajr* and *Asr* an exception. They say that praying optional prayers after *Fajr* and *Asr* is not allowed due to the periods following these prayers being the times in which it is not allowed to pray optional prayers. Also, they say that Maghrib should not be repeated, giving the same reasoning as has preceded.[3]

The Strongest Opinion: The strongest opinion is the first opinion due to the generality of the *ahaadeeth* concerning this matter and due to the absence of any proofs that would specify that these *ahaadeeth* refer to some prayers and not others.

---

[1] Abu Daawood (1/386), Maalik [Eng. Trans. Pg. 61 no. 290], an-Nasaa'ee (2/112), Ahmad (4/34), al-Haakim (1/244) and it is a *saheeb* hadeeth.
[2] Refer to *al-Kaafee* (1/218) by ibn Abdul Barr and *al-Mubdi`* (2/45).
[3] *al-Mabsoot* (1/152).

b) A Person Prays in Congregation and Then Finds Another Congregation

The scholars differ as to whether or not it is permissible for this person to repeat the prayer, falling into two opinions:

The First Opinion: The prayer is not to be repeated a second time. This is the chosen opinion of the Hanafee and Maalikee schools and a reported opinion of the Shaafi`ee school.[1]

The Second Opinion: The prayer can be repeated but with the condition that this prayer be established while the person is in the mosque or he enters the mosque and the people are praying. This is the chosen opinion of the Hanbalee, Shaafi`ee and Dhaahiree schools.[2]

The Proofs for the First Opinion: The first opinion is supported by the hadeeth of ibn Umar who said: I heard the Messenger of Allah (peace be upon him) saying,

$$ لَا تُصَلُّوا صَلَاةً فِي يَوْمٍ مَرَّتَيْنِ $$

"Do not pray the same prayer twice in one day.'"[3]

Therefore, the Prophet (peace be upon him) prohibited that the prayer be repeated another time. This hadeeth is taken to refer to the one who has already prayed in congregation, in order to reconcile it with the (previously mentioned) *ahaadeeth* that order that the prayer be repeated.

There is also the previously mentioned hadeeth of Jaabir bin Yazeed al-Aswad,

$$ إِذَا صَلَّيْتُمَا فِي رِحَالِكُمَا ثُمَّ أَتَيْتُمَا مَسْجِدَ جَمَاعَةٍ فَصَلِّيَا $$
$$ مَعَهُمْ فَإِنَّهَا لَكُمَا نَافِلَةٌ $$

---

[1] Refer to *al-Mabsoot* (1/135), *al-Mudawwanah* (1/88) and *al-Majmoo`* (4/223).

[2] *al-Mughnee* (2/519).

[3] Abu Daawood [Eng. Trans. 1/152 no. 579], an-Nasaa'ee (2/114) and Ahmad (2/19) with a *hasan* chain.

"If you have prayed in your houses and then come to the mosque to find a congregation there, pray with them, for it will be counted as an optional prayer for you."

There is also the previously mentioned hadeeth of Yazeed bin Aamir,

إِذَا جِئْتَ إِلَى الصَّلَاةِ فَوَجَدْتَ النَّاسَ فَصَلِّ مَعَهُمْ وَإِنْ كُنْتَ قَدْ صَلَّيْتَ تَكُنْ لَكَ نَافِلَةً وَهَذِهِ مَكْتُوبَةٌ

"When you come for prayer and find the people praying, pray with them, even if you have already prayed. It will count as an optional prayer for you and this will be counted as the obligatory prayer."

These two *ahaadeeth* prove that he commanded the one who prayed alone at home to repeat the prayer in congregation and this further proves that that the one who has already prayed in congregation should not repeat the prayer. 1

They also depend upon a rational proof, saying: The reason behind the person who has previously prayed alone repeating his prayer in congregation is so that he can gain the reward of the congregation that he has missed. On the other hand, the one who has already prayed in congregation has already gained the reward of the congregation. Therefore, there is no reason for him to repeat the prayer. If it were permissible for this person to repeat his prayer a second time in congregation, it would also be permissible for him to repeat the prayer a third, fourth and fifth time and so on. Such a thing has not been said by anyone.2

The Proofs for the Second Opinion: The proponents of the second opinion rely upon proofs from the Sunnah, narrations, the underlying reasoning and analogy.

From the Sunnah they quote the following: The previously mentioned hadeeth of Jaabir bin Yazeed al-Aswad,

---

1 *al-Mughnee* (2/519f) by ibn Qudaamah.
2 [Ash-Shawkaanee quoted this reasoning from ibn al-Arabee al-Maalikee in *Nayl al-Awtaar*. - Trans.]

إِذَا صَلَّيْتُمَا فِي رِحَالِكُمَا ثُمَّ أَتَيْتُمَا مَسْجِدَ جَمَاعَةٍ فَصَلِّيَا
مَعَهُمْ فَإِنَّهَا لَكُمَا نَافِلَةٌ

"If you have prayed in your houses and then come to the mosque to find a congregation there, pray with them. It will be counted as an optional prayer for you."

They also quote the hadeeth reported by Abu Daawood from Abu Mahjan ad-Du`lee that has previously been mentioned,

إِذَا جِئْتَ فَصَلِّ مَعَ النَّاسِ وَإِنْ كُنْتَ قَدْ صَلَّيْتَ

"When you come, pray with the people even if you have already prayed."

There is also the hadeeth of Abu Dharr al-Ghifaaree,

فَإِنْ أُقِيمَتِ الصَّلَاةُ وَأَنْتَ فِي الْمَسْجِدِ فَصَلِّ وَلَا تَقُلْ إِنِّي قَدْ
صَلَّيْتُ فَلَا أُصَلِّي

"And if the prayer is established while you are in the mosque, pray and do not say, 'I have already prayed and so I will not pray again.'"

They also refer to the action of Mu`aadh bin Jabal, wherein he used to pray *Ishaa* in congregation behind the Prophet (peace be upon him) and then return to his people and pray this same prayer again with them. The narration is explicit that he prayed *Ishaa* in congregation on both occasions and the Prophet (peace be upon him) did not object to his action. Hence, this proves the permissibility of repeating the prayer in congregation for the one who has already prayed in congregation.[1]

The reason for using these *ahaadeeth* is that their general sense includes the sanctioning of repeating a prayer for the one who has prayed alone and the one who has prayed in congregation.

---

[1] Refer to *al-Mughnee* (2/519f), and *al-Majmoo`* (14/223).

They depend also on the actions of the Companions, wherein it is reported that they used to pray in congregation and then go to the mosque and pray another time.

An example of this nature is what is reported from Anas who said, "Abu Musaa al-Ash`aree prayed the afternoon prayer with us at Murbad, then we ended up at a mosque and found that the prayer had been in process of starting and we prayed behind Mugheerah bin Shu`bah."[1]

As for reference to the underlying reasoning, if one were not to repeat the prayer with the congregation, this would make him deserving of the accusation of turning away from the congregational prayer. But when one prays with the congregation, such a danger no longer exists.

As for analogy, they argue that just as the one who has previously prayed alone can repeat his prayer in a congregation, similarly the one who has previously prayed with a congregation can also repeat prayer in congregation.

The Strongest Opinion: The second opinion is the strongest. Therefore, whoever is in the mosque and the prayer is established or whoever enters the mosque while the prayer is in progress should pray with the congregation even if he has already prayed in congregation. This is due to the generality of the texts that do not differentiate between the one who has prayed alone or in congregation and also to repel the accusation of turning away from the congregational prayer. Allah knows best.

2. The Follower Repeats the Prayer Because He Was Standing in the Wrong Place

If the person stands alone behind the last row or he stands to the left of the Imaam (and not his right when praying alone with him) [what should then be done]?

In the case where the follower prays standing alone behind the last row, he has performed something prohibited by agreement (*ittifaaq*). However, the Jurists differ as to whether or not his prayer is acceptable, holding two opinions:

First Opinion: His prayer is valid and he should not repeat it. This is the opinion of the majority of the scholars.

---

[1] *al-Mughnee* (2/521) by ibn Qudaamah.

This is the chosen opinion of the Hanafee, Maalikee and Shaafi`ee schools and a reported opinion from the Hanbalee school. It is also the opinion of Hasan al-Basree, al-Awzaa`ee and ibn al-Mundhir. [1]

Second Opinion: His prayer is not valid and it is necessary for him to repeat the prayer if he has performed one complete *rak`ah* in this state. This is the chosen opinion of the Hanbalee and Dhaahiree schools and it is the opinion of an-Nakha`ee and others. [2]

Shaykh al-Islam ibn Taymiyyah said, "This was the opinion of a group of the early companions of Ahmad, the opinion of some of the later Hanbalees and the opinion of a group of the Salaf."[3]

The Proofs for the First Opinion: Anas said,

فَقَامَ رَسُولُ اللَّهِ صَلَّى اللَّهُ عَلَيْهِ وَسَلَّمَ وَصَفَفْتُ أَنَا وَالْيَتِيمُ وَرَاءَهُ وَالْعَجُوزُ مِنْ وَرَائِنَا فَصَلَّى لَنَا رَسُولُ اللَّهِ صَلَّى اللَّهُ عَلَيْهِ وَسَلَّمَ رَكْعَتَيْنِ

"The Messenger of Allah (peace be upon him) stood and an orphan and I made a row behind him and the old woman stood behind us. He prayed two *rak`ah*s with us."[4] The old woman was Umm Sulaym, the mother of Anas bin Maalik. The Messenger of Allah (peace be upon him) allowed her to stand alone in a row following his lead. Therefore, this hadeeth proves that the prayer of one who prays on his own in a row is correct and it is not necessary for him to repeat the prayer.

There is also the hadeeth of Abu Bakra. He performed the initial *takbeer* behind the last row, bowed and walked to the last row. The Prophet (peace be upon him) said,

زَادَكَ اللَّهُ حِرْصًا وَلَا تَعُدْ

---

[1] Refer to *al-Mubdi`* (2/87) and *al-Mughnee* (2/211).
[2] Refer to *al-Mughnee* (1/211), *al-Insaaf* (2/289) and *al-Muhallaa* (4/52).
[3] *Mukhtasar Fataawaa al-Misriyyah* (p. 50).
[4] *Saheeh Muslim* [Eng. Trans. 1/320 no. 1387].

"May Allah increase you in eagerness, do not repeat [it]."[1]

Al-Baghawee said, "His saying, 'Do not repeat,' is a prohibition with the intent of showing the best course, not the prohibition of forbiddance. Had it been the prohibition of forbiddance, he would have ordered him to repeat the prayer."[2]

The hadeeth proves that Abu Bakra performed some of the prayer on his own behind the last row—this being the opening *takbeer*—yet despite this the Prophet (peace be upon him) did not order him to repeat the prayer. This proves that the prayer was valid and accepted.[3]

They also use a rational proof, saying: Standing alone behind the last row is the place for a woman when she prays in congregation with men. Therefore, it can also be the place for a man.

The Proofs for the Second Opinion: Al-Baghawee recorded via his chain that Waabisah bin Ma`bad said,

أَنَّ رَسُولَ اللَّهِ صَلَّى اللَّهُ عَلَيْهِ وَسَلَّمَ رَأَى رَجُلاً صَلَّى وَحْدَهُ خَلْفَ الصَّفِّ فَأَمَرَهُ أَنْ يُعِيدَ صَلاَتَهُ

"The Messenger of Allah (peace be upon him) saw a man praying on his own behind the last row and ordered him to repeat the prayer." Al-Baghawee said that the chain was *hasan*. Abu Daawood and at-Tirmidhee reported it.[4] It was declared *saheeh* by ibn Hajr in *al-Fath*, and by ibn Khuzaymah and ibn Hibbaan who said, "Those who do not necessitate the repetition take the command in the hadeeth of Waabisah bin Ma`bad to mean a recommendation."

There is also the hadeeth in which the Prophet (peace be upon him) prayed with his Companions and when he had completed the prayer and turned around, he saw a man alone behind the last row. The Prophet (peace be upon him)

---

[1] [*Sunan Abu Daawood* (Eng. Trans. 1/176 no. 683) and others - Trans.]

[2] *Sharh as-Sunnah* (3/378 no. 822) by al-Baghawee.

[3] Refer to *al-Mabsoot* (1/192), *Fath al-Qadeer* (1/309) and *al-Majmoo`* (4/296).

[4] Abu Daawood [Eng. Trans. 1/176 no. 682], Tirmidhee (no. 231), *Sharh as-Sunnah* (2/378-379).

remained where he was until the man had completed his prayer and then said,

اسْتَقْبِلْ صَلَاتَكَ فَلَا صَلَاةَ لِرَجُلٍ فَرْدٍ خَلْفَ الصَّفِّ

"Repeat your prayer for their is no prayer for the one who prays alone behind the last row."

This hadeeth contains the command to repeat the prayer for the one who has prayed alone behind the last row due to therebeing no prayer for him.

The Strongest Opinion: A third opinion concerning this issue is considered to be the strongest. This is that one's prayer is not valid if one were to pray alone behind the last row without a valid reason. However, if there were a valid reason the prayer would be valid, such as the last row being full and there being no place for the person to stand, or the Imaam already being in *ruku`* and the person is close to the last row, so he also performs *ruku`* in order to have attained that *rak`ah* and then walks to the last row while being in the state of bowing.

This is the opinion of al-Awzaa`ee and az-Zuhree and this is the opinion that is supported by the principles of the *Sharee`ah*.[1]

b) The Person Repeating the Prayer Because He Stood on the Left Side of the Imaam

The sunnah has clarified the place of standing for the Imaam and the follower. The regulations concerning the rows of a congregational prayer are as follows:

The Imaam stands opposite the middle of the first row when he is leading more than one person.

If there is only one person with the Imaam, he stands on the right side of the Imaam, parallel to him.

If there are three people, one of them [the Imaam] is to stand in front of the other two.

Children are to stand with the men. But if there are a large number of men and children, the men stand in front of

---

[1] Refer to *Sharh as-Sunnah* (3/379-380) by al-Baghawee.

the children. If there are women present, they stand behind the children.

If there are only men and women, the men stand behind the Imaam and the women stand behind the men. This is what the sunnah has described.

In the lengthy hadeeth narrated by Jaabir bin Abdullaah al-Ansaaree there occurs,

فَقَامَ رَسُولُ اللَّهِ صَلَّى اللَّهُ عَلَيْهِ وَسَلَّمَ لِيُصَلِّيَ وَجِئْتُ فَقُمْتُ
عَنْ يَسَارِهِ فَأَخَذَ بِيَدِي فَأَدَارَنِي حَتَّى أَقَامَنِي عَنْ يَمِينِهِ ثُمَّ
جَاءَ جَبَّارُ بْنُ صَخْرٍ فَتَوَضَّأَ ثُمَّ جَاءَ فَقَامَ عَنْ يَسَارِ رَسُولِ اللَّهِ
صَلَّى اللَّهُ عَلَيْهِ وَسَلَّمَ فَأَخَذَ رَسُولُ اللَّهِ صَلَّى اللَّهُ عَلَيْهِ وَسَلَّمَ
بِيَدَيْنَا جَمِيعًا فَدَفَعَنَا حَتَّى أَقَامَنَا خَلْفَهُ

"...So the Messenger of Allah stood to pray and I came and stood on his left side. He took me by my hand and directed me to stand on his right side. Then Jabbaar bin Sakhr came, performed *wudu`* and stood on the left side of the Messenger of Allah (peace be upon him). The Messenger of Allah (peace be upon him) took hold of both our hands and pushed us back until we stood behind him..."[1]

Anas bin Maalik said,

صَلَّيْتُ أَنَا وَيَتِيمٌ فِي بَيْتِنَا خَلْفَ رَسُولِ اللَّهِ صَلَّى اللَّهُ عَلَيْهِ
وَسَلَّمَ وَأُمُّ سُلَيْمٍ خَلْفَنَا

"An orphan and I prayed with the Messenger of Allah (peace be upon him) in our house and Umm Sulaym was behind us."[2]

Al-Baghawee said, "In this hadeeth, there is proof that men stand ahead of women in prayer and that the child stands with the men because it is possible for the child to lead the

---

[1] *Saheeh Muslim* [Eng. Trans. 4/1547 no. 7149].
[2] *Saheeh Muslim* [Eng. Trans. 1/321 no. 1387].

men. But if there are a large number of men and children, the men stand ahead of the children and the women at the back."[1]

Al-Mardaawee wrote in *al-Insaaf*, "If all the different types of people gather, then the men stand in front, then the boys, then the hermaphrodites, and then the women. This is by way of recommendation and this is the chosen opinion that is followed by the majority of the followers (of the Hanbalee school). This was the chosen opinion of ibn Adroos in his *Tadhkirah* and ibn Tameem."[2]

The prayer is a presence before Allah, the Glorious and Exalted. Therefore, it is necessary that the Imaam and the follower follow the correct mannerisms of worship, such as tranquillity and solemnity, standing in their correct places, and having the *taqwaa* of Allah in their prayers, so that Allah may unite their hearts upon the truth and guidance.

But what is the ruling of the one who stands in the wrong place in prayer. For example, he stands on the left side of the Imaam when he should have stood on the right? What is the ruling of his prayer with respect to its validity and having to repeat it?

There are a number of possible cases that can occur:

The follower stands to the left of the Imaam when there is already a follower behind him or on his right.

The follower stands to the left of the Imaam while there is a row behind the Imaam.

The follower stands to the left of the Imaam when there is no one behind him or on his right.

In the first two cases, his prayer is valid.

As for the third case, the Jurists have differed. There are two opinions:

First Opinion: His prayer is valid and there is no need to repeat it. This is the opinion of the majority of the scholars—the Hanafees, Maalikees and Shaafi'ees and it is an opinion reported from the Hanbalees. [3]

Second Opinion: His prayer is not valid and it is to be repeated if he completes one *rak'ah* while standing on the left

---

[1] *Sharh as-Sunnah* (3/no.829).
[2] *al-Insaaf* (2/283).
[3] Refer to *al-Badaa'i as-Sanaa'i* (1/159), *al-Mudawwanah al-Kubraa* (1/82), *al-Majmoo'* (4/188), and *al-Insaaf* (2/282).

side of the Imaam. This is the chosen opinion of the Hanbalee School. [1]

The Proofs for the First Opinion: First, there is the hadeeth reported by ibn Abbaas who said,

بتُّ عِنْدَ خَالَتِي فَقَامَ النَّبِيُّ صَلَّى اللّٰهُ عَلَيْهِ وَسَلَّمَ يُصَلِّي مِنْ اللَّيْلِ فَقُمْتُ أُصَلِّي مَعَهُ فَقُمْتُ عَنْ يَسَارِهِ فَأَخَذَ بِرَأْسِي فَأَقَامَنِي عَنْ يَمِينِهِ

"I spent the night at my aunt's. The Messenger of Allah (peace be upon him) stood to pray the night prayer. I stood and prayed on his left side. He took hold of my head and made me stand on his right side."

This hadeeth shows that ibn Abbaas stood for the beginning part of his prayer, wherein he performed the opening *takbeer*, on the left side of the Messenger of Allah (peace be upon him) who was the Imaam. The Prophet (peace be upon him) allowed him to continue the prayer and did not order him to repeat the opening *takbeer*. Hence, this proves that the prayer of the one who stands on the left side of the Imaam is valid.

There is also the hadeeth of Jaabir and Jabbaar that was previously mentioned wherein the Messenger of Allah (peace be upon him) did not order them to repeat the opening *takbeer*. Again, this proves that the prayer of the one who prays on the left side of the Imaam is valid and is not to be repeated. This is so because the validity of the prayer is dependent upon its conditions and pillars being fulfilled and all of these are fulfilled by the person who stands on the left side of the Imaam. Therefore, there is no need to repeat it because it is considered valid. Furthermore, that is a valid place to stand if there is someone to the right of the Imaam. Hence, it is one of the acceptable places to stand in the prayer.

The Proofs for the Second Opinion: There is the hadeeth reported by ibn Abbaas who said,

---

[1] *al-Mughnee* (2/212).

بِتُّ عِنْدَ خَالَتِي فَقَامَ النَّبِيُّ صَلَّى اللَّهُ عَلَيْهِ وَسَلَّمَ يُصَلِّي مِنْ
اللَّيْلِ فَقُمْتُ أُصَلِّي مَعَهُ فَقُمْتُ عَنْ يَسَارِهِ فَأَخَذَ بِرَأْسِي
فَأَقَامَنِي عَنْ يَمِينِهِ

"I spent the night at my aunt's. The Messenger of Allah (peace be upon him) stood to pray the night prayer. I stood and prayed on his left side. He took hold of my head and made me stand on his right side." There is also the hadeeth of Jaabir that has preceded.

These *ahaadeeth* show that the Prophet (peace be upon him) rejected the actions of ibn Abbaas, Jaabir and Jabbaar when they stood on his left side, thereby proving that it is not lawful to stand on the left side of the Imaam. Building upon this premise, whoever stands in this position has invalidated his prayer, as otherwise the Prophet (peace be upon him) would have left them to stand where they were.

The Strongest Opinion: The first opinion, that the prayer of the one who stands on the left side of the Imaam is valid, is the stronger opinion. This is especially so because the Prophet (peace be upon him) did not order ibn Abbaas, Jaabir and Jabbaar to repeat their opening *takbeer* due to their having performed it while standing on his left side and the soundness of the evidences concerning this.

Ash-Shaykh Abdurrahmaan as-Sa`dee said, "The correct opinion is that the persons' standing on the right side of the Imaam is a stressed Sunnah (*Sunnah Mu`akkadah*) and not obligatory, such that it would invalidate the prayer if he were not to stand on the Imaam's right. Therefore, the prayer of the one who stands to the left of the Imaam is valid even if there is no one standing on his right side. This is because the prohibition only occurred with respect to the one who stands alone in a row. As for his (peace be upon him) directing ibn Abbaas to stand on his right, all that does is prove that this is more excellent and it does not prove that this is obligatory since he did not forbid that this action be done. Actions of the Prophet (peace be upon him) prove that the action is a Sunnah (when not accompanied by an order). The same applies to his moving Jaabir and Jabbaar behind him after they had stood on his left and right sides, for this is equivalent to his directing ibn Abbaas and proves only that this position is more excellent."[1]

I say: This is the best opinion concerning this issue. If there is only one follower and he stands on the left side of the Imaam, it is necessary for the Imaam to direct him to his right side, thereby following what the Prophet (peace be upon him) did with ibn Abbaas. Allah Knows best.

4. The Person Repeating His Prayer Because He Has Prayed Behind a Sinning Imaam

Leading the Muslims in prayer is a great position and an excellent action that was carried out by the Prophet (peace be upon him) for the duration of his life and after him by the four Rightly Guided *Khaleefahs*. There is no doubt that the role of the Imaam in society is important. Indeed, how could it be otherwise when he leads the people in the greatest pillar of Islam after the two testimonies? This is why it is desired that the one who has been appointed as Imaam have praiseworthy characteristics that befit the requirements of his position and its importance. The Jurists do not differ with regards the fact that praying behind a just, knowledgeable, God-fearing Imaam is better than praying behind one who does not have those characteristics.

Al-Haakim recorded from Marthad bin Abee Marthad al-Ghanawee, who was one of the Companions who fought at Badr, that the Messenger of Allah (peace be upon him) said,

إِنْ سَرَّكُمْ أَنْ تُقْبَلَ صَلَاتُكُمْ فَلْيَؤُمّكم خِيارُكُمْ، فَإِنَّهُمْ وَفْدُكُمْ فِيما بَيْنَكُم وَبَيْنَ رَبّكُم عَزَّ وَجَلَّ

"If your desire is that your prayers be accepted, then let the best of you lead you, for indeed the [the Imaams] are your representative between yourselves and your Lord, the Mighty and Magnificent."[2]

[1] *al-Mukhtaaraat al-Jaliyyah min Masaa`il al-Fiqhiyyah* (pp. 61-62).
[2] *al-Mustadrak* (3/222). [This hadith is definitely weak. In fact, it can be found in a number of collections of fabricated hadith. See, for example, Muhammad

Imaam Ahmad wrote in his *Kitaab as-Salaah*, "From the obligatory duties upon the Muslims is that their best and most religious people lead them—those who have knowledge of Allah, those who fear Allah and those who supervise and are attentive to their duties to Him. This is due to the hadeeth,

إِذَا أَمَّ الرَّجُلُ الْقَوْمَ وَفِيهِمْ مَنْ هُوَ خَيْرٌ مِنهُ لَم يَزَالُوا فِي ثِفَالٍ

'When a person leads a people while there is someone else better than him, they will remain in perdition.'"[1]

There is no difference among the Jurists that it is disliked to pray behind a sinning Imaam due to the lack of confidence that he will fulfil the conditions of prayer and that making such a person an Imaam will decrease the congregation by diminishing their desire to pray behind him.[2]

But if one were to pray behind a sinning Imaam, is his prayer valid such that he has no need to repeat it or is it invalid such that he would have to repeat it? The discussion concerning this revolves around two different cases:

The First Case: The Imaam is a sinner with respect to his actions, such as the one who has performed a major sin, like fornication, stealing and drinking alcohol, or one who persists in performing a minor sin, such as shaving the beard or smoking.

The Second Case: The Imaam is a sinner with respect to his beliefs, such as being a Mu`tazili or Shee`a, especially the extremists from among them.

The Imaam Who is a Sinner With Respect to his Actions

The Jurists differed about the validity of the prayer of a person who prays behind such an Imaam. There are four opinions on this question:

Naasir al-Deen al-Albaani, *Silsilat al-Ahaadeeth al-Dhaeefah* (Riyadh: Maktabah al-Maarif, 1988), vol. 4, pp. 303-305.—JZ]
[1] Refer to *Faydh al-Qadeer* (6/88) by al-Munaawee. [This hadith is also definitely weak. It is recorded by al-Uqaili in *al-Dhuafaa* and declared weak by scholars such as al-Munaawee (in the reference the author refers to) and al-Albaani.—JZ]
[2] *Badaa`i as-Sanaa`i* (1/55).

First Opinion: His prayer is valid and should not be repeated. This is the chosen opinion of the Hanafee and Shaafi`ee schools and a reported position of the Hanbalee and Maalikee schools. [1]

Second Opinion: His being an Imaam is not valid and therefore those who prayed behind him should repeat their prayer. This is the chosen opinion of the Hanbalee school and a reported position of the Maalikee school. [2]

Third Opinion: If the Imaams' evil is linked to the prayer, his leading is not valid and whoever prayed behind him should repeat the prayer in its time as a recommendation. This is the depended upon position of the Maalikee school.

Fourth Opinion: If the Imaam openly sins, his leading is invalid and those who prayed behind him have to repeat their prayer. As for the one who does not openly sin, it is valid to pray behind him. This is a reported position of the Hanbalee school. [3]

The Proofs for the First Opinion: There is the hadeeth of Abu Dharr who said,

قَالَ لِي رَسُولُ اللَّهِ كَيْفَ أَنْتَ إِذَا كَانَتْ عَلَيْكَ أُمَرَاءُ
يُؤَخِّرُونَ الصَّلَاةَ عَنْ وَقْتِهَا قَالَ قُلْتُ فَمَا تَأْمُرُنِي قَالَ صَلِّ
الصَّلَاةَ لِوَقْتِهَا فَإِنْ أَدْرَكْتَهَا مَعَهُمْ فَصَلِّ فَإِنَّهَا لَكَ نَافِلَةٌ

"The Messenger of Allah (peace be upon him) said to me, 'How will you be when you will be governed by leaders who delay the prayers beyond their times?' I asked, 'What do you enjoin me to do?' He said, 'Pray the prayer at its time, and if you come across the prayer with them, pray the prayer and it will be counted as a supererogatory prayer.'"[4]

This hadeeth proves that the Messenger of Allah (peace be upon him) allowed one to pray behind them and made it as a supererogatory prayer. The apparent meaning of

---

[1] Refer to *al-Mabsoot* (1/40), *at-Taaj wa al-Ikleel* (2/93), *al-Majmoo`* (4/134), and *al-Mughnee* (2/187).
[2] Refer to the preceding references and *al-Insaaf* (2/252).
[3] *al-Insaaf* (2/252).
[4] *Saheeh Muslim* [Eng. Trans. 1/313 no. 1353].

the hadeeth shows that if they were to lead the prayers in their correct times, it would have been obligatory to pray behind them. There is no doubt that the one who misses the prayer and prays it in the wrong time has been unjust.

Also Abu Hurayrah narrated that the Messenger of Allah (peace be upon him) said,

يُصَلُّونَ لَكُمْ فَإِنْ أَصَابُوا فَلَكُمْ وَلَهُمْ وَإِنْ أَخْطَئُوا فَلَكُمْ وَعَلَيْهِمْ

"The Imaams pray for you, so if they pray correctly then both you and they [will be rewarded]. But if they make a mistake, you will be rewarded and [the sin] will be on them."[1] The Messenger of Allah (peace be upon him) permitted the prayer behind the rulers and clarified that if what they did was correct, all would be rewarded. However, if they did something wrong, it would be upon them only and not upon the followers. The permissibility of praying behind them indicates the permissibility of praying behind evil-doing people.

Abu Hurayrah reported that the Messenger of Allah (peace be upon him) said,

الصَّلاةُ الْمَكْتُوبَةُ وَاجِبَةٌ خَلْفَ كُلِّ مُسْلِمٍ بَرًّا كَانَ أَوْ فَاجِرًا وَإِنْ عَمِلَ الْكَبَائِرَ

"The obligatory prayer is obligatory behind every pious or sinning Muslim even if he commits major sins."[2]

It is also recorded that ibn Umar used to pray behind al-Hajjaaj who was an oppressive ruler and a sinner. However, ibn Umar never repeated his prayers, nor did any other Companion who prayed behind him. Hence, this constitutes a consensus from them that it is permissible to pray behind a sinning Imaam.

---

[1] *Saheeh al-Bukhaaree* [Eng. Trans. 1/375 no. 663].

[2] *Sunan Abu Daawood* [Eng. Trans. 1/156 no. 594] and its chain is broken.

The Proofs for the Second Opinion: There is the hadeeth of Jaabir that states,

خَطَبَنَا رَسُولُ اللَّهِ صَلَّى اللَّهُ عَلَيْهِ وَسَلَّمَ فَقَالَ يَا أَيُّهَا النَّاسُ
تُوبُوا إِلَى اللَّهِ قَبْلَ أَنْ تَمُوتُوا ... أَلَا لَا تَؤُمَّنَّ امْرَأَةٌ رَجُلًا وَلَا
يَؤُمَّ أَعْرَابِيٌّ مُهَاجِرًا وَلَا يَؤُمَّ فَاجِرٌ مُؤْمِنًا إِلَّا أَنْ يَقْهَرَهُ بِسُلْطَانٍ
يَخَافُ سَيْفَهُ وَسَوْطَهُ

"The Messenger of Allah (peace be upon him) addressed us saying, 'O people! Repent to Allah before you die...'" At the end of the hadeeth there occurs, "Do not let women lead men, or a bedouin lead the Muhaajir, or the sinner lead the believer unless he be strengthened with authority such that the believer fears his sword or whip."[1]

Therefore, a sinner leading the prayer is not valid just as it is not valid to appoint him to lead and whoever prays behind an unbeliever or the likes must repeat his prayer.

The scholars of this opinion also depend upon the fact that the duty of leading is a trust and responsibility. The Imaam recites on behalf of those he is leading. The sinner, though, is suspect and it is not guaranteed that he will recite anything, just as it is possible that he omit one of the conditions of the prayer, such as purity and there may be no indication to suggest that he has performed ablution. Therefore, for as long as he is suspect, it is not correct to have him lead. Whoever prays behind such a person should repeat his prayers due it not being allowed to take such a person as a leader of the prayer in the first place.

The Proofs for the Third Opinion: If the person's sin is not connected to the prayer, he would perform the prayer completely and his sin would not affect its validity. This is

---

[1] Reported by ibn Maajah (1/128-129 #1081, Book: Iqaamah as-Salaah, Chpt: Fard al-Jumu`ah). Its chain contains Abdullaah bin Muhammad al-Adawee and he is abandoned, it also contains Alee bin Zayd bin Jud'aan who is weak. [For an excellent discussion concerning the various routes of narration and wordings of this hadeeth refer to Muhammad Naasir al-Deen al-Albaani, *Irwaa al-Ghaleel fi Takhreej Ahaadeeth Manaar al-Sabeel*, #591. - trans.]

because the validity of prayer is dependent upon its conditions, pillars and obligations being fulfilled, and this person is able to fulfill them. As for the case of his sins being connected to prayer, it is not valid to have him lead because it will be largely assumed that his prayer would be invalid due to his not fulfilling one of the conditions or pillars.

The Proofs for the Fourth Opinion: The one who openly sins is not deserving of leading the prayer. Therefore, it is not correct to have him lead. Hence, the prayer of whoever prays behind him is invalid. This is also true because there is no excuse left for one to pray behind him when his condition has become absolutely clear for all to see. As for the case of the one who conceals his sin, it is permissible to pray behind him due to the excuse of not knowing his state of affairs.

The Strongest Opinion, and Allah Knows Best: The prayer behind one who is sinning in actions is valid and is not to be repeated. However, it is desired that such a person not be appointed as an Imaam so that maybe he will check himself and stop performing the sin. But if such a person were to be appointed as an Imaam, the prayer of the one who prays behind him is valid and is not to be repeated, in order to remove any harm or difficulty from the Muslims.

b. Repeating the Prayer Due to Praying Behind an Imaam Who is Evil With Respect to His Beliefs

The Jurists have differed as to whether or not one should repeat his prayer after praying behind an Imaam who is evil with respect to beliefs. There are four opinions on this question:

First Opinion: The prayer is valid although disliked. It is not necessary to repeat it. This is the chosen opinion of the Shaafi`ee and Hanafee schools, and a reported opinion of the Hanbalee school.[1]

Second Opinion: The prayer is valid. However, if there is time remaining, it is recommended to repeat the prayer. This is the chosen opinion of the Maalikee school.

---

[1] Refer to *Fath al-Qadeer* (1/304), *Jawaahir al-Ikleel* (1/…), and *al-Majmoo* (4/143).

Third Opinion: The prayer is unrestrictedly void and whoever prayed behind such an Imaam has to repeat his prayer. This is the chosen opinion of the Hanbalee school and a reported opinion of the Hanafee school.[1]

Fourth Opinion: If he is calling to innovations, openly manifesting his evil, the prayer is not valid behind him and is to be repeated. However, if he is not calling to his innovation nor openly manifesting his evil, the prayer prayed behind him is not to be repeated and it is valid. This is a reported opinion of the Hanbalee school.[2]

The Proofs for the First Opinion: The Prophet (peace be upon him) is reported to have said,

$$\text{صَلُّوا خَلْفَ مَنْ قَالَ لاَ إِلهَ الاَّ اللهُ}$$

"Pray behind whoever says, 'There is none worthy of worship save Allah.'"[3]

There is also the hadeeth in which the Prophet (peace be upon him) said,

$$\text{صَلُّوا خَلْفَ كُلِّ بَرٍّ وَفَاجِرٍ}$$

"Pray behind every pious and sinning person."[4]

There is also the hadeeth of Abu Dharr that was quoted earlier,

$$\text{فَإِنْ أَدْرَكَتْكَ الصَّلَاةُ مَعَهُمْ فَصَلِّ وَلَا تَقُلْ إِنِّي قَدْ صَلَّيْتُ فَلا أُصَلِّي}$$

"And if you come across the prayer, pray with them and do not say that, 'I have already prayed and so I will not pray again.'"

---

[1] Refer to *al-Kaafee* (1/182) by ibn Qudaamah and *al-Badaa`i as-Sanaa`i* (1/157).

[2] Refer to *al-Kaafee* (1/182-183).

[3] *Sunan ad-Daaruqutnee* (2/56-57) and he said (after mentioning other ahaadeeth with similar wordings), "None of these ahaadeeth are confirmed." Refer to *Nasb ar-Raayah* (2/27-28).

[4] Ibid and *Sunan Abu Daawood* [Eng. Trans. 1/156 no. 594].

The validity of prayer is linked to its pillars being fulfilled and the sinning Imaam is able to fulfill these pillars. Therefore, the prayer behind him is valid even though it may be disliked. However, something being disliked does not render it invalid. If the prayer is valid behind such an Imaam, it is not to be repeated.

They also make analogy to the fact that if such a person were to pray on his own, his prayer would be valid. Therefore his leading other people in prayer, by extension, would also be valid. And if his leading other people in prayer is valid then the prayer itself is valid and is not to be repeated.

The Proofs for the Second Opinion: The prayer behind such an Imaam is valid but disliked. Therefore, if there remains time, it should be repeated in order to pray it in a more complete form in which there is no factor that is disliked. This is done by praying it behind a just Imaam.

The Proofs for the Third Opinion: One proof is Allah's statement,

أَفَمَنْ كَانَ مُؤْمِنًا كَمَنْ كَانَ فَاسِقًا لَا يَسْتَوُونَ

"So is the one who believes no better than the one who is rebellious and wicked? They are not equal" [as-Sajdah (32):18]. This noble verse proves that the believer is not the same as the sinner. In fact, the condition of the believer is better than that of the sinner. Therefore, if this is the case, it is not correct to have the sinner lead the believer, and if his leading is not correct, the prayer of whoever prays behind him is not valid and is to be repeated.

There is also the hadeeth of the Prophet (peace be upon him) in which he said,

اجعلوا أئمتكم خياركم فإنهم وفدكم بينكم وبين ربكم

"Appoint the best of you to be your Imaams, for indeed they are your representative between yourselves and your Lord."[1] And the sinner is not the best of us.

"Also because the sinner is suspect and censured with regards to his religion, he is not trusted with the duty of

---

[1] *Sunan al-Bayhaqee* (3/90).

leading the prayer or fulfilling its conditions, in this way he resembles the unbeliever. Therefore, when his leading is not valid, the prayer of whoever prays behind him is not valid and is to be repeated. This is because he has been led by one concerning whom it is not valid for him to lead, just as if he were to be led by a woman."[1]

The Proofs for the Fourth Opinion: The innovator who calls to innovations and manifests his sin is not deserving of the duty of leading. Hence, it is not correct for him to do so. Therefore, the prayer of whoever prays behind him is invalid. This is not true of the one who keeps his innovation and sin to himself. Therefore, it is not necessary to repeat one's prayer if the Imaam is not open about his innovation.

This resembles the case of one who prays behind an Imaam who was broken his *wudu`* but the follower does not know of this. In such a case, the prayer is not to be repeated. But if one was to pray behind an unbeliever or one who cannot recite, it is necessary to repeat the prayer due to the condition of such people being apparent in most cases.

The Strongest Opinion: If there is none but a sinner to lead the prayer, even if his evil is with respect to his beliefs, his leading is valid and whoever prayed behind him is not to repeat the prayer. This is in order to remove harm or difficulty from the Muslims. Allah knows best.

5. The Reciter Repeating his Prayer Because He Has Prayed Behind One Who Cannot Recite Correctly

The meaning of *Ummee* is one whose recitation in prayer is poor regardless of which part of the Qur`aan it may be.[2] According to the Shaafi`ees and Hanbalees, it means the one who cannot recite the whole of *al-Faatihah* well, he leaves out a word or letter, or makes grammatical mistakes such that the meaning is altered.[3]

There is no doubt that the one who can recite well is more privileged than the one who cannot, especially in the case of leading prayer. It is obligatory that only the one who

---

[1] *al-Mubda* (2/65).
[2] Refer to *al-Mutla`* (pg. 10), and *ash-Sharh as-Sagheer* (1/437).
[3] Refer to *al-Mughnee* (2/195-197) and *al-Majmoo`* (4/166).

can recite well be allowed to lead the people in prayer, as the Prophet (peace be upon him) said,

$$يَؤُمُّ الْقَوْمَ أَقْرَؤُهُمْ لِكِتَابِ اللَّهِ$$

"Let the most proficient of the people in reciting the Book of Allah lead them [in prayer]."[1]

But if someone whose recitation of the obligatory part of the prayer was poor were to lead the prayer, what would be the ruling of the prayer of those who prayed behind him with respect to its validity and having to repeat it? The Jurists differed about this, expressing four opinions:

First Opinion: The prayer is not valid behind him and whoever has been led has to repeat the prayer. This was the opinion of Abu Haneefah, Maalik, ash-Shaafi`ee and Ahmad.[2]

Their proof lay in his (peace be upon him) saying,

$$لاَ صَلاَةَ لِمَنْ لَمْ يَقْرَأْ بِفَاتِحَةِ الْكِتَابِ$$

"There is no prayer for the one who has not recited the Opening Chapter of the Book."[3]

This hadeeth proves that it is obligatory to recite *Surah al-Faatihah*. Whoever is deficient in his recitation of it is not considered to have recited in a complete way and, therefore, whoever prayed behind him has to repeat their prayer.

Second Opinion: Praying behind him is permissible. Since it is permissible, it is not necessary to repeat one's prayer. This is the opinion of `Ataa bin Abee Rabaah, Qataadah, al-Muzanee, Abu Thawr, and ibn al-Mundhir.

They reasoned that he is not able to fulfill a pillar of the prayer and it is permissible to pray behind him just as in the case where the follower prays behind an Imaam who cannot stand.[4]

---

[1] *Saheeh Muslim* [Eng. Trans.1/326 no. 1420].

[2] Refer to *al-Bahr ar-Raa`iq* (1/382), *at-Taaj wal-Ikleel* (2/98), *al-Majmoo`* (4/166-167) and *al-Insaaf* (2/268).

[3] *Saheeh al-Bukhaaree* [Eng. Trans. 1/404 no. 723], *Saheeh Muslim* [Eng. Trans.1/215 no. 773].

[4] *al-Majmoo`* (4/167-168).

Third Opinion: It is permissible for the reciter of the Qur'aan to pray behind one who cannot recite correctly in those prayers that are prayed silently but not in those that are prayed aloud. This is a reported opinion of the Shaafi'ee and Hanbalee schools.

They reasoned that (in the silent prayers) everyone is commanded to recite for themselves and, therefore, their prayer is valid and there is no need to repeat it.[1]

Fourth Opinion: If the one who cannot recite correctly was to lead those who cannot recite correctly, their prayer is valid. This is the chosen opinion of the Hanbalee School. If the one who cannot recite correctly were to lead a mixture of those who can and cannot recite, then the prayer of those who cannot recite is valid, but the prayer of those who can recite is not valid and needs to be repeated. If one person who cannot recite correctly were to lead another who can, the prayer of both of them is not valid and needs to be repeated. This is because the one who could not recite correctly intended to lead while, in fact, he prayed by himself.[2]

The Strongest Opinion: The strongest opinion is the fourth opinion but some conditions need to be met:

(1) It is not permissible that the one who cannot recite be appointed as the permanent Imaam when there is a person in the congregation who can recite.

(2) It is not permissible for the reciter to start his prayer while being led by one who cannot recite correctly.

(3) If the one who can recite is led by one who cannot recite while not knowing his condition, his prayer is valid due to the generality of his saying,

$$صَلُّوا خَلْفَ مَنْ قَالَ لاَ إِلَهَ الاَّ اللهُ$$

"Pray behind whoever says, 'None has the right to be worshipped save Allah.'"

---

[1] Refer to *al-Majmoo'* (4/167), and *al-Mughnee* (2/30 - new edition).
[2] Refer to *al-Insaaf* (2/268-270) and *al-Mughnee* (3/30-41 Egypt edition).

6. The One Who Has Intended an Obligatory Prayer Repeating his Prayer Because He Prayed Behind One Who Had Intended an Optional Prayer

There are three possible situations that the follower may find himself in with respect to the Imaam:

(1) The follower and Imaam are in complete agreement inwardly and outwardly, such as both of them are praying *Dhuhur* or *Asr*.

(2) The follower and Imaam are in agreement outwardly but not inwardly, such as someone praying an obligatory prayer behind one who is praying an optional prayer.

(3) The follower and Imaam differ outwardly and inwardly, such as the one who is praying *Dhuhur* behind one who is praying *Maghrib*.

The Researching Scholars have differed about these issues. This difference is based on whether or not it is a condition that both the Imaam and follower be in agreement both inwardly and outwardly or whether it is sufficient that they be in agreement outwardly only. The outset of this difference is based upon a difference in understanding the meaning of some *ahaadeeth,* such as the Prophet's (peace be upon him) saying,

إِنَّمَا جُعِلَ الإِمَامُ لِيُؤْتَمَّ بِهِ

"Indeed the Imaam has been appointed only to be followed."[1] There is also the hadeeth of Mu'aadh bin Jabal in which he prayed with the Messenger of Allah (peace be upon him) and then led his people in prayer.[2]

What follows is a detailed analysis concerning this difference of opinion:[3]

First Opinion: The famous opinion of the Hanafee and Maalikee schools is that it is obligatory that the Imaam

---

[1] *Saheeh al-Bukhaaree* [Eng. Trans. 1/372 no. 656, 657], Saheeh Muslim [Eng. Trans. 1/226 no. 817].

[2] *Saheeh al-Bukhaaree* [Eng. Trans. 1/378 no. 669].

[3] *an-Niyyah wa Atharuhaa fee al-Ahkaam ash-Shar'iyyah* (1/364) by the author, Saalih as-Sadlaan.

and follower be in agreement both outwardly and inwardly. Therefore, it is not permissible for the one who intends to pray an obligatory prayer to pray behind someone who is praying an optional prayer. This opinion is also one of the two reported positions of the Hanbalee school and it is their chosen opinion.[1] Based on this, whoever prays an obligatory prayer behind someone praying an optional prayer must repeat his prayer.

Second Opinion: The Shaafi`ee school is of the opinion that it is permissible for the follower and the Imaam to differ both inwardly and outwardly. They said that it is permissible for someone praying an obligatory prayer to pray behind one who is praying an optional prayer and vice-versa. This opinion is the second of the two reported opinions of the Hanbalee school and it is the chosen opinion of the Dhaahiree school. The Dhaahiree school, however, only deems it permissible that the follower differ with the Imaam in the inward matters and not the outward.[2]

The Proofs for the First Opinion: The Prophet (peace be upon him) said,

$$ إِنَّمَا الأَعْمَالُ بِالنِّيَّاتِ وَإِنَّمَا لِكُلِّ امْرِئٍ مَا نَوَى $$

"Indeed actions are by intention, and for every person is what he intended."[3]

There is also the hadeeth,

$$ إِنَّمَا جُعِلَ الإِمَامُ لِيُؤْتَمَّ بِهِ فَلا تَخْتَلِفُوا عَلَيْهِ $$

"Indeed, the Imaam has been appointed only to be followed, so do not differ from him."

They replied to the action of Mu`aadh by saying that either it was specific to him or Mu`aadh prayed an optional prayer behind the Prophet (peace be upon him) and the

---

[1] Refer to *Tabyeen al-Haqaa`iq* (1/141-142), *al-Muwaahib al-Jaleel* (2/126), and *al-Mughnee* (2/126).

[2] Refer to *Fath al-Baaree* (2/195), *Tabyeen al-Haqaa`iq* (1/141-142), and *al-Muhallaa Sharh al-Mujallaa* (3/411) by ibn Hazm.

[3] *Saheeh al-Bukhaaree* [Eng. Trans.1/1 no. 1], *Saheeh Muslim* [Eng. Trans. 3/1056 no. 4692].

obligatory prayer with his people. Building upon this explanation, the adherents of this opinion say that it is permissible for one to pray optional prayers behind one who is praying an obligatory prayer (but not the opposite).

They also relied upon the fact that the intention of the follower is independent of the intention of the Imaam and, therefore, the Imaam cannot carry the intention of the follower. This is why it is not allowed to follow an Imaam while having a different intention [because then it cannot be considered a congregation, for all the people would not be praying the same prayer and hence would not have gathered for the same purpose]. For example, it is not acceptable for someone to pray *Jumu`ah* behind one praying *Dhuhur*.[1]

The Proofs for the Second Opinion: There is the story of Mu`aadh, reported by Jaabir, that Mu`aadh used to pray *Ishaa* with the Prophet (peace be upon him) and then return to his people and lead them in the same prayer. There occurs in some reports of this hadeeth,

$$ هِىَ لَهُ تَطَوُّعٌ وَلَهُمْ مَكْتُوبَةٌ $$

"It is counted as an optional prayer for him and an obligatory prayer for them." [2]

They also relied upon the fact that the intentions of the Imaam and follower differing do not prevent the validity of following in prayer. With regards to differing in the outward matters, they relied upon two points:

The two prayers are in conformity with respect to their form, although they may be different with regards to number of *rak`ahs*.

It is permissible for the follower to enter the prayer with an intention of splitting off from the Imaam. They took the hadeeth, "Indeed, the Imaam has been appointed only to be followed," to refer to the majority of situations and not all.[3]

---

[1] Refer to *Fath al-Baaree* (2/195), *Tabyeen al-Haqaa`iq* (1/141) and *an-Niyyah* (1/465).

[2] [Reported in the *Musnad ash-Shaafi`ee* and others. Declared to be *saheeh* by an-Nawawee and ibn Hajr. Refer to *Majmu`* (4/170) and *Fath* (2/249) - Trans.]

[3] [For example, it is permissible for the follower to be praying *Maghrib* behind an Imaam praying *Ishaa* knowing full well that after the third *rak`ah* he will no longer be following the Imaam. – Trans.]

The Strongest Opinion: The strongest opinion is that of the Dhaahiree school and the reported opinion of the Hanbalee school: It is obligatory that the Imaam and follower agree in the outward matters but not the inward. Therefore, it is not allowed that the follower pray `Asr behind an Imaam praying *Maghrib*, or pray the prayer of Eclipse behind an Imaam praying *Eed*, or the opposite. It is permissible for the follower to differ with the Imaam in the inward matters. Hence, it is allowable to pray *Dhuhur* behind an Imaam praying `Asr, or one who is praying a prayer in its time behind one who is making up a missed prayer, or one who is praying an obligatory prayer behind one who is praying an optional prayer and other similar instances.

They say it is possible to reconcile the hadeeth, "Indeed, the Imaam has only been appointed to be followed," with the story of Mu`aadh by the fact that the hadeeth proves that it is not permissible to differ with the Imaam in the outward matters. As for differing of the inward matters, we can understand this from the story of Mu`aadh. Also, there is no way to know the intention of a person because it is from the hidden matters and, therefore, the legally responsible person cannot be enjoined to do things that he cannot know about. Therefore, the prohibition is only with regards to one who differs with the Imaam in outward matters and this is why the Prophet (peace be upon him) exemplified the hadeeth by saying, "When he says the *takbeer*, say the *takbeer*. When he performs the *ruku`*, perform the *ruku`*..." and he did not mention any of the inward matters.[1]

---

[1] Refer to *al-Muhallaa* (3/411) and *an-Niyyah* (1/463-465) by the author.

Prayer in Congregation After the Time Has Expired

The continuous practice of the Prophet (peace be upon him) was to pray the prayers at the beginning of their times. This was practiced by him throughout his life. None who is versed in the Sunnah differs over this. There are number of sayings from him (peace be upon him) that prove this, such as his saying,

أَفْضَلُ الأَعْمَالِ الصَّلاةُ لِوَقْتِهَا

"The best actions is the prayer at its correct time." Other *ahaadeeth* have the same meaning.

But it is possible that for some reason or other the individual or congregation, due to a valid reason, misses a single prayer or a number of prayers. It is also possible that one misses a prayer deliberately out of laziness or apathy. In these cases, is the prayer to be made up or not? If we say that it permissible to make up the prayers, how are they to be made up?

The Obligation to Make Up Missed Prayers

"The Jurists of the Four Schools of Thought are agreed that it is obligatory to make up the missed obligatory prayers, regardless of whether one left them due to a valid reason, such as sleep or forgetfulness, or out of negligence and laziness."[1]

As for the legislated prayers that are due to a specific event, such as the prayer for rain and the prayer for the eclipse,

---

[1] *al-Istidhkaar li Madhaahib Fuqahaa al-Amsaar wa Ulamaa al-Aqtaar* (1/107f) by ibn Abdul Barr al-Qurtobee.

it is not sanctioned to make them up. On this point, there is no difference of opinion.[1]

The Manner in Which Prayers are Made Up

1) It Is Recommended to Pray in Congregation

This is the opinion of the majority of the scholars except al-Layth bin Sa'd, who only allowed it for making up *Jumu`ah* prayer and who held that only the *iqaamah* is to be said for the remainder of the prayers. Authentic *ahaadeeth* and the consensus of the scholars rebuke his opinion.[2]

Imaam Muslim recorded from Abu Hurayrah that,

أَنَّ رَسُولَ اللَّهِ صَلَّى اللَّهُ عَلَيْهِ وَسَلَّمَ حِينَ قَفَلَ مِنْ غَزْوَةِ خَيْبَرَ سَارَ لَيْلَهُ حَتَّى إِذَا أَدْرَكَهُ الْكَرَى عَرَّسَ وَقَالَ لِبِلالٍ اكْلأْ لَنَا اللَّيْلَ فَصَلَّى بِلالٌ مَا قُدِّرَ لَهُ وَنَامَ رَسُولُ اللَّهِ صَلَّى اللَّهُ عَلَيْهِ وَسَلَّمَ وَأَصْحَابُهُ فَلَمَّا تَقَارَبَ الْفَجْرُ اسْتَنَدَ بِلالٌ إِلَى رَاحِلَتِهِ مُوَاجِهَ الْفَجْرِ فَغَلَبَتْ بِلالاً عَيْنَاهُ وَهُوَ مُسْتَنِدٌ إِلَى رَاحِلَتِهِ فَلَمْ يَسْتَيْقِظْ رَسُولُ اللَّهِ صَلَّى اللَّهُ عَلَيْهِ وَسَلَّمَ وَلا بِلالٌ وَلا أَحَدٌ مِنْ أَصْحَابِهِ حَتَّى ضَرَبَتْهُمُ الشَّمْسُ فَكَانَ رَسُولُ اللَّهِ صَلَّى اللَّهُ عَلَيْهِ وَسَلَّمَ أَوَّلَهُمْ اسْتِيقَاظًا فَفَزِعَ رَسُولُ اللَّهِ صَلَّى اللَّهُ عَلَيْهِ وَسَلَّمَ فَقَالَ أَيْ بِلالُ فَقَالَ بِلالٌ أَخَذَ بِنَفْسِي الَّذِي أَخَذَ بِأَبِي أَنْتَ وَأُمِّي يَا رَسُولَ اللَّهِ بِنَفْسِكَ قَالَ اقْتَادُوا فَاقْتَادُوا

---

[1] *Bidaayah al-Mujtahid* (1/175) and *Sharh an-Nawawee `alaa Saheeh Muslim* (5/181).
[2] *Fath al-Baaree* (2/70) and *al-Majmoo`* (4/88).

رَوَاحِلَهُمْ شَيْئًا ثُمَّ تَوَضَّأَ رَسُولُ اللَّهِ صَلَّى اللَّهُ عَلَيْهِ وَسَلَّمَ

وَأَمَرَ بِلَالاً فَأَقَامَ الصَّلَاةَ فَصَلَّى بِهِمْ الصُّبْحَ فَلَمَّا قَضَى الصَّلَاةَ

قَالَ مَنْ نَسِيَ الصَّلَاةَ فَلْيُصَلِّهَا إِذَا ذَكَرَهَا فَإِنَّ اللَّهَ قَالَ أَقِمْ

الصَّلَاةَ لِذِكْرِي قَالَ يُونُسُ وَكَانَ ابْنُ شِهَابٍ يَقْرَؤُهَا

لِلذِّكْرَى

"While returning from the expedition of Khaybar, the Messenger of Allah (peace be upon him) became sleepy when night fell and so stopped to rest. He said to Bilaal, 'Remain on guard for us during the night.' Bilaal prayed as much as he could while the Messenger of Allah (peace be upon him) and his Companions slept. When the time for dawn approached, Bilaal leaned against his camel facing the direction in which the dawn was to appear. He was overcome with sleep. Neither the Messenger of Allah (peace be upon him), Bilaal nor any of his Companions awoke until the sun shone on them. The Messenger of Allah (peace be upon him) was the first to awake and became startled. He called to Bilaal. Bilaal replied, 'May my father and mother be sacrificed for you, O Messenger of Allah! The same thing overpowered me that overpowered you.' The Prophet (peace be upon him) said, 'Lead the beasts on.' So they led their camels to some distance. The Messenger of Allah (peace be upon him) performed ablution and ordered Bilaal to pronounce the *iqaamah* and then led them in the Morning Prayer. When he had finished he said, 'Whoever forgets to pray should pray when he remembers. Allah said,

وَأَقِمِ الصَّلَاةَ لِذِكْرِي

"And observe the prayer for My remembrance" [*Taa Haa* (20): 14].'"[1] Yunus said, "Ibn Shihaab used to recite the verse, '…for remembrance.'"

An-Nawawee said in *Sharh Saheeh Muslim*,

---

[1] *Saheeh Muslim* [Eng. Trans. 1/331 no. 1448].

This hadeeth contains evidence that the obligatory prayer which has been missed must be made up, regardless if one left it due to a valid excuse, such as sleep or forgetfulness or, due to no valid excuse. The hadeeth mentions only the excuse of forgetfulness due to it being said after the occurrence of a specific event but (is to be applied generally). If it is necessary for one who has a valid excuse to make up the prayer, it is even more so required for the one who has no valid excuse. Therefore, the hadeeth is informing us of this by means of using the lesser thing to alert to the greater thing.[1]

Al-Bukhaaree records that Imraan bin Husayn said,

سِرْنا مَعَ رَسُولِ اللّهِ صَلَّى اللّهُ عَلَيْهِ وَسَلَّمَ فَعَرَّسَ بِنا مِنَ السَّحَرِ، فَما اسْتَيْقَظْنا إلاَّ بِحَرِّ الشَّمْسِ فَقامَ الْقَوْمُ فَزِعِينَ مُسْرِعِينَ لِما فاتَهُمْ مِنَ الصَّلاةِ، فَقالَ رَسُولُ اللّهِ صَلَّى اللّهُ عَلَيْهِ وَسَلَّمَ ارْكَبُوا فَرَكِبْنا فَسِرْنا حَتَّى طَلَعَتِ الشَّمْسُ ثُمَّ نَزَلَ وَنَزَلْنا وَقَضَى الْقَوْمُ حَوائِجَهُمْ وَتَوَضَّأُوا، فَأَمَرَ بِلالاً فَأَذَّنَ وَصَلَّى رَكْعَتَيِ الْفَجْرِ وَصَلَّيْنا ثُمَّ أَمَرَهُ فَأَقامَ فَصَلَّى بِنا فَقُلْنا: يا رَسُولَ اللّهِ أَلاَ نُصَلِّي هَذِهِ الصَّلاةَ لِوَقْتِها، قالَ لاَ يَنْهاكُمُ اللّهُ عَنِ الرِّبا وَيَقْبَلُهُ مِنْكُمْ

"We went on an expedition with the Messenger of Allah (peace be upon him) and we lay down to sleep and we did not wake until we felt the heat of the sun. The people stood in alarm and haste due to their missing the *Fajr* prayer. The Messenger of Allah said, 'Mount your steeds and ride.' So we

---

[1] *Sharh Saheeh Muslim* (5/181f).

rode until the sun had risen. Then he got off his mount and so did we. The people relieved themselves and performed ablution. The Messenger of Allah ordered Bilaal to call the *adhaan* and he prayed the two Sunnahs of *Fajr*. Then he ordered Bilaal to perform the *iqaamah* and he led us in the prayer. We said, 'O Messenger of Allah should we not pray this prayer at its correct time?' He replied, 'Allah would not forbid you from dealing with interest and then accept it from you.'"[1]

Ibn Qudaamah said after mentioning the various reports concerning this story, "All of these reports show that he prayed the two *rak`ahs* of *Fajr* in congregation with his Companions. Therefore it is recommended to make up missed prayers in congregation."[2]

Al-Bukhaaree reports from Jaabir bin Abdullaah:

أَنَّ عُمَرَ بْنَ الْخَطَّابِ جَاءَ يَوْمَ الْخَنْدَقِ بَعْدَ مَا غَرَبَتْ الشَّمْسُ فَجَعَلَ يَسُبُّ كُفَّارَ قُرَيْشٍ قَالَ يَا رَسُولَ اللَّهِ مَا كِدْتُ أُصَلِّي الْعَصْرَ حَتَّى كَادَتْ الشَّمْسُ تَغْرُبُ قَالَ النَّبِيُّ صَلَّى اللَّهُ عَلَيْهِ وَسَلَّمَ وَاللَّهِ مَا صَلَّيْتُهَا فَقُمْنَا إِلَى بُطْحَانَ فَتَوَضَّأَ لِلصَّلاةِ وَتَوَضَّأْنَا لَهَا فَصَلَّى الْعَصْرَ بَعْدَ مَا غَرَبَتْ الشَّمْسُ ثُمَّ صَلَّى بَعْدَهَا الْمَغْرِبَ

"On the Day of al-Khandaq, Umar bin al-Khattaab came cursing the disbelievers of Quraysh after the sun had set and said, 'O Messenger of Allah, I have not been able to offer the *`Asr* prayer until the sun had almost set.' The Prophet (peace be upon him) said, 'By Allah, I have not prayed it.' So we stood facing But-haan and the Prophet (peace be upon him) performed ablution and so did we. He offered the prayer after the sun had set and then he offered the Maghrib prayer."[3]

---

[1] *Saheeh al-Bukhaaree* (4/232-233).

[2] *al-Mughnee* (2/348-349).

[3] *Saheeh al-Bukhaaree* [Eng. Trans. 1/327 no. 570].

Al-Haafidh ibn Hajr said,

A-Kirmaanee said, "If you were to ask: How does this hadeeth prove that the prayer was done in congregation? I would reply: It is possible that the wording of the hadeeth has been summarized, or the proof lies in the fact that the hadeeth has used the same wording for praying the missed prayer— `Asr— as was done for the prayer that was to be prayed in its time—*Maghrib*. There is no doubt that he prayed *Maghrib* in congregation because this is what is known from his habit. The first possibility is what ibn Muneer Zayn ad-Deen declared with certainty. If it is said: The hadeeth is not explicit that he prayed in congregation. I would reply: The content of the chapter heading is derived from his saying, 'The Prophet (peace be upon him) performed ablution and so did we.'" I [ibn Hajr] say: It is the first possibility that actually occurs; in the report of al-Ismaa`eelee there occurs that which would dictate that he (peace be upon him) prayed with them. He reports this hadeeth via the route of Yazeed bin Zaree` from Hishaam with the wording, "and so he led us in the `Asr prayer."[1]

I [Shaikh Saalih] say: A similar report has been reported by ibn Khuzaymah in his *Saheeh* from `Imraan bin Husayn who said, "We were on a journey with the Messenger of Allah (peace be upon him)...," mentioning the hadeeth concerning their sleeping until the sun had risen and then he said,

$$ ثُمَّ نَادَى بِالصَّلَاةِ فَصَلَّى النَّاسُ $$

"Then he called the *adhaan* and the people prayed." Ibn Khuzaymah then said, "This hadeeth is evidence to the contrary of the opinion of those who think that missed prayers

---

[1] *Fath al-Baaree* (2/68-70).

should not be prayed in congregation and instead should be prayed individually."[1]

It is also permissible to delay the congregational performance of the prayer that is to be made up if this is done for a valid reason.[2]

2) The Ruling of Praying Aloud or Silently in Congregation for the Made Up Prayers

If the prayer being made up in congregation is one in which the recitation is silent, meaning *Dhuhur* and `*Asr*, the Imaam is not to recite aloud, irrespective of whether this prayer is made up during the day or night. The author of *al-Insaaf* said, "I know of no difference concerning this."[3]

If the prayer being made up in congregation is one in which the recitation is aloud and is being prayed at some time during the night, then the Imaam should recite aloud. The author of *al-Insaaf* said, "I know of no difference concerning this as well."

If the prayer being made up in congregation is one in which the recitation is aloud and is being prayed at some time during the day, the Imaam should recite silently according to the correct opinion of the Hanbalee school.[4]

I say: This does not apply to the *Fajr* prayer because although *Fajr* is a prayer of the day from the point of view that it is prayed after the appearance of the dawn, its ruling is that of a night prayer from the point of view that one recites aloud in it. Therefore, when taking this into consideration, it is closer to the truth that it be prayed aloud when making it up. This opinion is supported by what Muslim and others report from Abu Qataadah concerning the story of their sleeping past the time of *Fajr*,

---

[1] *Saheeh ibn Khuzaymah* (2/98-99 nos. 987, 997).
[2] *az-Zawaa`id fee Fiqh al-Imaam Ahmad bin Hanbal* (1/116) by ibn Husayn.
[3] *al-Insaaf fee Ma`rifah al-Raajih min al-Khilaaf* (2/67) by al-Mardaawee.
[4] *al-Insaaf* (2/57).

ثُمَّ أَذَّنَ بِلَالٌ بِالصَّلَاةِ فَصَلَّى رَسُولُ اللَّهِ صَلَّى اللَّهُ عَلَيْهِ وَسَلَّمَ
رَكْعَتَيْنِ ثُمَّ صَلَّى الْغَدَاةَ فَصَنَعَ كَمَا كَانَ يَصْنَعُ كُلَّ يَوْمٍ

"...Then Bilaal called the *adhaan* for prayer and the Messenger of Allah (peace be upon him) prayed two *rak'ahs* and then said the morning prayer in the same manner as he did everyday."[1]

The grandfather of Ibn Taymiyyah, may Allah have mercy upon him, said, "This hadeeth contains evidence that the recitation of *Fajr* prayer is done aloud when made up during the day."[2]

3) The Ruling of Praying the Missed Prayers in Their Proper Order When There Is a Fear of Missing the Congregational Prayer (of the Present Prayer)

To pray the obligatory prayers in order is an obligatory. None of the Jurists differ about this.[3] Hence, it is not permissible to pray *Dhuhur* before *Fajr* or *'Asr* before *Dhuhur* because the prayer does not become obligatory before the onset of its time of observance.

But if the time for prayer has come and gone, and the person has not prayed that prayer, and the time of the next prayer has started, is praying the prayers in order considered obligatory such that the person has to make up the missed prayer before he prays the prayer whose time has started?

The Jurists have differed about this and their opinions are summarized below:

(1) Making up the missed prayers in order is obligatory, but the obligation is lifted due to forgetfulness, due to there being the fear that the time of the present prayer will end, or there being the fear that the prayer in congregation for the present prayer will be missed. This is the opinion of Sa'eed bin al-Musayyib, al-Hasan, ath-Thawree, Ishaaq, al-Awzaa'ee,

---

[1] *Saheeh Muslim* [Eng. Trans. 1/332 no. 1450].
[2] *al-Muntaqaa* (1/237 no. 613).
[3] *Tuhfatul Fuqahaa* (2/231).

the *Ashaab al-Ra'i* and the chosen opinion of the Hanbalee school.

Therefore, if one were to have started praying the prayer whose time it was and remembered that he still had to make up a missed prayer and there is not much time remaining for the present prayer, or he has not started the present prayer but there is not enough time left of the present prayer for him to pray the missed prayer and the present prayer without the time for the present prayer expiring, he should start with the present prayer and then pray the missed prayer. Similarly, if he has forgotten to pray the missed prayers, all the prayers he prayed afterwards are valid.[1]

(2) Making up the missed prayers in order is obligatory no matter what the circumstances, whether the missed prayers are small in number or large. This is reported from Imaam Ahmad[2] and Zufar from the Hanafee scholars.[3]

(3) Making up the missed prayers in order is obligatory as long as they do not exceed the number that is prayed in a night and day. This was the opinion of Abu Haneefah[4] and Maalik.[5]

This is because having to make up a number exceeding the prayers of a day and night in order becomes difficult and falls under having to repeat the same prayers. Therefore, the case becomes the same as that of making up the missed fasts of Ramadaan [in that one does not have to make them up in order].[6]

(4) Making up the missed prayers in order is recommended. This is the opinion of Taawoos, Hasan al-Basree, Shurayh, Muhammad bin al-Hasan, Abu Thawr, Daawood and it is the chosen opinion of the Shaafi'ee school.[7] They said: These are all to be considered as his debts and as such it is not obligatory that he pay them off in order unless

---

[1] Refer to *al-Insaaf* (1/444), *al-Mughnee* (2/344), *as-Salaah wa Hukm Taarikihaa* (pp. 133-134) by ibn al-Qayyim, *al-Majmoo`* (3/75), *az-Zawaa'id fee Fiqh al-Imaam Ahmad* (1/117-118), *Bidaayah al-Mujtahid* (1/187) by ibn Rushd, and *Majmoo` Fataawaa* (2/106).
[2] *al-Insaaf* (1/444).
[3] *al-Mabsoot* (1/188).
[4] *al-Mabsoot* (1/188).
[5] *Bidaayah al-Mujtahid* (1/187) by ibn Rushd.
[6] Refer to *al-Majmoo`* (3/75) and *al-Mughnee* (2/37).
[7] *al-Majmoo`* (3/75).

there be a clear evidence that proves this. In this case there is no such evidence. If a person were to pray them without following their order, he has still performed the prayer that he has been commanded to pray. Therefore, it is not necessary to perform something additional to this without clear evidence.[1]

The Strongest Opinion: The first opinion is the strongest due to its conforming to all of the authentic texts concerning this issue. Therefore, praying the missed prayers in order is obligatory irrespective of whether the person prays them in congregation or individually. If a person forgets or fears that there is not enough time left before the time of the present prayer expires, then he prays the present prayer first. The same applies to the one who fears that he will miss the congregation if he were to pray his missed prayers first and he has no hope that there will be a second congregation—this holds true even if their is plenty of time remaining before the time of the present prayer expires, according to the correct opinion of the scholars.[2]

The Prophet (peace be upon him) missed four prayers on the Day of al-Khandaq and he made them up in order. At-Tirmidhee reports with his chain of narration from Naafi` bin Jubayr bin Mut`am from Abu `Ubaydah bin `Abdullaah from `Abdullaah that he said,

إِنَّ الْمُشْرِكِينَ شَغَلُوا رَسُولَ اللَّهِ صَلَّى اللَّهُ عَلَيْهِ وَسَلَّمَ عَنْ
أَرْبَعِ صَلَوَاتٍ يَوْمَ الْخَنْدَقِ حَتَّى ذَهَبَ مِنَ اللَّيْلِ مَا شَاءَ اللَّهُ
فَأَمَرَ بِلالاً فَأَذَّنَ ثُمَّ أَقَامَ فَصَلَّى الظُّهْرَ ثُمَّ أَقَامَ فَصَلَّى الْعَصْرَ ثُمَّ
أَقَامَ فَصَلَّى الْمَغْرِبَ ثُمَّ أَقَامَ فَصَلَّى الْعِشَاءَ قَالَ وَفِي الْبَابِ عَنْ
أَبِي سَعِيدٍ وَجَابِرٍ

---

[1] Ibid.

[2] Refer to *al-Masaa`il al-Fiqhiyyah min Kitaab ar-Riwaayatayn wa al-Wajhayn* (1/133) by Qaadee Abu Ya`laa, *al-Insaaf* (1/444), *Majmoo` Fataawaa ibn Taymiyyah* (22/106), *al-Mabsoot* (1/188) by as-Sarkhasee, and *al-Mukhtaaraat al-Jaliyyah* (p. 29) by ibn as-Sa`dee.

"The polytheists distracted the Messenger (peace be upon him) from four prayers on the Day of al-Khandaq until whatsoever Allah wished of the night had passed. He ordered Bilaal to call the *adhaan*. Then he called the *iqaamah* and they prayed *Dhuhur*; then he called the *iqaamah* and they prayed `Asr*; then he called the *iqaamah* and they prayed *Maghrib*; then he called the *iqaamah* and they prayed `Ishaa*."

At-Tirmidhee said, "*Ahaadeeth* concerning this have been reported from Abu Sa`eed and Jaabir bin `Abdullaah.*"[1]

Imaam ibn al-`Arabee said, "The scholars differ as to the meaning of this hadeeth—if a legally responsible person were to miss a number of prayers, is he to pray them in order or pray them in whatever order he wishes? Imaam Maalik, Abu Haneefah—and it is the meaning of the saying of Ahmad and Ishaaq—said that praying them in order is obligatory as long as he remembers; but the obligation is lifted if he forgets [their order]. This applies as long as he has not missed the same prayer more than once or the number of missed prayers is not large."

Ash-Shaafi`ee and Abu Thawr said that there is no need to make them up in order. A similar opinion is reported from al-Hasan al-Basree, Taawoos and Shurayh.

Ibn Qudaamah said, "They are obligatory prayers that should have been prayed in their respective times. Therefore, it is obligatory to pray them in order just as five daily prayers are prayed. The Messenger of Allah (peace be upon him) said,

$$ وَصَلُّوا كَمَا رَأَيْتُمُونِي أُصَلِّي $$

'Pray as you have seen me praying.'"[2]

Shaykh al-Islam ibn Taymiyyah said, "Praying the missed prayers in order is obligatory according to the majority of scholars as long as their number is small. This was the opinion of Abu Haneefah, Maalik and Ahmad—indeed in a report from Ahmad, he considers it to be obligatory to pray the

---

[1] Reported by at-Tirmidhee (no. 179 - 1/291 in `Aaridah al-Ahwadhee) and an-Nasaa`ee (1/297-298). The chain to the hadeeth has some weakness but it has supporting evidence that convey the same meaning and strengthen it to a level that it can be used as evidence.
[2] *al-Mughnee* (2/237).

missed prayers in order whether they are small or great in number. Furthermore, these scholars differ among themselves as to what constitutes a small number."[1]

Addendum: There is another issue linked to this one. Suppose a person is praying the present prayer and then, during the prayer, he remembers that he has still to make up a missed prayer. This person falls into one of two cases: Either there is still plenty of time remaining for the present prayer or there is not.

If there is still plenty of time remaining, the person should complete the prayer with the intention of having prayed an optional prayer. He should then perform the missed prayer and then perform the present prayer. This applies whether the person was the Imaam or follower or praying on his own. This is the strongest opinion of the two opinions of the scholars concerning this issue.[2]

If there is a small amount of time remaining, the question is whether he should he begin with the missed prayer even if the time for the present prayer expires or is he free to choose? The scholars differed over this. Imaam Maalik said that he should commence with the missed prayer. The opinion of ash-Shaafi`ee, the *Ashaab ar-Ra`i*, and the correct opinion of the Hanbalee school as has preceded, is that one commences with the present prayer. Ash`hab said that one is free to choose.[3]

Al-Haafidh said, "`Ayaadh said, 'The controversy is when there are only a small number of prayers to be made up. If, however, there are a large number of prayers to be made up, there is no difference of opinion that one should start with the present prayer. The scholars differed as to what constitutes a small number—some saying four prayers and other saying the prayers of one whole day.'"[4]

---

[1] *Majmoo` Fataawaa* (22/107-108).
[2] Refer to *al-Mughnee* (2/338) and `*Aaridah al-Ahwadhee* (1/292-293).
[3] Refer to *Fath al-Baaree* (2/70) and *al-Mughnee* (2/340-341).
[4] *al-Fath* (2/70).

4) The Ruling of Making the *Adhaan* and *Iqaamah* for the Missed Prayers

The prayers fall into a number of different types with respect to the *adhaan* and *iqaamah*:[1]

There is a type for which the *adhaan* and *iqaamah* is called—these being the five prescribed daily prayers.

There is a type for which the *adhaan* and *iqaamah* is not called—these being the supererogatory prayers and the Funeral prayers.

There is a type for which the call *as-Salaah Jaami`ah* is made—these being the prayers of the eclipse, seeking rain, and the two Eeds.[2]

There is a type over which there is a difference of opinion—these being the missed prescribed prayers. The clarification of this matters follows.

The Jurists expressed five different opinions with regards the ruling of calling the *adhaan* and *iqaamah* for the missed (obligatory) prayers:

The First Opinion: "The Sunnah is to call the *adhaan* and *iqaamah* for a single missed prayer, this being the opinion of the Hanafee and Hanbalee schools and the established opinion of the Shaafi`ee school. This is with regards to making up the prayer in congregation.[3]

If the person is making up the missed prayers on his own, the recommendation is of a lesser degree of importance with respect to him. This is because the purpose of the *adhaan* and *iqaamah* is to publicly announce the prayer and there is no need to do so here."[4]

The Second Opinion: If there are a number of prayers that need to be made up, then, according to the Hanafee school, it is best that the *adhaan* and *iqaamah* be called

---

[1] *Al-Ashbaah wa an-Nadhaa`ir* (p. 434) by as-Suyutee.

[2] What as-Suyutee mentions here that there is a call for the two Eed prayers and the prayer for seeking rain, he contradicts the position of the generality of scholars. We have mentioned it here only to truthfully and completely quote what as-Suyutee says. All that is reported with regards to their being a call for the two Eeds is unauthentic, be it from the Prophet (peace be upon him) or the Companions. Refer to *Nayl al-Awtaar* (3/295-296).

[3] Refer to *al-Mughnee* (2/76) and *Mawsoo`ah al-Fiqhiyyah* (2/369).

[4] Refer to *Badaa`i as-Sanaa`i* (1/154), *al-Muhadhdhab* (1/62), *Majmoo`* (3/91), and *Kashshaaf al-Qinaa`* (1/232).

separately for every prayer. According to the Hanbalee school, and this is also the established opinion of the Shaafi`ee school, it is recommended to call the *adhaan* (and the *iqaamah*) for the first prayer and then only the *iqaamah* for the remaining prayers. This is permissible according to the Hanafee school.[1]

The Third Opinion: Whoever misses a prayer or prayers should call the *iqaamah* only for every prayer and not call the *adhaan*. This is the opinion of the Maalikee school and an opinion of the Shaafi`ee school.[2]

The Fourth Opinion: If one hopes that people would join him in the prayer, he should call the *adhaan* and *iqaamah;* if he has no hope of this, he should call the *iqaamah* only. This is because the purpose of the *adhaan* is to gather the people for congregation and if there is no hope of gathering the people, there is no need to call the *adhaan*. This is an opinion of the Shaafi`ee school.[3]

The Fifth Opinion: One does not perform the *adhaan* or the *iqaamah* when making up missed prayer. This is the opinion of Sufyaan at-Thawree.[4]

The Strongest Opinion: It is recommended for whoever misses a single prayer to pray it after calling the *adhaan* and *iqaamah*; if he does not do this and prays, his prayer is still considered valid and complete—this applies if he is praying alone. If he has missed a number of prayers, it is recommended that he call the *adhaan* for the first prayer only and the *iqaamah* for the rest. Therefore, the *adhaan* would be called once, and the *iqaamah* for each missed prayer. It is permissible to leave the *adhaan* and suffice with the *iqaamah* only, even if these prayers are prayed in congregation.[5]

Addendum: After deciding that this is the strongest opinion, the person must be careful when he calls the *adhaan* and *iqaamah* not to cause any disturbance among the people. For example, one who is making up a missed prayer at the time of *Duhaa* or after `Asr should make the *adhaan* in such a way as to fulfil the Sunnah, but not to cause confusion.

---

[1] *al-Mawsoo`ah al-Fiqhiyyah* (2/370).
[2] *al-Istidhkaar* (1/111).
[3] *al-Majmoo`* (3/90) and *al-Mugnee* (2/76).
[4] *al-Istidhkaar* (1/111-113).
[5] Refer to *Saheeh ibn Khuzaymah* (2/87 no. 973 2/99 no. 997), *al-Istidhkaar* (1/111) and *al-Mughnee* (2/75).

Waiting for the Appointed Imaam and the Forbiddance of Establishing the Congregation Before Him Without Authority

The role of Imaam for the prayer is considered to be one of the best actions in Islam. The best of the people should be given the responsibility of carrying it out. "The best people" refers to those who possess noble characteristics, such as knowledge, piety, good recitation, and justice. The Jurists have agreed that the appointed Imaam of a mosque has the most right to lead the prayer.[1] This applies even if there are others who are more knowledgeable, better reciters than him or more pious than him. It is not permissible to commence the prayer before him, overruling his authority. Similarly, it is not permissible for anyone to be an Imaam in a mosque that has an appointed Imaam except with his prior permission.

What follows is some of the statements of the Imaams concerning this:

Imaam al-Haskafee from the Hanafee scholars said, "Know that the owner of a house (in his house) and the Imaam of a mosque have the greatest right to be the Imaam, unrestrictedly so—unless there be present the Sultaan or judge, in which case they should lead."[2]

The annotator to his work, ibn Aabideen said, "The meaning of his saying, 'unrestrictedly' is that this holds true even if there be present those who have more knowledge and are more proficient in reciting the Qur'aan than he."[3] The reason behind this is to close off the avenues that lead to splitting and argumentation.

---

[1] *Risaalah fee Iqaamah al-Hujjah `alaa al-Musallee Qabl al-Imaam ar-Raatib* (p. 21),
[2] *Radd al-Muhtaar `alaa ad-Darr al-Mukhtaar* (1/375-376) by ibn Aabideen.
[3] Ibid.

Ibn Qayyim al-Jawziyyah said, "The Legislator has commanded that the people gather behind one Imaam with respect to the *Khaleefate*, the *Jumu`ah* (Friday Prayer), the Two *Eid*s, the prayer for seeking rain and the prayer of fear. The reason behind this is to close off the means that lead to disunity and difference and in order to unite the hearts and words. This is from the greatest intentions of the *Sharee`ah* for the *Sharee`ah* has closed all doors that would lead to disunity and mutual hatred, to the extent that it has ordered that the rows of prayer be straightened so that hearts do not differ. The evidences concerning this are too many to be mentioned."[1]

Ibn Furhoon from the Maalikee scholars wrote in his *Tabsirah*, "Issue: If a mosque has an appointed Imaam who leads some of the prayers, it is not allowed to pray behind other than him in those prayers. Ibn al-Basheer said, 'There is no difference with regards the prohibition of this.'"[2]

Imaam ibn Abee Zayd al-Qayrawaanee said in his *Risaalah*, "It is disliked that a second congregation be held in any mosque that has an appointed Imaam." The commentator to his words, al-Manoofee said, "Meaning before the congregation of the appointed Imaam, alongside him or after him. This is because this leads to mutual hatred and dispute among the Imaams. If such is the outcome, the action deserves to be prohibited."[3]

The Shaafi`ee scholars said, as mentioned in *Minhaaj at-Taalibeen*, "The one who is the most knowledgeable and most proficient in reciting the Qur`aan should be made the Imaam.... Ibn Hajr said in *at-Tuhfah fee Sharh al-Minhaaj*, 'That is in the case where there is no appointed Imaam. If there is an appointed Imaam, he is the one who takes precedence over all others in leading because he is the one who has been given the legitimate authority to be the Imaam.'"[4]

Ar-Raheebaanee al-Hanbalee said,

---

[1] *I`laam al-Muwaqqi`een* (3/157).
[2] *Tabsirah al-Hukkaam fe Usool al-Aqdiyyah wa Manaahij al-Ahkaam* by ibn al-Firhawn al-Maalikee al-Madanee.
[3] Refer to *Risaalah fee Iqaamah al-Hujjah `alaa al-Musallee Jamaa`atan qabl al-Imaam ar-Raatib min al-Kitaab wa as-Sunnah wa Aqwaal Saa`ir al-A`immah al-Madhaahib* (p. 20) by Jamaal ad-Deen al-Qaasimee.
[4] Ibid (p. 27).

It is forbidden for one who meets the requirements of being an Imaam to lead the prayer in a mosque for which there is already an appointed Imaam without his permission. This is because the appointed Imaam is of the same standing as the owner of a house about whom the Prophet (peace be upon him) said,

لَا يُؤَمُّ الرَّجُلُ الرَّجُلَ فِي بَيْتِهِ إِلاَّ بِإِذْنِهِ

"Let not a person lead another person in his house except with his permission." This is also because it leads to hatred and moving away from the appointed Imaam. It also invalidates the benefit of appointing a specific Imaam in the first place. Therefore, it is not valid that one be an Imaam in a mosque in which there is an appointed Imaam before the appointed Imaam, without his permission. This is the clear sense derived from the words of the Hanbalee scholars. It is not prohibited that one lead after the appointed Imaam has led because he has fulfilled his duty and therefore his right is no longer transgressed. The author of *al-Iqnaa*` said, 'Except for the one who hates the Imaam, meaning that it is not permissible for him to lead after the Imaam because his intention is to cause harm to the Imaam and, therefore, he resembles the one who leads before the appointed Imaam."[1]

The preceding quotes show us the important position that the Imaam holds. They also show that what some people do in following up and broadcasting the mistakes of the Imaam in order to cause confusion and dislike of him is a serious mistake and transgression of due right. It is as if, to these people, the prayer consists merely of outward actions. So where are they with regards to its inner aspects, such as the

---

[1] *Mataalib Ulee an-Nahee Sharh Ghaayah al-Muntahaa* (5/614-615).

khushoo` and submission, and the uniting of the ranks under the flag of one Imaam in this noble action of worship?

No matter what the case, the evidence is against these people [who spread such evil] regardless of which sect or *madh-hab* they may adhere to. If they had only carefully considered the guidance of the Messenger of Allah (peace be upon him) and his companions, may Allah be pleased with them, and the Righteous Salaf, then never would they have taken this route of causing disunity in the mosques by turning away from the congregation of the appointed Imaam and, hence, dividing the congregation.

Abu Daawood reports in his *Sunan* from a number of the Companions of the Messenger of Allah (peace be upon him) that he said,

$$لَقَدْ أَعْجَبَنِي أَنْ تَكُونَ صَلاةُ الْمُسْلِمِينَ أَوْ قَالَ الْمُؤْمِنِينَ وَاحِدَةً$$

"Indeed it pleases me that the prayer of the Muslims—or he said believers—be one."[1]

The one who causes people to become averse to the Imaams should consider the Prophet's (peace be upon him) pleasure and delight that the prayer of the Muslims is united and one. Through this, we come to know that the one who expends his efforts in fragmenting this unity has opposed the Messenger of Allah (peace be upon him), has turned away from that which delights him and has actively disobeyed him—and refuge is sought with Allah from that.

Abdur-Razzaaq reports in his *Musannaf* from Naafi` who said, "The prayer was commenced in a part of Madeenah wherein Abdullaah bin Umar owned a piece of land. The Imaam of that mosque was a slave and ibn Umar came in order to attend the prayer. The Imaam said, 'Proceed and lead us.' Ibn Umar replied, 'You have the most right to lead in your mosque' and so the slave led the prayer."

Such was ibn Umar whose ranking in knowledge and excellence far exceeded that of the Imaam, yet he had him lead

---

[1] *Sunan Abu Daawood* [Eng. Trans. 1/130 no. 506].

due to his being the appointed Imaam. The aid of Allah is sought [to fix our current situation].

Nobody is denying that there may occur disputes between man and man regarding worldly and religious matters throughout this life. Allah has decreed this through His Wisdom. The reason behind this is that humans have been created with different intellects and understanding, just as they have been created having different goals, ideals and temperaments. However, when we consider the Companions, we find that they too had their differences and we find that some chose the opinion of one companion and others chose the opinion of another. Despite this, their mosque was one, their Imaam was one and their *Khateeb* was one.

Is it not a tremendous calamity that some rash and thoughtless people spend their time in discovering and exposing the faults of the scholars and Imaams and it does not distress them that their actions are foolish and transgressing the rights of others? To these people and those who think like them we say: Withdraw your hands from that which does not concern you and concerning which you have no right to delve into. Do not delve into that which you have nothing to do with and will not be questioned about. The Messenger of Allah (peace be upon him) said,

مِنْ حُسْنِ إِسْلامِ الْمَرْءِ تَرْكُهُ مَا لا يَعْنِيهِ

"From the excellence of the Islam of a person is his leaving that which does not concern him."[1]

We do not deny the fact that there are Imaams who do not fulfil their responsibilities and who are lax in performing their obligations. For example, you could see one of them neglecting his mosque and not being constant in performing his duty of leading the prayers, nor does he respond to the advice of his followers. This is a grave error that should be

---

[1] Reported by at-Tirmidhee (no. 2317), ibn Maajah (no. 3976) and it is a *hasan* hadeeth when taking into account its supporting evidence. [This hadith is on the borderline between *hasan* and weak. However, most likely, it is a weak hadith. For a detailed discussion of this hadith, see Jamaal al-Din Zarabozo, *Commentary on the Forty Hadith of al-Nawawi* (Boulder, CO: Al-Basheer Company for Publications and Translations, 1999), vol. 2, pp. 580-88.—JZ]

realized and corrected. Everyone should know the rights and duties upon him. So fear Allah as He should be feared. Know that Allah is the One Who Knows the true intentions of people and he is the One who guides to the Straight Path.

Closely Following the Imaam

It is a must upon the follower to closely follow the Imaam, irrespective of whether it be at the beginning or end of the prayer. This is due to what Abu Daawood reports in his *Sunan* from the hadeeth of Abu Hurayrah that the Prophet (peace be upon him) said,

إِذَا جِئْتُمْ إِلَى الصَّلَاةِ وَنَحْنُ سُجُودٌ فَاسْجُدُوا وَلَا تَعُدُّوهَا شَيْئًا وَمَنْ أَدْرَكَ الرَّكْعَةَ فَقَدْ أَدْرَكَ الصَّلَاةَ

"When you come to the prayer and we are in prostration, prostrate and do not count it as (a complete *rak`ah*). Whoever catches a *rak`ah* has caught the prayer."[1]

Sa`eed bin Mansoor reports in his *Sunan* from a group of the People of Madeenah that the Prophet (peace be upon him) said,

مَنْ وَجَدَنِي قَائِماً أَوْ رَاكِعاً أَوْ سَاجِداً فَلْيَكُنْ مَعِي عَلَى الْحَالِ الَّتِي أنا عَلَيْها

"Whoever finds me standing, bowing, or prostrating, let him join me in the same state that he finds me in." [2]

This holds true for everyone who comes to the mosque and finds that the prayer has been started. He should not busy himself with making up missed prayers, praying the prayer for greeting the mosque or praying optional prayers, be it in his house or in the mosque.

The reason for this is that when the *Mu`addhin* starts calling the *iqaamah* for prayer, it is one of the causes that prevents the performance of optional prayers.[3] Muslim reports

---

[1] *Sunan Abu Daawood* [Eng. Trans. 1/228 no. 892].
[2] Refer to *Nayl al-Awtaar* (3/173) and *Sayl al-Jarraar* (1/267).
[3] *al-Mawsoo`ah al-Fiqhiyyah* (12/168-169).

in his *Saheeh* from Abu Hurayrah that the Prophet (peace be upon him) said,

$$\text{إِذَا أُقِيمَتْ الصَّلاةُ فَلا صَلاةَ إِلاَّ الْمَكْتُوبَةُ}$$

"When the *iqaamah* for the prayer has been said, there is no prayer except the obligatory prayer."[1] Ahmad, may Allah have mercy upon him, has the wording,

$$\text{إِذَا أُقِيمَتْ الصَّلاةُ فَلا صَلاةَ إِلاَّ الَّتِي أُقِيمَتْ}$$

"When the *iqaamah* for the prayer has been said, there is no prayer except the one that has been established."[2]

There are three points that need to be discussed here:

(1) The ruling of what one should do when one enters the mosque and the prayer has been started.

(2) What to do if the *iqaamah* is called while one is praying an optional prayer.

(3) What to do if one has started praying an obligatory prayer, one that has been missed or the present one, either alone or in congregation, and the *iqaamah* is called.

The scholars have a detailed analysis of these three points. I will summarize them here and mention the strongest opinions—and the Aid of Allah is sought.

The Maalikee Opinion

It is forbidden for the one who arrives late to start praying an optional or obligatory prayer after the *iqaamah* has been called for the prayer that is to be led by the appointed Imaam. When the *iqaamah* has been called in the mosque while one is praying an obligatory or optional prayer in the mosque or in his home, then, if he fears that he will miss a *rak'ah* with the Imaam, he, without any exception, should discontinue his prayer and join the prayer with the Imaam. He should discontinue his prayer by saying the *salaam* or by doing

---

[1] *Saheeh Muslim* [Eng. Trans. No. 710, no. 63].
[2] *Musnad Ahmad* (2/353).

something that would invalidate the prayer, such as talking or making the intention to invalidate the prayer.

If, however, he does not fear that he will miss a *rak'ah,* he should complete his prayer as an optional prayer and as two *rak'ahs.* It is recommended that he pray it sitting down.

If he is praying the very same prayer that has been commenced—for example, he was praying the *'Asr* prayer and then the *iqaamah* for the *'Asr* prayer was called for the congregational prayer—he should finish the prayer before he reaches the odd numbered *rak'ahs* and not complete the prayer. If he has only prayed one *rak'ah,* he should add to it a second. If he is praying his second *rak'ah,* he should complete it. If he is praying his third *rak'ah* but has not completed it, meaning that he has not yet performed its prostrations, then he should sit again, say the *tashahhud* and then say the *salaam.* This holds true for the case when he is praying the prayers that consist of four *rak'ahs.*

If he is praying *Fajr* or *Maghrib* and the congregational prayer is commenced, he should discontinue his prayer and join the congregation, so that the possibility of its being considered an optional prayer being prayed at a prohibited time no longer remains. If, however, he has completed the second or third *rak'ah* of *Maghrib* or the second *rak'ah* of *Fajr,* he should complete the prayer with the intention of it being the obligatory prayer.[1]

The Shaafi'ee Opinion

If one is praying an optional prayer and the *iqaamah* for the congregational prayer is called, then, if he does not fear that he will miss the congregational prayer, he should complete his optional prayer and afterwards join the congregation. If he fears that he will miss the congregational prayer, he should cut off his prayer because the congregational prayer is better and more superior. One can also make the intention to enter the congregation without actually severing his (current prayer). If he enters the mosque and the prayer has already been

---

[1] Refer to *ash-Sharh as-Sagheer* (1/431) and *Qawaaneen al-Ahkaam al-Fiqhiyyah* (p. 68).

established, he is not to busy himself with praying optional prayers due to the Prophet's (peace be upon him) saying,

$$إِذَا أُقِيمَتْ الصَّلاةُ فَلا صَلاةَ إِلاَّ الْمَكْتُوبَةُ$$

"When the *iqaamah* for the prayer has been said, there is no prayer except for the obligatory prayer." 1

The Hanbalee Opinion

When the *Mu`adhdhin* starts calling the *iqaamah* for the congregational prayer, there is no prayer save the obligatory prayer. Therefore, one should not start praying any optional prayers whatsoever nor the regular sunnah prayers, be they the *sunnah*s of *Fajr* or any other prayer, be it in the mosque or in one's house. This due to the generality of the aforementioned hadeeth.

If one does pray an optional prayer after the *iqaamah* has been called, this prayer of his is not counted due to what the hadeeth mentions,

$$إِذَا أُقِيمَتْ الصَّلاةُ فَلا صَلاةَ إِلاَّ الْمَكْتُوبَةُ$$

"When the *iqaamah* for the prayer has been said, there is no prayer except the obligatory prayer." 2

Also, al-Bayhaqee reported in his *Sunan* that, "Umar bin al-Khattaab used to beat the people for praying after the *iqaamah* had been called."3

If the prayer has been commenced while one is praying optional prayers, even if he is not in the mosque, he should complete the prayer with quick *rak`ah*s, even if he misses a *rak`ah* of the congregational prayer. This is based on Allah's words,

$$وَلا تُبْطِلُوا أَعْمَالَكُمْ$$

1 *Saheeh Muslim* [Eng. Trans. No. 710, no. 63],
2 *Saheeh Muslim* [Eng. Trans. No. 710, no. 63].
3 *Sunan al-Kubraa* (2/483) and refer to *al-Muhallaa* (3/151, 308) by ibn Hazm adh-Dhaahiree.

"...And do not invalidate your actions" [Muhammad (47):33].

He should not pray more than two *rak`ahs*. If he had started a third *rak`ah* (when the *iqaamah* is called), he should complete the prayer as four *rak`ahs* because this is better than praying three. If, however, he were to end the prayer at the third *rak`ah* by saying the *salaam,* such is also permissible.

All of this holds true unless the one praying the optional prayer fears that he will miss the congregational prayer altogether. In that case, he discontinues his prayer and joins the congregation, because the obligatory prayer is more important.[1]

The Hanafee Opinion

If one starts praying the obligatory prayer, or is making up a missed prayer and the *iqaamah* for the congregational prayer is called, then, if he is praying *Fajr* or *Maghrib* and is still in the first *rak`ah*—even if this be after the prostration—it is upon him to discontinue his prayer by saying the *salaam* and join the congregation. If he is in the second *rak`ah* and has not yet performed the prostrations, it is also upon him to discontinue his prayer. However, if he has already performed the prostrations, he should complete the prayer.

If one is praying a prayer consisting of four *rak`ahs,* for example, *Dhuhur* or *`Asr* and if he is in the first *rak`ah* and before the prostration, he should discontinue his prayer and join the Imaam. If he has performed the prostrations of the first *rak`ah,* he should complete the prayer in two *rak`ahs* and join the congregation in order to attain the superiority and excellence of the congregation. What he prayed is counted as an optional prayer.

If he has stood for the third *rak`ah* and the *iqaamah* is called for the congregational prayer before his performing its prostrations, he should discontinue his prayer by saying one *salaam* while standing. If he has completed his third *rak`ah* of a four *rak`ah* prayer or *Maghrib,* he should complete his prayer (as it should be) because performing the majority has the same ruling as performing the totality. Then he should pray

---

[1] *Kashshaaf al-Qinaa`* (1/539f).

with the congregation. This prayer will be counted as an optional prayer because the obligatory prayer cannot be repeated in one time period. The evidence for this lies in what was said by Yazeed al-Aswad,

شَهِدْتُ مَعَ النَّبِيِّ صَلَّى اللَّهُ عَلَيْهِ وَسَلَّمَ حَجَّتَهُ فَصَلَّيْتُ مَعَهُ

صَلاةَ الصُّبْحِ فِي مَسْجِدِ الْخَيْفِ وَأَنَا غُلامٌ شَابٌّ فَلَمَّا قَضَى

صَلاتَهُ وَانْحَرَفَ إِذَا هُوَ بِرَجُلَيْنِ لَمْ يُصَلِّيَا مَعَهُ فَقَالَ عَلَيَّ

بِهِمَا فَجِيءَ بِهِمَا تُرْعَدُ فَرَائِصُهُمَا فَقَالَ مَا مَنَعَكُمَا أَنْ تُصَلِّيَا

مَعَنَا فَقَالا يَا رَسُولَ اللَّهِ إِنَّا قَدْ صَلَّيْنَا فِي رِحَالِنَا قَالَ لا

تَفْعَلا إِذَا صَلَّيْتُمَا فِي رِحَالِكُمَا ثُمَّ أَتَيْتُمَا مَسْجِدَ جَمَاعَةٍ

فَصَلِّيَا مَعَهُمْ فَإِنَّهَا لَكُمَا نَافِلَةٌ

"I accompanied the Prophet (peace be upon him) on his Hajj and I prayed *Fajr* with him in the Mosque of Khayf. At that time I was a young man. When he finished the prayer, he saw two people who had not prayed with him. He said, 'Bring them to me.' So they were summoned and came apprehensively. He asked them, 'What prevented you from praying with us?' They replied, 'O Messenger of Allah, we already prayed in our houses.' He said, 'Do not do this again. If you have prayed in your houses and then come to the mosque to find a congregation there, pray with them, for it will be counted as an optional prayer for you.'"[1]

Whoever enters the mosque and finds that the prayer has commenced, he is to join the congregation and he is not to perform any optional prayers, unless they be the *sunnah*s of *Fajr* which he should pray near the door of the mosque and then enter. This is when he does not fear that by doing this he will miss the congregational prayer. If he fears he will miss the prayer, he should join the Imaam in praying the obligatory

[1] *Sunan at-Tirmidhee* (2/18 - *Aaridah al-Ahwadhee*), *Sunan Abu Daawood* [Eng. Trans. 1/151 no. 575] and *Mustadrak al-Haakim* (1/244).

prayer. This is because the reward of the congregation is greater and the threat in leaving it is far more severe.[1]

The Correct Opinion

It is obligatory upon whoever hears the *iqaamah* that he not involve himself in reciting the Qur'aan, reciting words of remembrance of Allah, commencing a prayer, praying the sunnahs of *Fajr* or performing any other prayer, be this in his house or in the mosque. Instead, he must concern himself with going [to the prayer] and following the Imaam.

Ibn Hazm wrote in *al-Muhallaa,* "Issue: Whoever hears the *iqaamah* for the *Fajr* prayer and knows that were he to pray the sunnahs of *Fajr,* he will miss a portion of the Fajr prayer, even if only it be the opening *takbeer,* then it is not permissible for him to involve himself in praying them. Were he to pray them, he would have disobeyed Allah, the Exalted. When he has completed the prayer with the Imaam he can, if he wishes, pray the two sunnahs or he can leave them. This also applies to the one who is praying optional prayers and during them the *iqaamah* for the obligatory prayer has been called [that is, he should leave his optional prayer if he fears missing a part of the prayer.]"

Then he went on to say, "We do not know of any evidence from the Qur'aan, the authentic Sunnah or even the weak *ahaadeeth,* the consensus, analogy, and the saying of the Companions that would support the opinion of Abu Haneefah and Maalik. Hence, due to their opinion being devoid of proof, we make recourse to our opinion [previously mentioned] and found that the clear proofs lay with it."[2]

Then he mentioned a number of *ahaadeeth* and narrations concerning this, including he previously mentioned hadeeth of Abu Hurayrah,

$$\text{إِذَا أُقِيمَتِ الصَّلَاةُ فَلَا صَلَاةَ إِلَّا الْمَكْتُوبَةُ}$$

---

[1] Refer to *Fath al-Qadeer* (1/335-342) and *Tabyeen al-Haqaa`iq* (1/180-184).
[2] *al-Muhallaa* (3/143-152 no. 308).

"When the *iqaamah* for the prayer has been said then there is no prayer except for the obligatory prayer." [1]

There is also the hadeeth reported by ibn Buhaynah, Abdullaah bin Malik,

$$\text{أُقِيمَتْ صَلاةُ الصُّبْحِ فَرَأَى رَسُولُ اللَّهِ صَلَّى اللَّهُ عَلَيْهِ وَسَلَّمَ}$$

$$\text{رَجُلاً يُصَلِّي وَالْمُؤَذِّنُ يُقِيمُ فَقَالَ أَتُصَلِّي الصُّبْحَ أَرْبَعًا}$$

"The *Fajr* prayer was commenced and the Messenger of Allah (peace be upon him) saw a man praying while the *Mu`adhdhin* was calling the *iqaamah* and he said, 'Are you praying *Fajr* as four *rak`ahs*?'"[2]

Ibraaheem an-Nakha`ee said concerning the one who finds the Imaam praying while he has yet to pray the two sunnahs of *Fajr*, "He starts with the obligatory prayer."

Sa`eed bin Jubair said, "Discontinue your prayer at the time of *iqaamah*."

Similar other *ahaadeeth* and narrations come from a number of the Salaf, may Allah be pleased with them all. This is the opinion that Shaykh al-Islam ibn Taymiyyah determined to be the strongest,[3] as did his student, al-Allaamah ibn Qayyim al-Jawziyyah[4] and others. Allah Knows best.

---

[1] *Saheeh Muslim* [Eng. Trans. No. 710, no. 63].

[2] Reported by al-Bukhaaree [Eng. Trans. 1/357 no. 632] and Muslim [Eng. Trans. 1/346 no. 1536] and the wording is Muslim's.

[3] *Majmoo` Fataawaa* (23/264).

[4] *I`laam al-Muwaqqi`een* (2/356-357).

Conveying (the *Takbeers*) behind the Imaam in Congregational Prayer

First: From the sunnahs of the prayer is that the Imaam pronounces the *takbeer, tasmee`*, and the *salaam* as loudly as the need dictates so that the followers can hear him. It is disliked for the Imaam to raise his voice more than what is needed.

The *takbeer* and the statements made upon moving from position to position in prayer are to come from the Imaam. However, if his voice does not reach those who are behind him, it is desired that one of the followers convey his statements. The meaning of *takbeer* here is the opening *takbeer* and the *takbeers* said upon moving from position to position in the prayer.

Second: The linguistic meaning of *tableegh* (conveyance), being derived from the verb *ballagha,* is to convey and reach. It is said, "something *ballagha* to him" when it was made to reach him. "The *salaam* has been *ballagha,*" when it has reached him.[1]

The *Sharee`ah* meaning of this word is more specific than the linguistic meaning. It means to announce and inform, because one is conveying the information.[2]

The meaning of *tableegh* in congregational prayer is to convey the statements of *takbeer* made by the Imaam so that those led can hear it.[3]

The evidence for the sanctioning of *tableegh* lies in the hadeeth reported by al-Bukhaaree from Aa`ishah who said,

---

[1] *al-Misbaah al-Muneer* and *Mu`jam Lugha al-Fuqahaa* (1/120).
[2] *Radd al-Mukhtaar alaa ad-Darr al-Mukhtaar* (1/319) by ibn Aabideen.
[3] *Mu`jam Lugha al-Fuqahaa* (1/120).

لَمَّا مَرِضَ النَّبِيُّ صَلَّى اللَّهُ عَلَيْهِ وَسَلَّمَ مَرَضَهُ الَّذِي مَاتَ فِيهِ

أَتَاهُ بِلَالٌ يُؤذِنُهُ بِالصَّلَاةِ فَقَالَ مُرُوا أَبَا بَكْرٍ فَلْيُصَلِّ قُلْتُ إِنَّ

أَبَا بَكْرٍ رَجُلٌ أَسِيفٌ إِنْ يَقُمْ مَقَامَكَ يَبْكِي فَلَا يَقْدِرُ عَلَى

الْقِرَاءَةِ فَقَالَ مُرُوا أَبَا بَكْرٍ فَلْيُصَلِّ فَقُلْتُ مِثْلَهُ فَقَالَ فِي الثَّالِثَةِ

أَوِ الرَّابِعَةِ إِنَّكُنَّ صَوَاحِبُ يُوسُفَ مُرُوا أَبَا بَكْرٍ فَلْيُصَلِّ فَصَلَّى

وَخَرَجَ النَّبِيُّ صَلَّى اللَّهُ عَلَيْهِ وَسَلَّمَ يُهَادَى بَيْنَ رَجُلَيْنِ كَأَنِّي

أَنْظُرُ إِلَيْهِ يَخُطُّ بِرِجْلَيْهِ الْأَرْضَ فَلَمَّا رَآهُ أَبُو بَكْرٍ ذَهَبَ يَتَأَخَّرُ

فَأَشَارَ إِلَيْهِ أَنْ صَلِّ فَتَأَخَّرَ أَبُو بَكْرٍ رَضِيَ اللَّهُ عَنْهُ وَقَعَدَ النَّبِيُّ

صَلَّى اللَّهُ عَلَيْهِ وَسَلَّمَ إِلَى جَنْبِهِ وَأَبُو بَكْرٍ يُسْمِعُ النَّاسَ التَّكْبِيرَ

"When the Messenger of Allah (peace be upon him) fell ill with the illness from which he died, Bilaal came to him to inform him of the prayer. He said, 'Order Abu Bakr to lead the prayer.' I (Aa`ishah) said, 'Abu Bakr is a soft hearted man and were he to stand and lead the prayer in your place, he would weep so much that he would not be able to recite the Qur`aan.' The Prophet (peace be upon him) repeated the same request three or four times and on each occasion I repeated what I said. He then said, 'Indeed, you are like the companions of Yusuf; order Abu Bakr to lead the prayer.' So Abu Bakr led the prayer. In the meantime the Prophet (peace be upon him) [recovered slightly] and came out with the help of two men and it is if I can still see him dragging his feet on the ground. When Abu Bakr saw him, he tried to retreat but the Messenger of Allah (peace be upon him) indicated to him to continue leading. Abu Bakr retreated and the Prophet (peace be upon him) sat by his side and Abu Bakr repeated the *takbeer* of the Prophet (peace be upon him) for the people to hear."[1]

---

[1] *Saheeh al-Bukhaaree* [Eng. Trans. 1/383 no. 680].

The Opinions of the Jurists Concerning the *Tableegh*

The opinion of the Shaafi`ee[1] and Hanafee[2] scholars is that it is obligatory upon the one who is conveying—regardless of whether he is the Imaam or follower—to have the intention to enter the prayer when saying the initial *takbeer*. If his intention was only to convey, his prayer would not have been initiated. If his intention was to say the initial *takbeer* for entering the prayer and also to convey the wording, his prayer is valid.

The Maalikees are of the opinion that it is permissible to appoint a specific person to convey the announcements so that the people can hear, and his prayer is valid even if his intention was (solely) to convey when he said the *takbeer* and *tahmeed* (the saying of *sami-Allaahu liman hamidah*).[3]

The Hanbalees are of the opinion that "It is recommended that the Imaam say the announcements loud enough so that the followers can hear (and thereby know) when he moves from position to position in prayer, for example he says the opening *takbeer* aloud. If the words of the Imaam are not heard by all the followers, it is recommended that some of the followers raise their voices so the others can hear."[4]

Ibn Qudaamah, may Allah have mercy upon him, said, "It is recommended that the Imaam say the *takbeer* loud enough so the followers can hear him and then in turn say the *takbeer,* for it is not permissible for them to say the *takbeer* except after his pronouncement of the *takbeer*. If it is not possible for him to make all the followers hear, it is recommended for some of the followers to say the *takbeers* loudly so that the rest, who could not hear the Imaam, can hear them."[5]

From what has preceded we are able to establish the following regulations:

---

[1] *al-Majmoo`* (3/398).
[2] *Rasaa`il ibn Aabideen* (1/318).
[3] *Haashiyah ad-Dasooqee* (1/318).
[4] *al-Mughnee* (2/128-129).
[5] Ibid.

The Sunnah is that the Imaam should say the *takbeer*, *tahmeed*, and *salaam* aloud to the extent required, allowing those following to hear him.

If it is not possible for all of the followers to hear due to a reason linked with the Imaam, their being a large congregation, or their being some obstacle that prevents his voice from reaching them, is it permissible for one of the followers to convey the voice of the Imaam? The clear position arrived at from the Sunnah is that this is permissible and the evidence has preceded.

But when we look to the reality in many of today's mosques, we find that the *tableegh* has been used at other than its correct occasion and in a way that has not been legislated. This is because the *tableegh* in many Muslim lands has been taken as something necessary and is used without considering the wisdom and reason behind its legislation. Therefore, this matter has become something customary rather than something which is a Sunnah that is to be enacted due to specific reasons.

Conveying Behind the Imaam in the Two Holy Mosques

At this juncture it would be good to mention that it is not desired to perform the *tableegh* behind the Imaam in the Two Holy Mosques of Mecca and Madeenah. This is because there exists no need for it since loudspeakers are employed that fulfil the objective of the *tableegh* in a far more complete way.

The one who considers the words of the People of Knowledge that have preceded and their difference concerning this issue will find that they did not state the permissibility of the *tableegh* except in specific circumstances and on rare occasions. Indeed, some of them forbade the *tableegh* unrestrictedly. I wish to alert everyone to this so that we are able to distinguish our words and actions that are customary from those that are done as actions of worship in the most important pillar of Islam after the testimony of faith.

Shaykh al-Islam ibn Taimiyyah said,

> The *tableegh* and *takbeer* and raising the voice
> when saying the *tahmeed* and *tasleem* were not
> practiced during the time of the Messenger of
> Allah (peace be upon him), nor in the time of

his *Khaleefahs*, and not for a long time afterwards, except on two occasions. The first time was when the Messenger (peace be upon him) injured himself by falling off his horse and, therefore, prayed in his house sitting. Abu Bakr conveyed the *takbeer* from him as is reported by Muslim in his *Saheeh*. The second time was on the occasion of his illness from which he died and Abu Bakr conveyed from him, and this is well known.

There is no difference among the scholars that it is not recommended to do this *tableegh* when there is no need. Indeed, many of them explicitly stated that it was detestable and some of them said that doing this invalidates the prayer of the one doing it. This opinion is voiced in the school of thought of Maalik, Ahmad and others. The scholars have differed concerning the case when there is a need, such as (some of) the followers being far away from the Imaam, or due to the physical weakness of the Imaam or other such things. The well-known opinion among the Hanbalees is that the *tableegh* is permissible under this circumstance, and this is the most authentic opinion of the two opinions voiced by the Maalikees. It has reached me that Ahmad refrained from voicing an opinion concerning this. Given the opinion that it is permissible, it is conditional upon the fact that the one conveying omits none of the obligations of the prayer.

As for the case when the calmness and tranquillity of the one conveying is greatly disturbed, his prayer is rendered invalid according to the most of the scholars, as is proven by the Sunnah. Also, if the one conveying precedes the Imaam, this also renders his prayer invalid according to what is clear from the Hanbalee school of fiqh. This opinion is proven by the Sunnah and statements of the Companions. If the one conveying omits the *dhikr* performed in the bowing and prostrating, then there is a difference as whether or not his prayer is rendered invalid. The apparent stance of the Hanbalee school of thought is that it is invalid.

There is no doubt that conveying without any need is a *bid`ah*. Whoever believes that it is unrestrictedly an action which draws one close to Allah, then there is no doubt that he is either ignorant or an obstinate denier. All of the scholars have mentioned in their books, even in their books in which they do not delve into detail, that "none of the *takbeers* should be articulated aloud unless one is the Imaam."

Whoever persists upon his belief that the *tableegh* is unrestrictedly an action which draws one close to Allah should be punished for this act, due to his contradicting the consensus—this being the least possible stance taken against him. Allah Knows best.[1]

---

[1] *Majmoo` Fataawaa* (23/400-403).

The Ruling of Reciting Behind the Imaam in Congregational Prayer

The five obligatory prayers prayed in congregation are either of the type in which the recitation is silent, such as *Dhuhur* and *'Asr,* or where the recitation is aloud, such as *Fajr, Maghrib* and *'Ishaa.* The recitation in these latter prayers is considered to be aloud from the point of view that the Imaam recites *Surah al-Faatihah* and what comes afterwards in the first two *rak'ahs* aloud and silently in the remaining *rak'ahs* of *Maghrib* and *'Ishaa.*

This is with respect to the Imaam. With respect to the followers, should they recite behind the Imaam in congregational prayer? If so, when should they recite? What is the ruling of this recitation according to the Jurists? This is what we shall discuss here *inshaa'Allah.*

The Prayer in Which the Recitation is Silent

The majority of the People of Knowledge are of the opinion that the follower recites *al-Faatihah* silently behind the Imaam for *Dhuhur* and *'Asr* prayers, the third *rak'ah* of *Maghrib* and the last two *rak'ahs* of *'Ishaa.* However they differ as to whether this is recommended or obligatory.

The generality of the evidences stress the desirability that the follower recite and not be lax with regards to this, especially with respect to *Surah al-Faatihah.* This is due to what ibn Maajah reports with his chain of narrators from Jaabir bin Abdullah who said,

كُنَّا نَقْرَأُ فِي الظُّهْرِ وَالْعَصْرِ خَلْفَ الإِمَامِ فِي الرَّكْعَتَيْنِ الأُولَيَيْنِ بِفَاتِحَةِ الْكِتَابِ وَسُورَةٍ وَفِي الأُخْرَيَيْنِ بِفَاتِحَةِ الْكِتَابِ

"We used to recite *Surah al-Faatihah* and another *surah* in the first two *rak`ah*s of *Dhuhur* and `Asr, and *al-Faatihah* in the last two *rak`ah*s when praying behind the Imaam."[1]

The Sunnah is to recite silently and it is disliked to recite aloud.[2]

The evidence for this lies in what `Imraan bin Husayn reported:

أَنَّ رَسُولَ اللَّهِ صَلَّى اللَّهُ عَلَيْهِ وَسَلَّمَ صَلَّى الظُّهْرَ فَجَعَلَ رَجُلٌ يَقْرَأُ خَلْفَهُ بِسَبِّحِ اسْمَ رَبِّكَ الْأَعْلَى فَلَمَّا انْصَرَفَ قَالَ أَيُّكُمْ قَرَأَ أَوْ أَيُّكُمُ الْقَارِئُ فَقَالَ رَجُلٌ أَنَا فَقَالَ قَدْ ظَنَنْتُ أَنَّ بَعْضَكُمْ خَالَجَنِيهَا

The Messenger of Allah (peace be upon him) prayed *Dhuhur* and a person he was leading started reciting *Surah al-A`laa*. When the Messenger of Allah had completed the prayer, he said, "Which one of you was reciting," or, "Who was the reciter?" The man replied, "It was I." He said, "I thought that some of you were competing with me in it."[3]

The Prayer in Which the Recitation is Aloud

The scholars have differed concerning this issue.[4] It is reported from a group of the Companions that they obligated reciting behind the Imaam and it is reported from others that they did not use to recite behind the Imaam. Therefore the Jurists have divided into three opinions concerning this:

First Opinion: Reciting behind the Imaam is obligatory in both the aloud and silent prayers.

Second Opinion: The follower is not to recite behind the Imaam, be it the aloud or silent prayers.

---

[1] *Sunan ibn Maajah* (1/151 no. 827).
[2] *al-Mawsoo`ah al-Fiqhhiyah* (16/183).
[3] *Saheeh Muslim* [Eng, Trans. 1/218 no. 783].
[4] Refer to *Ma`aalim as-Sunan* by al-Khattaabee, with *Tahdheeb as-Sunan* by ibn al-Qayyim in the margin (1/394) and *Majmoo` Fataawaa* (22/294-296).

Third Opinion: The follower recites in those prayers in which the Imaam recites silently but does not recite in the prayers in which the Imaam recites aloud, regardless of whether he hears the recitation or not.

Before you is an analysis of each opinion along with its proponents and their evidence.

The First Opinion: Reciting Behind the Imaam is Obligatory in Both the Aloud and Silent Prayers

This is the opinion of ash-Shaafi`ee and a reported opinion of the Hanbalee school. It is also the chosen opinion of Imaam al-Bukhaaree, ash-Shawkaanee and others.

Their evidence lies in the following:

First is the hadeeth reported by Ubaadah bin Saamit that the Messenger of Allah (peace be upon him) said,

$$لَا صَلَاةَ لِمَنْ لَمْ يَقْرَأْ بِفَاتِحَةِ الْكِتَابِ$$

"There is no prayer for the one who does not recite the Opening Chapter of the Book."[1]

There is also the hadeeth of Abu Hurayrah in which the Prophet (peace be upon him) said,

$$مَنْ صَلَّى صَلَاةً لَمْ يَقْرَأْ فِيهَا بِأُمِّ الْقُرْآنِ فَهِيَ خِدَاجٌ ثَلَاثًا غَيْرُ تَمَامٍ$$

"Whoever prays a prayer in which he does not recite al-Faatihah, then it is deficient, it is deficient, it is deficient, it is incomplete."[2] This hadeeth is general and applies to the Imaam, the follower and the one praying alone.

Next there is the hadeeth of Anas that the Prophet (peace be upon him) asked (his Companions),

---

[1] al-Bukhaaree [Eng. Trans. 1/404 no. 723], Muslim [Eng. Trans. 1/214 no. 771], Abu Daawood [Eng. Trans. 1/210 no. 822], Tirmidhee (no. 247), Nasaa`ee (2/137-138), and al-Haakim in *al-Mustadrak* (1/238).

[2] Muslim [Eng. Trans. 1/215 no. 775].

187

أَتَقْرَأُونَ فِي صَلَاتِكُمْ وَالإِمَامُ يَقْرَأُ، فَسَكَتُوا فَقَالَهَا ثَلَاثَ
مَرَّاتٍ، فَقَالَ قَائِلٌ إِنَّا نَفْعَلُ، قَالَ فَلَا تَفْعَلُوا وَيَقْرَأُ أَحَدُكُمْ
بِفَاتِحَةِ الكِتَابِ فِي نَفْسِهِ

"Do you recite in your prayers while the Imaam is reciting?"
They remained silent and he repeated the question three times.
Then a person said, "Indeed we do so." He replied, "Do not do
so but let each of you recite the *Faatihah* of the Book to
himself."[1]

And there are many other *ahaadeeth* of this nature.
Also, there are a number of authentic and established
narrations from the Companions that cement the fact that
reciting *al-Faatihah* behind the Imaam is recommended. These
include:

Yazeed bin Shareek at-Tameemee said, "I asked Umar
bin al-Khattaab, 'Should I recite when praying behind an
Imaam, O Leader of the Believers?' He replied, 'Yes.' I asked,
'Even if you recited?' He said, 'Even if I recited.'"[2]

Imraan bin Husayn said, "Do not consider the prayer
of a Muslim to be correct except with purity, *ruku`* and the
Faatihah of the Book whether behind the Imaam or without
the Imaam."[3]

Abu ad-Dardaa said, "Do not leave reciting the
Faatihah of the Book behind the Imaam whether he recites
aloud or not." A similar statement was made by ibn Abbaas.[4]

---

[1] al-Haythamee said, "Reported by Abu Ya`laa and at-Tabaraanee in *al-Awsat*
and its narrators are trustworthy and precise." *Majma` az-Zawaa`id* (2/110).
[This hadith was recorded in a number of books, including *Saheeh ibn Hibbaan*
and *Sunan al-Baihaqi*. The chains of the hadith are at least *hasan*, as Shuaib al-
Arnaaoot and Khaldoon al-Ahdab have pointed out. It was also used as evidence
by al-Bukhari himself. Cf., for example, Shuaib al-Arnaaoot, footnotes to Ameer
Alaa al-Deen al-Faarisi, *al-Ihsaan fi Taqreeb Saheeh ibn Hibbaan* (Beirut:
Muassasat al-Risaalah, 1988), vol. 5, p. 153.—JZ]
[2] *at-Ta`leeq al-Mughnee `alaa Sunan ad-Daaruqutnee* (1/317).
[3] *al-Qiraa`ah Khalf al-Imaam* (pg. 6) by al-Bayhaqee.
[4] *as-Sunan al-Kubraa* (2/169) by al-Bayhaqee.

The Second Opinion: The Follower Does Not Recite in Either the Prayers Said Silently or Aloud

This is the opinion of the Hanafee School and the chosen opinion of the Hanbalee School and others.[1]

From their proofs is:

The *mursal* report of Abdullaah bin Shidaad that the Prophet (peace be upon him) said,

مَنْ كَانَ لَهُ إِمَامٌ فَقِرَاءَةُ الإِمَامِ لَهُ قِرَاءَةٌ

"Whoever has an Imaam, then the recitation of the Imaam is the recitation for him."[2]

From the narrations they depend upon are:

Ibn Umar, replying to a question posed to him about whether one should recite behind the Imaam, said, "When one of you prays behind the Imaam, the recitation of the Imaam suffices him. When one of you prays alone, let him recite."

---

[1] Refer to *Fath al-Qadeer* (1/294) and *al-Insaaf* (2/56) by al-Mardaawee.

[2] Reported by Ibn Maajah (1/105) and it is weak.. The author of *Misbaah az-Zujaajah fee Zawaa`id ibn Maajah* (1/105) said, "Its chain contains the liar Jaabir and the hadeeth contradicts what the six works report from the hadeeth of Ubaadah bin Saamit." Ibn Hajr said in *Talkhees al-Habeer* (1/232), "It is well-known from the hadeeth of Jaabir and he reports it via a number of routes from a group of the Companions and all the routes are defective." Ad-Daaruqutnee said in his *Sunan* (1/331), "Jaabir and Layth are both weak." Al-Allaamah ibn al-Qayyim said in *Tahdheeb as-Sunan* (1/349 in the margin of *Ma`aalim as-Sunan*), "They have no proof with this hadeeth because it is *mursal* and the *mursal* hadeeth is weak and cannot be taken to oppose a *saheeh* hadeeth that has its chain continuously linked back to the Prophet (peace be upon him). Also, the recitation of the Imaam cannot be considered to be the recitation of the follower unless he hears it. As for the case when he does not hear the recitation, the Imaam's recitation cannot be considered his recitation. So it becomes necessary for him to recite. This is alongside the multitude of *ahaadeeth* enjoining one to recite in the prayer. Also, it is not correct to remain silent when one should recite. It is truly amazing that we find the People of Opinion enjoining the follower to recite the opening supplication, the *tasbeeh* while in *ruku`* and *sujood*, and the *tashahhud* while forbidding him from reciting the Qur`aan thinking that the Imaam recites for all. Why is not the same true for the *takbeer*, *tasbeeh* and the other matters? This is from the strange consequences of blind and rigid following. May Allah guide us to the straight way."

And Abdullaah bin Umar did not use to recite behind the Imaam.[1]

Katheer bin Murrah said, "Abu ad-Dardaa was asked if there was recitation in every prayer to which he replied, 'When the Imaam leads a people, I do not see except that his recitation suffices them.'"[2]

The Third Opinion: The Follower Recites in the Prayers That Are Performed Silently but Not in Those Performed Aloud

The third opinion is that the follower only does not recite in the prayers said aloud, this is regardless of whether the follower hears the recitation of the Imaam or not. This is the opinion of Imaam Maalik and the majority of his companions, Abdullaah bin al-Mubaarak, Imaam Ahmad and the majority of his companions, Ishaaq bin Raahawayah and others.[3]

From their proofs is:

Allah says in the Quran,

$$\text{وَإِذَا قُرِئَ الْقُرْءَانُ فَاسْتَمِعُوا لَهُ وَأَنْصِتُوا لَعَلَّكُمْ تُرْحَمُونَ}$$

"When the Qur'aan is recited, listen and be silent so that perchance you may have Mercy bestowed upon you" [al-A'raaf (7):204].[4]

There is also the hadeeth of Abu Musa al-Ash'aree that the Prophet (peace be upon him) said,

$$\text{وَإِذَا قَرَأَ فَأَنْصِتُوا}$$

---

[1] *as-Sunan al-Kubraa* (2/161).

[2] *at-Ta'leeq al-Mughnee 'alaa Sunan ad-Daaruqutnee* (1/232 found in the margin of *Sunan ad-Daaruqutnee*).

[3] *Nayl al-Awtaar* (2/241).

[4] They say that this verse is general to *al-Faatibah* and other verses. But those who opine that it is necessary to recite say that the generality of this verse has been specified by the hadeeth of Ubaadah bin Saamit and the principle of building the general upon the specific is well established. Cf., *Nayl al-Awtaar* (2/241).

"...And when he recites, remain silent."[1]

They mentioned many more *ahaadeeth* but space does not allow that they be mentioned.

The Strongest Opinion

From what has preceded, it becomes clear that the reason behind the difference concerning this issue lies with the different methods that the scholars used in reconciling the various *ahaadeeth*.[2]

The Shaafi`ee scholars exempted the recitation of *al-Faatihah* from the general prohibition of reciting when the Imaam is reciting aloud, enacting the hadeeth of Ubaadah bin Saamit.

The Maalikee and Hanbalee scholars exempted the recitation of *al-Faatihah* in the prayers in which the Imaam recites aloud from the generality of the hadeeth, "There is no prayer for the one who does not recite the Faatihah of the Book." This is due to the prohibition contained in the hadeeth of Abu Hurayrah, "...and when he recites, remain silent" and due to the saying of Allah,

$$\text{وَإِذَا قُرِئَ الْقُرْءَانُ فَاسْتَمِعُوا لَهُ وَأَنْصِتُوا لَعَلَّكُمْ تُرْحَمُونَ}$$

"When the Qur`aan is recited, listen and be silent so that perchance you may have Mercy bestowed upon you" [al-A`raaf (7):204].

The Hanafee scholars exempted the obligation of reciting by the follower for any prayer when being led by an Imaam. They made the obligation of recitation to be upon the Imaam only, enacting the hadeeth of Jaabir reported by Muslim. So the hadeeth of Jaabir specifies the generality of the Prophet's saying, "and recite what is easy which you have." This is because they are not of the opinion that it is obligatory to recite *al-Faatihah* in the prayer. Instead, what is obligatory is that one recites a portion of the Qur`aan due to Allah's saying,

---

[1] [Referring to the hadeeth which has preceded, "Indeed the Imaam has only been appointed to be followed..." - Trans.]

[2] Refer to *Bidaayah al-Mujtahid* (1/149) by ibn Rushd to see the reasons behind the difference concerning this issue.

$$\text{فَاقْرَءُوا مَا تَيَسَّرَ مِنَ الْقُرْءَان}$$

"And recite what is easy thereof from the Qur'aan"
[*Muzzammil* (73) :20].[1]

I say: When the reason behind the difference becomes
clear to you with the resultant opinion and its evidence, it
behoves the Muslim that he take to every opinion that is
proven through evidence. Reconciling the evidences and
thereby enacting them all is better than acting upon some and
ignoring the rest. This is because the words of the Legislator
can never be contradictory; instead, they must be reconciled.

The opinion that the follower remains silent when the
Imaam recites aloud and recites when the Imaam recites
silently is the opinion that best reconciles the evidences.
Therefore, the texts commanding one to remain silent are to be
taken to refer to the prayer in which the Imaam recites aloud
and the texts commanding one to recite are to be taken to refer
to the prayer in which the Imaam recites silently.

However this matter will always fall into one of two
cases:

The first case is where the Imaam has periods of
silence (while reciting) to allow the follower to recite in those
periods. But this act of silence is not necessary.[2] In this case,
it is not permissible that the follower be lax in reciting *al-Faatihah*.

Al-Mardaawee said, "It is recommended that one
recite during the pauses of the Imaam. This is the preferred
opinion and this is what the majority adhere to. Many of them
decisively stated this and it is said that it is obligatory to recite
during the pauses of the Imaam."[3]

The second case is where the Imaam does not have
periods of silence. In this case, the correct position is that it is

---

[1] The hadeeth of Jaabir is reported by Muslim (1/304 no. 399 Kitaab as-Salaah, chpt. 13) and Ahmad (2/420). "Abu Daawood and a group of the scholars said that the hadeeth of Abu Musaa is not preserved and has been censured. Al-Bayhaqee said, 'The agreement of all of these hadeeth masters over the weakness of this hadeeth takes precedence over the authentication of Muslim.'" Refer to *Faydh al-Qadeer* (1/416 no. 793) of al-Munaawee.
[2] *Majmoo` Fataawaa* (23/272).
[3] *al-Insaaf* (2/228-229).

obligatory upon the follower to listen to the recitation of the Imaam and remain silent. This is due to the saying of Allah,

وَإِذَا قُرِئَ الْقُرْءَانُ فَاسْتَمِعُوا لَهُ وَأَنْصِتُوا

"When the Qur`aan is recited, listen and be silent" [*al-A`raaf* (7): 204].

The command to remain silent adjoining the order to listen stresses the importance of listening. Therefore, it is obvious that remaining silent in prayer is the more deserving course of action. If this were not the case, for whom is the Imaam reciting?

Furthermore, if the followers were to recite for themselves in the prayers read aloud, leaving the Imaam to recite for himself, this means that the Imaam is not being followed in this. This is incomprehensible because the Imaam has been appointed only to be followed.

However, it is possible that there be certain circumstances in which it is recommended for the follower to recite *al-Faatihah* (in the aloud prayers). For example, the follower may not be able to hear the Imaam due to being far away or his only making out the murmuring of the Imaam, not being able to understand the words. In such cases, he should recite *al-Faatihah,* as is reported from Ahmad in one narration.[1]

Shaykh al-Islam ibn Taymiyyah wrote,

> The scholars are in a state of difference and confusion over reciting behind the Imaam, despite the widespread need of understanding this issue. The principle opinions are three: two extremes and one balanced.
>
> The first extreme is that one never recites behind the Imaam. The second extreme is that one always recites behind the Imaam. The third view, being the opinion of the majority of the Salaf, is if one hears the recitation of the Imaam, he remains silent and does not recite. If he cannot hear the recitation of the Imaam, he recites for himself. Indeed his reciting is

---

[1] *al-Insaaf* (2/228-229).

better than his remaining silent. This is the opinion of the majority of scholars, from among them: Maalik, Ahmad bin Hanbal and the majority of their companions, a group of the companions of ash-Shaafi`ee and Abu Haneefah. It is the old opinion of ash-Shaafi`ee and it is the opinion of Muhammad bin al-Hasan.

Then he said, may Allah have mercy upon him,

When the Imaam recites aloud, the follower listens to his recitation. If he cannot hear due to being far away, he himself recites according to the most correct of the two opinions voiced—and it is the opinion of Ahmad and others. If he cannot hear due to deafness or he only hears the murmuring of the Imaam and cannot make out the words, then there are two opinions concerning this in the *madh-hab* of Ahmad and others. The most apparent opinion is that he should recite because he can either recite or listen, and in this case he cannot be considered to be listening for the purpose of listening is not being attained. Therefore his reciting is better than his remaining silent.[1]

---

[1] *Majmoo` Fataawaa* (23/265-288) [This then could be considered a fourth opinion in addition to the three that the Shaykh has already mentioned. – Trans.]

The States of the Follower with His Imaam in Congregational Prayer

The Imaam has only been appointed to lead and be followed. He is "followed" in that the novements of the follower occur after the movements of the Imaam, from one position to the next, and he does not differ with him in any action of the prayer. Furthermore, he observes his movements with order and precision. This is because the follower follows and the way of following is that he not precede the Imaam in any action. "The majority of the Jurists hold that the prayer of the follower is linked to and follows the prayer of the Imaam with respect to the outward actions of the prayer."[1]

When the follower precedes the Imaam or acts at the same time or (greatly) delays in following him, he has left the commanded following.

Therefore, these are the states that the follower could possibly be in with regards to his Imaam: (1) Preceding, (2) Agreeing, (3) Following or (4) Delaying. In what follows lies an explanation of each state and the ruling on the follower's prayer.

The First State: Preceding the Imaam

This means that the follower precedes the Imaam in saying the *takbeer,* bowing, rising from bowing, prostrating, or saying the *salaam.* The Jurists are agreed that it is prohibited to precede the Imaam.

Shaykh al-Islam ibn Taymiyyah said, "As for preceding the Imaam, this is unlawful by agreement of the Imaams. It is not permissible to go into *ruku`* before the Imaam or to prostrate before him."

The *ahaadeeth* of the Prophet (peace be upon him) show the prohibition of this act. The prohibition of something

---

[1] *Nayl al-Awtaar* (3/158) and *an-Niyyah wa Atharuhaa fee al-Ahkaam ash-Shar`iyyah* (1/423) by the author.

dictates forbiddance. From these *ahaadeeth* is the hadeeth reported by Muslim from Anas bin Maalik who said,

$$صَلَّى بِنَا رَسُولُ اللَّهِ صَلَّى اللَّهُ عَلَيْهِ وَسَلَّمَ ذَاتَ يَوْمٍ فَلَمَّا$$

$$قَضَى الصَّلَاةَ أَقْبَلَ عَلَيْنَا بِوَجْهِهِ فَقَالَ أَيُّهَا النَّاسُ إِنِّي إِمَامُكُمْ$$

$$فَلَا تَسْبِقُونِي بِالرُّكُوعِ وَلَا بِالسُّجُودِ وَلَا بِالْقِيَامِ وَلَا$$

$$بِالِانْصِرَافِ فَإِنِّي أَرَاكُمْ أَمَامِي وَمِنْ خَلْفِي$$

"The Messenger of Allah (peace be upon him) prayed with us one day and when we had finished, he turned, faced us and said, 'O people, I am your Imaam so do not precede me in the bowing, prostration, standing (from bowing and prostration) and leaving from the prayer. Indeed, I see all who are behind me and in front of me."[1]

Al-Bukhaaree reported from Abu Hurayrah that the Prophet (peace be upon him) said,

$$أَمَا يَخْشَى أَحَدُكُمْ أَحَدُكُمْ إِذَا رَفَعَ رَأْسَهُ قَبْلَ الْإِمَامِ أَنْ$$

$$يَجْعَلَ اللَّهُ رَأْسَهُ رَأْسَ حِمَارٍ أَوْ يَجْعَلَ اللَّهُ صُورَتَهُ صُورَةَ$$

$$حِمَارٍ$$

"Is not the one who raises his head before the Imaam afraid that Allah might transform his head into that of a donkey or disfigure his face to that of a donkey?"[2]

Ibn Hajr al-Asqalaanee said,

> The apparent meaning of the hadeeth dictates the prohibition of rising before the Imaam due to his being threatened with disfiguration and this is from the most severe of punishments. Imaam an-Nawawee declared this with certainty in *Sharh al-Muhadhdhab*. Despite

---

[1] *Saheeh Muslim* [Eng. Trans. 1/255 no. 857].
[2] *Saheeh al-Bukhaaree* [Eng. Trans. 1/374 no. 660].

the opinion that this is prohibited, the majority are of the opinion that although the one who does this is sinful, the prayer is still valid. It is reported from ibn Umar that he was of the opinion that the prayer is rendered invalid and this was the opinion of Ahmad in one of the reports from him and it is the opinion of the Dhaahirees, building upon the premise that prohibition necessitates *fasaad* (invalidity of that action). In *al-Mughnee* it is narrated from Ahmad that he said in his treatise on prayer, "There is no prayer for the one who precedes the Imaam due to this hadeeth, for if the prayer was to be considered valid then reward would be hoped for and punishment would not be feared for him."[1]

Deliberately preceding the Imaam invalidates the prayer. Hence, if the follower deliberately precedes the Imaam in a pillar of the prayer, such as the *ruku`* or *sujood* while knowing this ruling, his prayer is rendered invalid. This is the stronger of the two opinions voiced by the scholars. Indeed, Imaam Ahmad clearly stated this in his famous book on prayer.[2] It was also declared to be the strongest opinion by Shaykh al-Islam ibn Taymiyyah.[3]

As for the one who precedes the Imaam out of negligence, forgetfulness or ignorance, it is upon him to retract from that action and redo it after the Imaam. If he does not do this deliberately upon knowledge, his prayer is rendered invalid. However, Imaam Ahmad, in his book on prayer, was of the opinion that preceding the Imaam renders the prayer invalid in any case.

The Strongest Opinion

If one is negligent or forgets, or is ignorant of the ruling (of preceding the Imaam), his prayer is valid. This was

---

[1] *Fath al-Baaree* (2/182-183).
[2] *ar-Risaalah as-Sanniyyah fee as-Salaah wa maa Yalzimu feehaa.*
[3] *Majmoo` Fataawaa* (23/338).

the opinion voiced by the Permanent Committee for Scholarly Research and Legal Rulings.[1]

As for the case when the follower precedes the Imaam in the opening *takbeer,* his prayer has not been commenced and there is no difference among the scholars concerning this.

Al-Kasaanee said, "Upon this basis all of the issues concerning following are concluded. When one precedes the Imaam in saying the opening *takbeer,* his following is not correct. This is because the meaning of following—and that is the foundation—cannot be actualized here because building upon something that is absent is impossible."[2]

Al-Khaleel said, "(From the conditions of the prayer are) his following the Imaam in the opening *takbeer* and the *salaam.*"[3]

Ash-Shaafi'ee said, "For whoever enters the prayer before the Imaam, his prayer is rendered invalid."[4]

Abdur-Rahmaan bin Abu Umar bin Qudaamah said, "If he says the (opening) *takbeer* before the Imaam then his prayer has not commenced and it is upon him to say the *takbeer* again, this time after the Imaam."[5]

The Second State: Agreement with the Imaam

The reality of this is for both the Imaam and follower to move from one pillar to the next at the same time. Examples of this would be the performance of *ruku`* and *sujood* and saying the opening *takbeer* together. This is also erroneous because one cannot be said to be following the Imaam in the way that has been ordered in the Prophet's (peace be upon him) saying,

$$\text{إِنَّمَا جُعِلَ الإِمَامُ لِيُؤْتَمَّ بِهِ فَإِذَا كَبَّرَ فَكَبِّرُوا وَإِذَا سَجَدَ}$$

$$\text{فَاسْجُدُوا وَإِذَا رَفَعَ فَارْفَعُوا وَإِذَا قَالَ سَمِعَ اللَّهُ لِمَنْ حَمِدَهُ}$$

---

[1] Fatwa, no. 36, dated 2/3/1392.
[2] *Badaa`i as-Sanaa`i fee Tarteeb ash-Sharaa`i* (1/138).
[3] *Al-Mukhtasar* (p. 33).
[4] *al-Umm* (1/156).
[5] *Ash-Sharh al-Kabeer* (1/267).

فَقُولُوا رَبَّنَا وَلَكَ الْحَمْدُ وَإِذَا صَلَّى قَاعِدًا فَصَلُّوا قُعُودًا
أَجْمَعُونَ

"Indeed, the Imaam has only been appointed to be followed. When he says the *takbeer,* then say the *takbeer.* When he goes into prostration, then go into prostration. When he rises, then rise. When he says, 'Allah has heard the one who praised Him' say, 'O Allah! Our Lord to you belongs all praise.' When he prays sitting, then all of you pray sitting."[1]

Agreement can occur in sayings or actions.

Agreement in saying: If the follower says the opening *takbeer* with the Imaam and finishes saying it before the Imaam finishes, his prayer is invalid. The Jurists of the Four Schools of Fiqh have stated this.

Ar-Raheebaanee said, "As for the follower agreeing with the Imaam in the statements of the prayer, such that he says the opening *takbeer* with the Imaam or says it before the Imaam finishes, his prayer is not considered to be valid regardless of whether he does it deliberately or out of negligence because its condition is that it be said after the Imaam. He has missed this condition."[2]

Agreement in Action: Agreement in action occurs in cases such as the follower bowing or prostrating at the same time as his Imaam. The strongest opinion of the scholars concerning this is that it is disliked. Al-Bayhaqee reports with his chain from Hittaan bin Abdullaah ar-Riqaashee who said, "Abu Musaa addressed us and taught us our prayer, explaining to us the Sunnah that we should adhere to. He said, 'When you pray, straighten your rows and let one of you lead. When the Imaam says the *takbeer,* say the *takbeer.* When he says, 'Nor the path of those who have earned your Anger or gone astray,' say, '*Aameen*' and Allah will preserve you. When he says the *takbeer* and goes into *ruku`,* then say the *takbeer* and go into *ruku`*...'"[3]

Ibn Abdul Barr al-Qurtobee said, after mentioning this hadeeth, "The hadeeth proves that the actions of the follower

---

[1] *Saheeh Muslim* [Eng. Trans. 1/226 no. 817].
[2] *Mataalib Ulee an-Nahee* (1/627).
[3] *Sunan* (2/96).

occur immediately after the action of the Imaam, such that there is no time lapse. This is because the *faa* (and/then) in his saying 'when the Imaam says the *takbeer* then (*faa*) say the *takbeer*...' necessitates that this action occur quickly after the action of the Imaam. It is established from the point of view of narration and reason that the ruling of his saying, "when the Imaam says the *takbeer* then say the *takbeer*" with regards to the opening *takbeer* is that the follower start saying the *takbeer* after the Imaam and finish saying it after him. Due to this being the case, then, by analogy, the same applies to *ruku`*, *sujud* and, in fact, all the actions of the prayer."[1]

The Third State: Delaying in Following the Imaam[2]

The meaning of this is that the follower delays in following the Imaam to the extent of a *rak`ah* or two *rak`ahs*, more or less, regardless of whether this is due to a valid excuse or not.

If the follower delays due to a valid reason and the Imaam exceeds him by a complete *rak`ah* or more, he should (go to the point at which the Imaam is), continue following the Imaam and then make up what he missed. If the Imaam exceeds him by less then a *rak`ah*, he should catch up and continue following the Imaam and there is nothing that he has to do beyond that. Examples of a valid excuse are drowsiness, negligence and absent-mindedness, or the Imaam performing the prayer very quickly.

If the follower delays following the Imaam without a valid excuse, such that he delays deliberately, his prayer is invalidated because purposely he left following his Imaam.

The Fourth State: Following

This is what is desired from the follower. The reality of this is that the follower move after the Imaam has moved

---

[1] *at-Tambeed limaa fee al-Muwatta min al-Ma`aanee wa al-Asaaneed* (6/147-148).
[2] Refer to *al-Mughnee* (2/211-212) and *al-Majmoo` Sharh al-Muhadhdhab* (4/131-133).

such that the follower starts each movement after the Imaam has started [after his movement] but before he has completed the part of the prayer he is performing. The same applies for the statements. With respect to statements, the follower starts saying them after the Imaam has started. [1]

To be strictly correct: The statements of the follower and his actions should commence after the Imaam has completed his action or statement. This is due to what al-Baraa'a reports:

كَانَ رَسُولُ اللّهِ صَلَّى اللّهُ عَلَيْهِ وَسَلَّمَ إِذَا قَالَ سَمِعَ اللّهُ لِمَنْ حَمِدَهُ لَمْ نَزَلْ قِيَامًا حَتَّى نَرَاهُ قَدْ وَضَعَ وَجْهَهُ فِي الأَرْضِ ثُمَّ نَتَّبِعُهُ

"When the Messenger of Allah used to say 'Allah has heard the one who praises Him,' we remained standing until we saw him placing his face on the ground and then we followed him."[2]

Abu Musaa narrated that,"the Messenger of Allah (peace be upon him) addressed us and clarified to us our Sunnah and taught us our prayer. He said,

إِذَا صَلَّيْتُمْ فَأَقِيمُوا صُفُوفَكُمْ ثُمَّ لِيَؤُمَّكُمْ أَحَدُكُمْ فَإِذَا كَبَّرَ فَكَبِّرُوا ...فَإِنَّ الإِمَامَ يَرْكَعُ قَبْلَكُمْ وَيَرْفَعُ قَبْلَكُمْ

'When you pray, straighten your rows and let one of you lead. When he says the *takbeer,* then say the takbeer... for indeed the Imaam performs *ruku`* before you and rises before you.'"[3]

Abu Hurayrah reported that the Prophet (peace be upon him) said,

---

[1] Refer to *Majmoo` Sharh al-Muhadhdhab* (4/132) and *al-Mughnee* (2/161-1663).

[2] Al-Bukhaaree [Eng. Trans.1/374 no. 658] and Muslim [Eng. Trans. 1/252 no. 960].

[3] *Saheeh Muslim* [Eng. Trans. 1/221 no. 800].

إِنَّمَا جُعِلَ الإِمَامُ لِيُؤْتَمَّ بِهِ فَإِذَا كَبَّرَ فَكَبِّرُوا وَإِذَا رَكَعَ فَارْكَعُوا
وَإِذَا قَالَ سَمِعَ اللَّهُ لِمَنْ حَمِدَهُ فَقُولُوا رَبَّنَا وَلَكَ الْحَمْدُ وَإِذَا
سَجَدَ فَاسْجُدُوا وَإِذَا صَلَّى جَالِسًا فَصَلُّوا جُلُوسًا أَجْمَعُونَ

"Indeed, the Imaam has only been appointed to be followed. So when he says the *takbeer,* then say the *takbeer.* When he performs the *ruku`,* then perform the *ruku`.* When he says, 'Allah has heard the one who praised Him,' say, 'Our Lord! To you belongs praise.' When he performs the *sajda,* then perform the *sajda.* When he prays sitting, then all of you pray sitting."[1]

His words, "When he performs the *ruku`,* then perform the *ruku`*" dictates that the followers' *ruku`* happens after the *ruku`* of the Imaam. This is because the wording comes with the *faa* (then) which indicates that the action occurs afterwards. This is like saying, "Zayd came and then (*faa*) `Amr," that is, `Amr came after Zayd. "So these proofs are explicit statements that the follower starts his movements in the actions of prayer such as rising, *ruku`,* and *sujood,* after the Imaam has completed his action."[2]

There are a number of narrations from the Companions in which they said, "Indeed the Messenger of Allah (peace be upon him) used to stand straight while we were still in prostration."

Ibn Mas`ud saw someone preceding the Imaam and remarked, "You have not prayed on your own, nor have you followed your Imaam." Meaning that there is no prayer for him.

Ibn Umar saw someone preceding the Imaam and said, "You have not prayed on your own, nor have you prayed with the Imaam." Then he hit him and ordered him to repeat the prayer.[3] If this prayer were valid in the eyes of ibn Umar, he would not have ordered him to repeat it.

These are explicit proofs that the follower commences his actions of the prayer after the Imaam has completed his.

---

[1] The discussion of this hadith has already been given.
[2] *Al-Mughnee* (2/208-209).
[3] *Sharh Saheeh Muslim* (4/119).

Whoever considers the state of the majority of people today with respect to their prayers in the mosques will find that they do not establish the prayer in the way of the Prophet (peace be upon him) and his Companions—except for those upon whom your Lord bestows Mercy. For example, at the very point the Imaam starts saying the *takbeer,* they say the *takbeer;* indeed they precede him in it. The same applies to the *ruku`* and *sujood.* As for the following that is enjoined, this is rarely found. In this is proof that many of them are ignorant of the Sunnah and are distant from the guidance of the Messenger of Allah (peace be upon him) with respect to the prayer. And the Aid of Allah is sought!

The Principle of the Brevity or Elongation of the Congregational Prayer

The Wise Legislator has recommended that the congregational prayer be brief out of concern for the circumstances of the people and to make matters easy for them. The Imaams have been enjoined to make the congregational prayer brief and not to perform a lengthy recitation. This is a matter over which there is a consensus. It is a recommended act.

The meaning of brevity (*takhfeef*) is that the prayer be restricted to the least that would make it complete or perfect, by fulfilling its obligations and the sunan. It does not mean to decrease from this or to increase from this.

However, it is important to note that this does not mean that lengthening the prayer should be left altogether. Rather the followers should get accustomed to a longer prayer from their Imaam. He should lengthen the prayer on occasion in order to enact the Sunnah. In this way, there would be no harm in lengthening the prayer. It is in this light that we can understand the narrations that mention that the Prophet (peace be upon him) used to lengthen his prayer. The Companions did not use to consider the prayer to be long on those occasions due to their great eagerness and desire to attain the good.

Therefore being brief in prayer, without leaving off any obligations and sunan, and lengthening the prayer, without going to extremes, are both proven by the Sunnah. Whether one lengthens or prays briefly is dependent upon the state of the people, taking into account time, place and weather conditions. However, it is reprehensible for one to be so brief that he is deficient in performing the various parts of the prayers, for example, one does not have time to say the *tasbeeh* three times in *ruku`* and *sujood*.

If lengthening the prayer is hard upon the followers and they ask that it be shortened, it should be shortened. But if they do not find it hard or do not wish that the prayer be shortened, it is not disliked to lengthen the prayer.

The person who is praying on his own can lengthen the prayer as much as he likes, as long as this does not mean that he exceeds the period of that prayer.

Furthermore, the matter of lengthening the prayer differs with different prayers. The predominant case for the *Fajr* and *Dhuhur* prayers is that they be long. For `*Asr* and '*Ishaa,* the predominant case is that they not be too long nor too short. The predominant case for the *Maghrib* prayer is that it be brief. It is permissible to differ from these predominant cases sometimes as occurs in the texts.

Brevity is a relative matter that has no set definition in the language or the custom of people, rather it varies from person to person. Therefore, it is possible that some people pray what they see to be a brief prayer but what others see to be a lengthy prayer. Hence, it is recommended for the Imaam to predominantly do that which was predominantly done by the Prophet (peace be upon him), on occasion increasing in the length and on occasion shortening due to some benefit, as was sometimes done by the Prophet (peace be upon him). Hence, the reference point for this is the Sunnah and not the desire of the Imaam or the followers.

Here are some of the reports that describe this topic.

Abu Daawood reports in his *Sunan* with his chain from Umar, and he heard this from Jaabir, that,

كَانَ مُعَاذٌ يُصَلِّي مَعَ النَّبِيِّ صَلَّى اللَّهُ عَلَيْهِ وَسَلَّمَ ثُمَّ يَرْجِعُ فَيُصَلِّي بِقَوْمِهِ فَأَخَّرَ النَّبِيُّ صَلَّى اللَّهُ عَلَيْهِ وَسَلَّمَ لَيْلَةً الصَّلاةَ وَقَالَ مَرَّةً الْعِشَاءَ فَصَلَّى مُعَاذٌ مَعَ النَّبِيِّ صَلَّى اللَّهُ عَلَيْهِ وَسَلَّمَ ثُمَّ جَاءَ يَؤُمُّ قَوْمَهُ فَقَرَأَ الْبَقَرَةَ فَاعْتَزَلَ رَجُلٌ مِنْ الْقَوْمِ فَصَلَّى فَقِيلَ نَافَقْتَ يَا فُلانُ فَقَالَ مَا نَافَقْتُ فَأَتَى رَسُولَ اللَّهِ صَلَّى اللَّهُ عَلَيْهِ وَسَلَّمَ فَقَالَ إِنَّمَا نَحْنُ أَصْحَابُ نَوَاضِحَ وَنَعْمَلُ

بِأَيْدِينَا وَإِنَّهُ جَاءَ يَؤُمُّنَا فَقَرَأَ بِسُورَةِ الْبَقَرَةِ فَقَالَ أَفَتَّانٌ أَنْتَ اقْرَأْ

بِكَذَا اقْرَأْ بِكَذَا قَالَ أَبُو الزُّبَيْرِ بِسَبِّحْ اسْمَ رَبِّكَ الأَعْلَى وَاللَّيْلِ

إِذَا يَغْشَى فَذَكَرْنَا لِعَمْرٍو فَقَالَ أُرَاهُ قَدْ ذَكَرَهُ

"Mu`aadh used to pray with the Prophet (peace be upon him) and then return and pray with his people. One night the Prophet (peace be upon him) delayed the prayer—on one occasion the narrator said, 'The *Ishaa* prayer'—and Mu`aadh prayed with the Prophet (peace be upon him). Then Muadh went to his people and (prayed with them) reciting *al-Baqarah*. Due to this a person left the congregation and prayed on his own. It was said to him, 'You have become a hypocrite.' He replied, 'I have not become a hypocrite.' He went to the Prophet (peace be upon him) and said, 'We tend the camels used for watering and we work hard using our hands and he comes and recites *Surah al-Baqarah*.' The Prophet (peace be upon him) said (to Mu`aadh), 'Are you putting these people to trial? Recite such and such (*surah*) and such and such (*surah*).' Abu Zubayr said, '(He mentioned) *Surah al-A`laa* and *Surah al-Layl*.' We mentioned this to `Amr and he said, 'I think he mentioned (those *Surahs*).'"[1]

Ibn Hajr said, "Indeed, it was the lengthening that became the reason of their leaving the (congregational) prayer and disliking it."[2]

Al-Bukhaaree reports from the hadeeth of Abu Hurayrah that the Prophet (peace be upon him) said,

إِذَا صَلَّى أَحَدُكُمْ لِلنَّاسِ فَلْيُخَفِّفْ فَإِنَّ مِنْهُمْ الضَّعِيفَ وَالسَّقِيمَ

وَالْكَبِيرَ وَإِذَا صَلَّى أَحَدُكُمْ لِنَفْسِهِ فَلْيُطَوِّلْ مَا شَاءَ

"When one of you prays with the people, let him pray with brevity for indeed among them are the weak and the old. When

---

[1] Reported by al-Bukhaaree [Eng. Trans. 1/378 no. 669], Muslim [Eng. Trans.1/248 no. 936, 937], Abu Daawood [Eng. Trans. 1/203 no. 790] and an-Nasaa`ee (2/97-98).
[2] *al-Fath* (1/195).

one of you prays on his own, let him lengthen the prayer as much as he likes."[1]

In another narration, it sates,

$$\text{الْمَرِيضَ وَذَا الْحَاجَةِ}$$

"[And among them are] the ill and the one who has a pressing need."

Al-Bukhaaree also reports from the hadeeth of ibn Mas`ud that,

$$\text{أَنَّ رَجُلاً قَالَ وَاللَّهِ يَا رَسُولَ اللَّهِ إِنِّي لَأَتَأَخَّرُ عَنْ صَلاة الْغَدَاة}$$

$$\text{مِنْ أَجْلِ فُلَان مِمَّا يُطِيلُ بِنَا فَمَا رَأَيْتُ رَسُولَ اللَّهِ صَلَّى اللَّهُ}$$

$$\text{عَلَيْهِ وَسَلَّمَ فِي مَوْعِظَةٍ أَشَدَّ غَضَبًا مِنْهُ يَوْمَئِذٍ ثُمَّ قَالَ إِنَّ مِنْكُمْ}$$

$$\text{مُنَفِّرِينَ فَأَيُّكُمْ مَا صَلَّى بِالنَّاسِ فَلْيَتَجَوَّزْ فَإِنَّ فِيهِمْ الضَّعِيفَ}$$

$$\text{وَالْكَبِيرَ وَذَا الْحَاجَةِ}$$

A person said, "By Allah, O Messenger of Allah, indeed I do not attend the morning prayer due to such and such a person who lengthens it." I have not seen the Prophet (peace be upon him) giving an exhortation in which he displayed more anger than on that day. He said, "Indeed there are among you those who cause the people to become averse to attending the congregational prayer. Whoever prays with the people, let him take a middle course (in his recitation), for among them are the weak, the old, and those with a pressing need."[2]

Generally speaking, brevity is realized while in the state of standing in prayer because it is dependent upon the recitation of the Imaam. Due to this, Imaam al-Bukhaaree entitled the chapter containing the previously mentioned hadeeth, "Chapter: The Imaam being brief in the standing and his completing the *ruku`* and *sujud*."

---

[1] *Saheeh al-Bukhaaree* [Eng. Trans. 1/379 no. 671, 672].
[2] Ibid [1/379 no. 670].

Ibn Hajr said, "Al-Kirmaanee said, 'The word "and" (*waw*) here is taken to mean along with (*ma`a*) and it is as if (al-Bukhaaree) is saying: Chapter: Being brief without omitting any of the obligations. This is the explanation of his (peace be upon him) saying, "Let him take a middle course," because he could not enjoin anything that would lead to the invalidation of the prayer.' Ibn Munayyir, ibn Rasheed and others said, 'Being brief has been restricted to the standing in the chapter heading, even though the wording of the hadeeth is general, because the one who lengthens predominantly does this in the standing (through lengthy recitation). As for perfecting any other action, it does not burden the people. It is as if al-Bukhaaree took the hadeeth mentioned in the chapter to have the same meaning as that derived from the story of Mu`aadh, for the command for brevity mentioned therein was regards the recitation.'"[1]

Muslim reports in his *Saheeh* from the hadeeth of Anas bin Maalik that the Messenger of Allah (peace be upon him) said,

$$\text{إِنِّي لَأَدْخُلُ الصَّلَاةَ أُرِيدُ إِطَالَتَهَا فَأَسْمَعُ بُكَاءَ الصَّبِيِّ فَأُخَفِّفُ مِنْ شِدَّةِ وَجْدِ أُمِّهِ بِهِ}$$

"Indeed, I enter the state of prayer desiring to lengthen it but I hear the crying of a child and, therefore, shorten the prayer due to the severe anguish that its mother feels when it cries."[2]

It is reported from Makhool ad-Dimishkee that Abu ad-Dardaa` led the people in prayer. It was a rainy day and the roof of the mosque only covered the first row. When he had completed the prayer he saw that the people had become drenched in rain and said, "Was there no one of understanding in the mosque who could have said, 'O you who lengthen the prayer, be brief for the people are getting drenched'?"

Al-Baghawee said, "I say: This is the opinion of the majority of the scholars. They preferred the opinion that the Imaam not lengthen the prayer out of fear that this would be hard upon the weak and those who have a pressing need.

---

[1] *al-Fath* (2/197-198).
[2] *Saheeh Muslim* [Eng. Trans. 1/250 no. 952].

However, if all of the people wish that the prayer be lengthened, there is no harm in lengthening it."[1]

The Amount that the Prophet (peace be upon him) Used to Recite in the Prayer

Muslim reports in his *Saheeh* from Abu Sa`eed al-Khudree,

أَنَّ النَّبِيَّ صَلَّى اللَّهُ عَلَيْهِ وَسَلَّمَ كَانَ يَقْرَأُ فِي صَلَاةِ الظُّهْرِ فِي الرَّكْعَتَيْنِ الأُولَيَيْنِ فِي كُلِّ رَكْعَةٍ قَدْرَ ثَلَاثِينَ آيَةً وَفِي الأُخْرَيَيْنِ قَدْرَ خَمْسَ عَشْرَةَ آيَةً أَوْ قَالَ نِصْفَ ذَلِكَ وَفِي الْعَصْرِ فِي الرَّكْعَتَيْنِ الأُولَيَيْنِ فِي كُلِّ رَكْعَةٍ قَدْرَ قِرَاءَةِ خَمْسَ عَشْرَةَ آيَةً وَفِي الأُخْرَيَيْنِ قَدْرَ نِصْفِ ذَلِكَ

"The Prophet (peace be upon him) used to recite about thirty verses in each *rak`ah* of the first two *rak`ah*s of *Dhuhur* and in the last two about fifteen verses—or he said half that (of the first *rak`ah*). For `Asr, he used to recite about fifteen verses in each of the first two *rak`ah*s and in the last two half that amount."[2]

Muslim also reports from Anas and Abu Sa`eed al-Khudree,

لَقَدْ كَانَتْ صَلَاةُ الظُّهْرِ تُقَامُ فَيَذْهَبُ الذَّاهِبُ إِلَى الْبَقِيعِ فَيَقْضِي حَاجَتَهُ ثُمَّ يَتَوَضَّأُ ثُمَّ يَأْتِي وَرَسُولُ اللَّهِ صَلَّى اللَّهُ عَلَيْهِ وَسَلَّمَ فِي الرَّكْعَةِ الأُولَى مِمَّا يُطَوِّلُهَا

---

[1] *Sharh as-Sunnah* (3/409 no. 844) by al-Baghawee.
[2] *Saheeh Muslim* [Eng. Trans. 1/245 no. 911].

"When when the prayer for *Dhuhur* would be started, a person could go to al-Baqee`, relieve himself, perform *wudu`*, return and find the Messenger of Allah (peace be upon him) still in the first *rak`ah,* due to its length."[1]

Al-Bukhaaree reports in his *Saheeh* from the hadeeth of Abu Qataadah,

$$ أَنَّ النَّبِيَّ صَلَّى اللَّهُ عَلَيْهِ وَسَلَّمَ كَانَ يُطَوِّلُ فِي الرَّكْعَةِ الأُولَى مِنْ صَلَاةِ الظُّهْرِ وَيُقَصِّرُ فِي الثَّانِيَةِ وَيَفْعَلُ ذَلِكَ فِي صَلَاةِ الصُّبْحِ $$

"The Prophet (peace be upon him) used to lengthen the first *rak`ah* and pray the second *rak`ah* shorter in the *Dhuhur* prayer. He also used to do this in the *Fajr* prayer."[2]

And in a narration,

$$ كَانَ يَفْعَلُ ذَلِكَ فِي الظُّهْرِ وَالعَصْرِ وَالصُّبْحِ $$

"He used to do this in *Dhuhur*, `Asr and *Fajr*."

An-Nawawee reconciles the *ahaadeeth* regarding being brief in the prayer and those regarding lengthening it by saying,

> The scholars said: The prayer of the Messenger of Allah (peace be upon him) used to differ with respect to its length due to differing circumstances. When the followers preferred that the prayer be long and there was no work to distract them, he would lengthen it. In that case, it would not be a burden on them. If this were not the case, he would be brief in the prayer. Sometimes, it was possible that he desired to lengthen the prayer and then decided to shorten it due to something that called for this, such as the crying of a child. It

---

[1] Ibid [1/246 no. 916].
[2] *Saheeh al-Bukhaaree* [Eng. Trans. 1/405 no. 726, 1/413 no.743].

was also possible that he entered the prayer when there was not much time remaining before it expired and so he would shorten it. It is also said that he would lengthen the prayer sometimes, but mostly he would be brief. He lengthened it to show its permissibility; but he was mostly brief in it because this was the best course and he ordered that the prayer be brief in his saying,

إِنَّ مِنْكُمْ مُنَفِّرِينَ فَأَيُّكُمْ مَا صَلَّى بِالنَّاسِ فَلْيَتَجَوَّزْ فَإِنَّ فِيهِمْ الضَّعِيفَ وَالْكَبِيرَ وَذَا الْحَاجَةِ

"Indeed there are among you those who cause the people to become averse to attending the congregational prayer. When any of you prays with the people, be brief for there are among them the weak, the old and those who have a pressing need." It is also said that he lengthened the prayer on one occasion and shortened it on another to show that there is no necessary amount of recitation apportioned after the recitation of *al-Faatihah*; instead, it is permissible to recite a small or large amount. Indeed, all that is necessary to recite is *al-Faatihah*. This is why the narrations all concur on the recitation of *al-Faatihah* but differ as to the amount that was recited after it. In sum, the Sunnah is what the Prophet (peace be upon him) enjoined due to the reason that he explained. He only lengthened the prayer on some occasions due to the absence of the reasons that would dictate the need to be brief. So, if someone sees that the reason for being brief is absent, he can lengthen the prayer.[1]

---

[1] *Sharh Saheeh Muslim* (4/174).

The Ruling of Praying in Congregation behind Radio or Television Broadcasts

From the new issues that have arisen in our times is that some people's desire for going to the mosques and praying in them has slackened. Their desire for performing that which would multiply their good deeds and by which Allah would raise their ranks has decreased. These people have started praying behind radios or televisions [away from the congregation], following the broadcast of the Imaam thinking that by doing so they are praying in congregation. It is possible that some of the people do this out of ignorance or they do it out of laziness and considering this act from among the signs of Allah to be inconsequential. This act being the congregational prayer. Due to this fact it becomes necessary for us to issue a warning concerning this.

Praying behind a radio or television broadcast and following the Imaam while at home is invalid. Indeed, it is to be counted among the innovations in worship. The Prophet (peace be upon him) said,

$$ مَنْ أَحْدَثَ فِي أَمْرِنَا هَذَا مَا لَيْسَ فِيهِ فَهُوَ رَدٌّ $$

"Whoever introduces into this affair of ours that which is not part of it, it is rejected."[1]

The Standing Committee for Scholarly Discussion and Legal Verdicts gave a ruling on this, saying, "It is not permissible for men or women, the weak or strong, to pray alone or in congregation at home following the prayer of the Imaam through merely hearing his voice on the speaker. This is regardless of whether the prayer is an optional or obligatory prayer, whether it is the prayer of *Jumu`ah* or any other prayer,

---

[1] *Saheeh al-Bukhaaree* [Eng. Trans. 5/535 no. 861] and *Saheeh Muslim* [Eng. Trans. 3/931 no. 4266].

whether their house is behind the Imaam or in front of him. This is because it is obligatory upon healthy men to pray the obligatory prayers in the mosques while this obligation is lifted from women and the weak."[1]

---

[1] Fatwa no. 2437, dated 25/5/1399 A.H.

Ruling for the Congregational Prayer on a Ship

Prayers While Upon a Boat

The Jurists have differed about praying on a ship sitting when one is able to stand. There are two opinions:

The First Opinion: It is not correct to pray sitting when one is able to pray standing. This was the opinion of Abu Yusuf and Muhammad bin al-Hasan (the two students of Abu Haneefah), Maalik, Shaafi`ee and Ahmad.

They proved this by the hadeeth of Imraan bin Husayn who said,

فَسَأَلْتُ النَّبِيَّ صَلَّى اللهُ عَلَيْهِ وَسَلَّمَ عَنِ الصَّلاةِ فَقَالَ صَلِّ قَائِمًا فَإِنْ لَمْ تَسْتَطِعْ فَقَاعِدًا فَإِنْ لَمْ تَسْتَطِعْ فَعَلَى جَنْبٍ

"I asked the Prophet (peace be upon him) about the prayer and he replied, 'Pray standing. If you are not able to, pray sitting. And if you are not able to that, pray lying down.'"[1]

This hadeeth proves that if one is able to pray standing, he has to do so and cannot pray sitting unless there be a factor preventing him from standing.

The Second Opinion: It is correct for one to pray sitting despite the ability to pray standing. This was the opinion of Abu Haneefah.[2] He relied upon the hadeeth that is reported from Suwayd bin Ghafla that he said, "I asked Abu Bakr and Umar about praying on a ship. They replied, 'If it is moving, pray sitting; if it is still, pray standing.'"

---

[1] *Saheeh al-Bukhaaree* [Eng. Trans. 1/121 no. 218].
[2] *Badaa`i as-Sanaa`i* (1/109).

Al-Kaasaanee gave the reasoning behind this by saying, "The movements of the ship cause dizziness. Therefore, one should pray while sitting."[1]

The Strongest Opinion: After considering the two opinions and their respective evidences, it becomes clear, and Allah knows best, that the first opinion is the stronger of the two. This is due to it being supported by an authentic hadeeth and because standing is a pillar from the pillars of the prayer. Its obligation cannot be lifted unless one is incapable of performing it.

As for the saying of Abu Bakr and Umar that Abu Haneefah uses as evidence, it is possible that it is referring to a case where there is no valid excuse or one where there is a valid excuse. When an evidence is open to a number of possible explanations it is no longer possible to use it as an evidence.

As for the rational argument, no attention is paid to it because it contradicts the hadeeth of Imraan bin Husayn which is a *saheeh* hadeeth. Hence, the evidence of Abu Haneefah is replied to and the first opinion is determined to be the strongest: it is not permissible to pray on a ship sitting when one is capable of standing.

Building upon what has preceded, praying on a ship is permissible according to the Four Imaams. One should pray standing; if he is unable to, he can pray sitting.

The Ruling of Praying in Congregation on a Ship

The Hanbalee scholars have unequivocally stated that the prayer prayed on a ship should be in congregation. The actions of the Companions indicate this; Jaabir bin Abdullaah, Abu Sa`eed al-Khudree and Abu Hurayrah were on a ship and they prayed in congregation, while standing, some of them leading the rest, even though they were capable of praying on the shore.[2]

---

[1] *Badaa`i as-Sanaa`i* (1/109).
[2] Reported by Sa`eed bin Mansoor in his *Sunan* as mentioned in *al-Muntaqaa min Akhbaar al-Mustafaa* by Majd ad-Deen Abu al-Barakaat ibn Taymiyyah (1/662 no. 1509, 1/326 no. 784 with the *tahqeeq* by Muhammad Haamid al-Fiqhee).

This applies if those on a ship can pray in congregation while standing. If they cannot pray in congregation while standing but they can pray standing individually, should they all pray individually or should they pray in congregation while sitting?

There are two reported opinions concerning this in the Hanbalee school of fiqh.

The First Narration: Everybody prays individually, standing.

The Second Narration: If the Imaam prays sitting, those behind him pray sitting.

The reasoning behind the first opinion is that praying standing is more important. If one were to pray sitting while being able to pray standing, his prayer is not valid. However, if one were to pray individually while being able to pray in congregation, his prayer is still valid.

The reasoning behind the second opinion is that if the Imaam prays sitting, the followers should pray sitting and their prayer would be valid.[1]

---

[1] Refer to *Badaa`i al-Fawaa`id* (4/144-145) by ibn al-Qayyim. [This is because according to the Hanbalee school it is sanctioned for the followers to pray sitting if the Imaam prays sitting due to a valid reason, this being the better course in their eyes. – Trans.]

The Ruling of Congregational Prayer in a Car, Train or Plane

It is possible for the one driving a car to get out of it so that he can pray the obligatory prayer on the ground. If, however, for some reason he cannot stop and get out of the car, he can pray in the car if he fears that he will miss the time of that prayer. The same applies to trains.

As for a plane, it does not stop except at the destination airport. Therefore, if the journey is long and one fears that the time for prayer will expire before he reaches the destination, he should pray in the plane and not delay the prayer beyond its set time. This is something that is not impossible and it is not difficult. We ourselves have experienced it, and all praise is due to Allah.

However, if the areas between the aisles and by the doors are too small to accommodate all the people who wish to pray, it is possible to pray a congregation with the number that space does allow and then pray another congregation after this. This is based on Allah's saying,

فَاتَّقُوا اللَّهَ مَا اسْتَطَعْتُمْ

"Fear Allah as much as you are able" [*at-Taghaabun* (64):16].

The Ruling for Women Praying in a Congregation

Women Attending the Mosques and Praying in Congregation with the Men

It is not obligatory upon women to attend the obligatory prayers in congregation. There is no difference of opinion on this point.[1]

However, in general, it is permissible for women to attend the prayer in the mosque due to what is established in the Prophetic Sunnah that the women used to pray in the mosque.

Aa`ishah said,

لَقَدْ كَانَ رَسُولُ اللّهِ صَلَّى اللّهُ عَلَيْهِ وَسَلَّمَ يُصَلِّي الْفَجْرَ
فَيَشْهَدُ مَعَهُ نِسَاءٌ مِنْ الْمُؤْمِنَاتِ مُتَلَفِّعَاتٍ فِي مُرُوطِهِنَّ ثُمَّ
يَرْجِعْنَ إِلَى بُيُوتِهِنَّ مَا يَعْرِفُهُنَّ أَحَدٌ

"The Messenger of Allah (peace be upon him) used to pray *Fajr* and the believing women used to attend, covered with their veiling sheets. After the prayer was finished, they would return and not one of them would be recognized."[2]

The Prophet (peace be upon him) said,

لَا تَمْنَعُوا نِسَاءَكُمْ الْمَسَاجِدَ وَبُيُوتُهُنَّ خَيْرٌ لَهُنَّ

---

[1] *Mawsoo`ah al-Ijmaa* (2/622) by Sa`dee Abu Jaib.
[2] *Saheeh al-Bukhaaree* [Eng. Trans. 1/225 no. 368].

"Do not prevent your women from attending the mosques. And their homes are better for them."[1]

Abu Daawood reports in his *Sunan* from Abu Hurayrah that the Messenger of Allah (peace be upon him) said,

لَا تَمْنَعُوا إِمَاءَ اللَّهِ مَسَاجِدَ اللَّهِ وَلَكِنْ لِيَخْرُجْنَ وَهُنَّ تَفِلَاتٌ

"Do not prevent the female slaves of Allah from the mosques of Allah, but let them go out without having perfumed themselves."[2]

However, the best course for women, in general, is to pray in their homes. Umm Salamah narrated that the Messenger of Allah (peace be upon him) said,

خَيْرُ مَسَاجِدِ النِّسَاءِ قَعْرُ بُيُوتِهِنَّ

"The best mosques for women are in the depths of their houses."[3]

We will summarize the opinions of the Jurists on this issue.

Abu Haneefah and his two companions said, "It is disliked for young women to attend the congregation in any case, due to the fear of *fitna* (alluring others). There is no problem if an old woman were to attend the *Fajr*, *Maghrib* and *Ishaa* prayers. This is because the rebellious sinners are generally asleep for *Fajr* and *Ishaa* and busy eating at *Maghrib*."[4]

The chosen opinion of the later Hanafees is, "it is disliked for women to attend the congregation, even if this be for *Jumu`ah*, *Eed* or any lecture, in any case, even if she be an old women attending by night. This is because of the corruption of the times and prevalence of sin."[5]

---

[1] *Sunan Abu Daawood* [Eng. Trans. 1/149 no. 567].
[2] Ibid [1/149 no. 565].
[3] *Mustadrak al-Haakim* (1/209).
[4] *Fath al-Qadeer* (1/352).
[5] *al-Fiqh al-Islamee wa Adillatuhu* (2/154) by Wahbah az-Zuhaylee.

From the Maalikee scholars, ibn Rushd said, "The detailed analysis of this issue in my opinion shows that women are of four types:

a) The old woman for whom men find no urges. Therefore, she has the same ruling as men in that she can go to the mosque and gatherings of *dhikr*...

b) The middle-aged woman towards whom the men find no desire, although one cannot say that such is always the case. Such a woman can go to the mosques for the obligatory prayers and the gatherings of knowledge and *dhikr*. However, she should not frequently go out in fulfilling her daily needs.

c) The young woman who is not beautiful or of noble lineage can go to the mosque for the congregational prayer or the funeral prayer of a close relative only.

d) The young woman who is beautiful and of noble lineage may make her choice. In general, she is free not to go out at all."[1]

The Shaafi`ee and Hanbalee scholars said, "It is disliked for beautiful women, be they young or old, to attend the congregation because this could lead to *fitna*. Instead, they should pray in their houses. As for those women who are not beautiful, then, as long as they do not perfume themselves, they can go with the permission of their husbands. But their houses are still better for them."

The Correct Opinion concerning this is that if the woman goes out, not having perfumed herself, adorned herself, or worn decorative clothes, and she will not fall into *fitna* or cause others to fall into *fitna* and she wishes to go out to the mosques, then one must not prevent her. However, her house is better for her.[2]

Women Praying in Congregation by Themselves With One of Them Leading

"Congregational prayer for women is sanctioned and there is no difference of opinion concerning this. The most proficient in reciting the Qur`aan should lead them according

---

[1] *ash-Sharh as-Sagheer* (1/446-447) by ad-Dardeer.
[2] Refer to *Majmoo Fataawaa Shaykh al-Islam ibn Taymiyyah* (29/296) and *Nayl al-Awtaar* (3/96) by ash-Shawkaanee.

to the most correct opinion. Every prayer which is sanctioned as a congregation for men is also sanctioned for women, be it obligatory or optional."[1]

Ibn al-Mundhir records the validity of congregational prayer for women as being narrated from Aa'ishah, Umm Salamah, Hamnah, 'Ataa, ath-Thawree, al-Awazaa'ee, Ahmad, Ishaaq and Abu Thawr. There is no opposing opinion known from the Companions.[2]

It is better for women to pray in congregation in their houses rather than praying in the mosque in congregation with the men. This is because it is better for a woman to pray alone in her house rather then attend the congregational prayer in the mosque. Therefore, praying in congregation at home would be even better as long as this action does not lead to something forbidden.

If it comes about that women gather in a house, school or university or other such abodes, it is recommended for them to pray in congregation. The woman leading stands in front of them or stands in the middle of their (first row). She recites aloud in the prayers to be read aloud, being careful not to pray too loudly if men can hear her.

The *ahaadeeth* and narrations proving the sanctioning of congregational prayer for women, with one of them leading, are many, including:

The hadeeth reported by al-Haakim and ibn Khuzaymah from Umm Waraqah al-Ansaaree that the Prophet (peace be upon him),

أَمَرَها أَنْ تُؤَمَّ أَهْلَ دَارِها

"Ordered her to lead the people of her house in prayer."

There is also the report of Abdur-Rahmaan bin Khallaad from Umm Waraqah that the Prophet (peace be upon him) said,

---

[1] *al-Majmoo'* (4/96).
[2] *al-Muhalla* (3/171-172).

$$\text{اِنْطَلِقُوا بِنَا نَزُورُ الشَّهِيدَةَ وَأَذِنَ لَهَا أَنْ يُؤَذَّنَ لَهَا وَأَنْ تُؤَمَّ أَهْلَ}$$

$$\text{دَارِهَا فِي الفَرِيضَةِ وَكَانَتْ قَدْ جَمَعَتْ القُرْآنَ}$$

"Come let us visit a female martyr." He gave permission that the *adhaan* be said for her and that she lead the people of her household in the obligatory prayers, for she had memorized the Qur`aan.[1]

Aa`ishah led the women in the *Maghrib* prayer, standing in the middle of (their first row). She made the recitation aloud.[2]

Hujayrah bint Husayn said, "Umm Salamah—the Mother of the Believers—led us in the `Asr prayer and stood among us."[3]

It is reported from ibn Umar that he ordered a slave girl of his to lead the women (of his household) in prayer on the nights of Ramadaan.[4]

These *ahaadeeth* and narrations bear testimony to the fact that it is recommended for women to pray in their own congregation. This is the opinion of Abu Haneefah, ash-Shaafi`ee, Ahmad bin Hanbal, Daawood adh-Dhaahiree and their followers.[5]

As for whoever voices an opposing opinion, it is rejected since it has no evidence to certify its correctness. The Authentic Sunnah has ruled that it is recommended for women to pray in congregation and not individually. Even if there were no evidence concerning this issue except the generality of the Prophet's saying,

$$\text{صَلَاةُ الْجَمَاعَةِ تَفْضُلُ صَلَاةَ الْفَذِّ بِسَبْعٍ وَعِشْرِينَ دَرَجَةً}$$

---

[1] *Sunan Abu Daawood* [Eng. Trans. 1/156 no. 592], al-Haakim (1/203) and *Saheeh ibn Khuzaymah* (3/89 no. 1676 chpt. 168).
[2] *al-Muhalla* (3/171) by ibn Hazm.
[3] Ibid.
[4] *al-Muhalla* (3/173).
[5] *al-Muhalla* (3/171-172).

"The congregational prayer is twenty seven times more excellent than the prayer of the individual," that would have sufficed. Allah knows best.[1]

---

[1] Refer to *I`laam al-Muwaqqi`een `an Rabbil Aalameen* (3/357-358) and *al-Muhalla* (3171-174) by ibn Hazam adh-Dhaahiree.

Excuses for Not Attending the Congregational Prayer

There is no reason for anyone to miss the congregational prayer unless he has a valid excuse, be it general or specific.

Examples of general excuses are: severe rain during the night or day, a strong wind on a dark night, snow, severe cold, severe muddiness, severe heat at *Dhuhur* time and other such things.

This is based on what is reported from ibn Umar that he called the *adhaan* on a cold and windy night and announced, "Pray in your homes." Then he said,

$$\text{أَنَّ رَسُولَ اللَّهِ صَلَّى اللَّهُ عَلَيْهِ وَسَلَّمَ كَانَ يَأْمُرُ مُؤَذِّنًا يَقُولُ أَلَا}$$

$$\text{صَلُّوا فِي الرِّحَالِ فِي اللَّيْلَةِ الْبَارِدَةِ الْمَطِيرَةِ}$$

"On a cold and rainy night the Messenger of Allah (peace be upon him) used to order the *Mu'adhdhin* to say, 'Pray in your homes.'"[1]

Ibn Battaal said, "The scholars are unanimously agreed that it is permissible to remain away from the congregational prayer due to heavy rain, darkness, wind and other such things."[2]

Examples of specific excuses are:

1. **Illness.** The meaning of illness here is that illness which would make it difficult for one to attend the congregational prayer. This does not hold true for slight illness, such as a slight headache or the like. This excuse also applies to one who is attending to another, even if the person is not a relative.

This is based on the verse,

---

[1] *Tarh at-Tathreeb fee Sharh at-Taqreeb* (2/317-318) by al-Haafidh al-Iraaqee. [This hadith is recorded by Muslim and others.—JZ]
[2] Ibid.

$$\text{هُوَ اجْتَبَاكُمْ وَمَا جَعَلَ عَلَيْكُمْ فِي الدِّينِ مِنْ حَرَجٍ}$$

"He has chosen you and has imposed no difficulties on you in the religion" [*Hajj* (22):78].

The Prophet (peace be upon him) said, when he became severely ill and left off praying with the people for many days,

$$\text{مُرُوا أَبَا بَكْرٍ فَلْيُصَلِّ لِلنَّاسِ}$$

"Command Abu Bakr to lead the people in prayer."[1]

Therefore, the congregational prayer is not obligatory upon the sick, the one who has a chronic disease, the one who has his hand and foot cut off or foot only cut off, the paralyzed, and the old man who is not able to attend and the likes.

Ibraaheem an-Nakha`ee said, "They did not use to allow anyone to miss the congregational prayer unless he were sick or in fear."[2]

Ibn Hazm said, "There is no difference of opinion concerning this."[3]

2. Fear. Fear here means that that he fears for himself, his property or his honor.[4]

Allah says,

$$\text{لَا يُكَلِّفُ اللَّهُ نَفْسًا إِلَّا وُسْعَهَا}$$

"Allah does not burden a soul beyond what it can bear" [*al-Baqarah* (2):286].

Ibn Abbaas reported that the Prophet (peace be upon him) said,

$$\text{مَنْ سَمِعَ النِّدَاءَ فَلَمْ يَجِبْ فَلَا صَلَاةَ لَهُ إِلَّا مِنْ عُذْرٍ قَالُوا يَا}$$

$$\text{رَسُولَ اللَّهِ وَمَا الْعُذْرُ قَالَ خَوْفٌ أَوْ مَرَضٌ}$$

---

[1] *Saheeh al-Bukhaaree* [Eng. Trans. 1/386 no. 684].
[2] *al-Musanaaf* (1/351) by ibn Abee Shaybah.
[3] *al-Muhallaa* (4/285).
[4] *al-Mughnee* (1/451) by ibn Qudaamah.

"Whoever hears the call to prayer and does not respond, then there is no prayer for him unless he has an excuse." They asked, "What constitutes an excuse O Messenger of Allah?" He replied, "Fear or illness."[1]

Ibn Maajah reported with a *saheeh* chain from ibn Abbaas that the Prophet (peace be upon him) said,

$$ مَنْ سَمِعَ النِّدَاءَ فَلَمْ يَأْتِهِ فَلَا صَلَاةَ لَهُ إِلاَّ مِنْ عُذْرٍ $$

"For whoever hears the call to prayer and does not come to it, there is no prayer, unless he has an excuse."[2]

3. Repressing the urge to go to the toilet. This refers to restraining oneself from excreting or urinating because this prevents one from completing the *khushoo`* in prayer.

This is based on what Muslim reports from Aa`ishah who said, "I heard the Messenger of Allah (peace be upon him) saying,

$$ لَا صَلَاةَ بِحَضْرَةِ الطَّعَامِ وَلَا هُوَ يُدَافِعُهُ الأَخْبَثَانِ $$

'There is no prayer when the food has been served or when one is repressing the urge to go to the toilet.'"[3]

4. When the food has been served. This is based on the previously mentioned hadeeth,

$$ لَا صَلَاةَ بِحَضْرَةِ الطَّعَامِ $$

"There is no prayer when the food has been served..."

Naafi` reported that ibn Umar said, "When one of you is eating food, do not hurry [but eat] until your need has been fulfilled, even if the prayer is commenced."[4]

5. Eating something that has a foul smell. The obligation of attending the congregational prayer is lifted from the one who has eaten radish, onion, leek, garlic, or meat that has a foul smell which one is unable to remove. This is

---

[1] *as-Sunan al-Kubraa* (1/185) by al-Bayhaqee.
[2] *Sunan ibn Maajah* (no.793).
[3] *Saheeh Muslim* [Eng. Trans. 1/278 no. 1139].
[4] *as-Sunan al-Kubraa* (3/74) and refer to *Fath al-Baaree* (2/161-162).

because the smell that comes out of the mouth due to having eaten these foods harms the people that the person is talking to and makes them averse to being close to him.

Muslim reports in his *Saheeh* from Jaabir that the Prophet (peace be upon him) said,

مَنْ أَكَلَ ثُومًا أَوْ بَصَلاً فَلْيَعْتَزِلْنَا أَوْ لِيَعْتَزِلْ مَسْجِدَنَا وَلْيَقْعُدْ فِي بَيْتِهِ

"Whoever eats garlic or onion should stay away from us or let him stay away from our mosque and instead sit in his home."[1]

The same applies to a butcher who has a foul smell and anyone else who has a foul smell because the underlying reasoning has been given to be the harming of other Muslims. The one who has leprosy or any other contagious disease that causes harm has the same rule apply to him by analogy.[2]

6. The Imaam lengthening the prayer to the point that it becomes hard upon the followers. This is based on the report from ibn Mas`ud reports that a man said, "By Allah, O Messenger of Allah, indeed I remain away from the morning prayer due to such and such a person who lengthens it." I have not seen the Prophet (peace be upon him) giving an exhortation in which he displayed more anger than on that day. He said,

إِنَّ مِنْكُمْ مُنَفِّرِينَ فَأَيُّكُمْ مَا صَلَّى بِالنَّاسِ فَلْيَتَجَوَّزْ فَإِنَّ فِيهِمْ الضَّعِيفَ وَالْكَبِيرَ وَذَا الْحَاجَةِ

"Indeed, there are among you those who cause the people to become averse to attending the congregational prayer. When any of you prays with the people be brief, for there are among them the weak, the old and those who have a pressing need."[3]

---

[1] *Saheeh Muslim* [Eng. Trans. 1/279 no. 1146].
[2] *Haashiyah ar-Rawd al-Marba`* (2/356) by ibn Qaasim.
[3] Reported by al-Bukhaaree [Eng. Trans. 1/379 no. 670].

7. Being overcome with sleep. This is based on the hadeeth from Abu Qataadah that the Messenger of Allah (peace be upon him) said,

$$\text{إِنَّهُ لَا تَفْرِيطَ فِي النَّوْمِ إِنَّمَا التَّفْرِيطُ فِي الْيَقَظَةِ فَإِذَا سَهَا}$$
$$\text{أَحَدُكُمْ عَنْ صَلَاةٍ فَلْيُصَلِّهَا حِينَ يَذْكُرُهَا وَمِنْ الْغَدِ لِلْوَقْتِ}$$

"There is no negligence in sleep. Negligence exists only in the state of wakefulness. Therefore, if one of you forgets to pray, let him pray as soon as he remembers and let him pray the prayers of the next day at their correct times..."[1]

8. Being naked and destitute, having no clothes to wear.[2]

9. Being on a journey and fearing that one's travelling party will leave him behind.[3]

10. Attending to the dead person and preparing him for burial.

11. A grave concern that prevents one having *khushoo`* in prayer.

Abu ad-Dardaa` said, "From the understanding of a person is that he fulfils his need so that he can devote his attention to prayer, as his heart would then be free of his concern."[4]

Examples of this are: craving for something that one has not yet attained, searching for something lost that one has hope of finding, striving to regain a belonging that has been forcibly taken, extreme depression, the existence of one who would harm the person on the road to the mosque or in it, and the fear of falling into *fitnah* or causing *fitnah*.[5]

---

[1] Muslim [ng. Trans. 1/332 no.1450], Abu Daawood [Eng. Trans. 1/114 no. 436], Tirmidhee (no. 177), an-Nasaa`ee (1/294). The hadeeth occurs as part of a story the basis of which is mentioned in al-Bukhaaree [Eng. Trans. 1/327 no. 659].

[2] Mentioned by an-Nawawee in *Rawdah at-Taalibeen* (1/345-346).

[3] Mentioned by ibn Qudaamah in *al-Mughnee* (2/453).

[4] *Haashiyah ar-Rawd al-Marba`* (2/357) by ibn Qaasim.

[5] Ibid (2/361).

As-Suyutee wrote in *al-Ashbaahu wa al-Nadhaair*, "The excuses that allow one to leave the congregational prayer number about forty."[1]

Ibn al-Qayyim also mentions one of the reasons that would allow one to leave the congregational prayer, saying, "The Muslims boycotting a person excuses that person from attending the congregational prayer. Meaning their boycotting him for a legitimate reason, this is because Hilaal bin Umayyah and Maraarah bin ar-Rabee' remained in their homes, praying in their homes and they did not attend the congregational prayer."[2]

An-Nawawee said in *ar-Rawdah* after mentioning the excuses for not attending *Jumu'ah* and the congregational prayer, "...from the conditions of the prayer is that one knows and understands what he is doing. The excuses mentioned prevent one from actualizing this. When these excuses disappear, one then performs the prayer having complete *khushoo'*. Performing the prayer with *khushoo'* after missing the congregational prayer is better than praying in congregation with no *khushoo'*."[3]

The Undesirability and Sin Is Lifted Due to These Excuses and the Person Attains the Reward of Congregational Prayer

The scholars have differed concerning the excuses that allow one to miss the congregational prayer: Is the sin[4] or undesirability[5] lifted from this person without his attaining the reward and excellence of congregation or is the sin or undesirability lifted with his attaining the reward of congregational prayer?

The scholars have two opinions concerning this.

---

[1] *Al-Ashbaah wa an-Nadhaa'ir* (pp. 439-440).
[2] *Zaad al-Ma'aad* (3/20).
[3] *Rawdah at-Taalibeen* (1/346) and *Haashiyah ar-Rawd al-Marba'* (2/364 fn. 2).
[4] If one takes to the opinion that attending the congregational prayer is obligatory.
[5] If one take to the opinion that it is recommended.

The First Opinion: Only the sin is lifted. This was the opinion that an-Nawawee declared with certainty.[1]

The Second Opinion: The sin is lifted and one attains the superiority of the congregational prayer. This is the correct opinion.[2] Therefore, if one leaves attending the congregational prayer due to a valid excuse, he attains the reward of the congregational prayer.

The proofs for this are many, including:

The hadeeth of Abu Musa that the Prophet (peace be upon him) said,

$$ إِذَا مَرِضَ الْعَبْدُ أَوْ سَافَرَ كُتِبَ لَهُ مِثْلُ مَا كَانَ يَعْمَلُ مُقِيمًا صَحِيحًا $$

"If the servant becomes ill or embarks on a journey, what is written for him (of reward) is the same as if he were healthy and resident."[3]

There is also the hadeeth of ibn Umar which states that the Prophet (peace be upon him) said,

$$ إِنَّ الْعَبْدَ إِذَا كَانَ عَلَى طَرِيقَةٍ حَسَنَةٍ مِنَ الْعِبَادَةِ ثُمَّ مَرِضَ قِيلَ لِلْمَلَكِ الْمُوَكَّلِ بِهِ اكْتُبْ لَهُ مِثْلَ عَمَلِهِ إِذَا كَانَ طَلِيقًا حَتَّى أُطْلِقَهُ أَوْ أَكْفِتَهُ إِلَيَّ $$

"If the servant is upon a good way of worship and then he becomes ill, it will be said to the angel appointed over him, 'Write for him the actions he would have done were he healthy until I cause him to regain his health or take him to Myself.'"[4]

`Ataa bin Yasaar narrated that the Prophet (peace be upon him) said,

---

[1] *Majmoo`* (4/100) and also see *Haashiyah ar-Rawd al-Marba`* (2/365).
[2] *Fath al-Baaree* (6/136-137).
[3] *Saheeh al-Bukhaaree* [Eng. Trans. 4/149 no. 239].
[4] *Musnad Ahmad* (2/203).

إِذَا مَرِضَ الْعَبْدُ قَالَ اللهُ لِلْكِرَامِ الْكَاتِبِينَ اكْتُبُوا لِعَبْدِي مِثْلَ

الَّذِي كَانَ يَعْمَلُ حَتَّى أَقْبِضَهُ أَوْ أُعَافِيهِ

"When the servant becomes ill, it is said to the two recording Angels, 'Write for my servant what he would have done had he been healthy until I cause him to die or become healthy once again.'"[1]

I say: When it becomes clear to you that it is not possible to miss the congregational prayer unless one has a valid excuse, then what can be said of those who hear the call to prayer yet do not attend it while being healthy and well? What excuses would they give when they stand before Allah, the Magnificent and Exalted? Does such a person not take heed from the fact that leaving the congregational prayer is from the signs of hypocrisy?[2]

Does he not desire what all these people who regularly attend the congregational prayer desire? Among these people are those who cannot come to the mosque unless in some form of transport, or those who walk to the mosque leaning on their walking stick, or those who have a pain but they endure this hoping for reward.

We ask Allah that He guides the misguided Muslims and that He rewards the obedient Muslims.

---

[1] Reported by ibn Abee Shaybah (2/230) as a *saheeh mursal* report. There are many more *abaadeeth* concerning this. Refer to *Irwaa al-Ghaleel* (2/346), *Rawdah at-Taalibeen* (1/334-346) and *Fath al-Baaree* (6/136-137).
[2] [Ibn Mas`ud said, "None remained away from the congregational prayer except a hypocrite whose hypocrisy was well known." (Saheeh Muslim) – Trans.]

Innovations, Errors and Evil Actions That Are Done in Congregational Prayer

Our Muslim nation has become submerged into various forms of blind following and following of customs and habits that have reached the point of affecting the realm of beliefs and the lawful and prohibited. Habits, blind following, errors and evils have been faithfully preserved by many of the children of this nation to the point that they no longer have the ability to distinguish between habitual actions and actions of worship, between that which is legislated and that which is forbidden. One can add to this the ignorance of many people with regards the rules and regulations of the actions of worship, especially the outward actions, the most important of which are the five daily prayers.

The general course with actions of worship and mannerisms of worship is that they are to be done exactly as the *Sharee`ah* has ordered. This most definitely applies to the prayer as well. It is obligatory that you safeguard yourself from adding to it any actions that have not been sanctioned and not omit anything of its pillars and obligations.

I shall list some of the errors and evil actions that are done by the Imaam and the followers to alert one to them and warn about them.

Articulating the Intention Aloud Before the Opening *Takbeer*: Some people say, "I intend to pray such and such a prayer facing the *Qiblah* consisting of four *rak`ahs* as the Imaam/follower, praying the prayer at its time/making up a missed prayer as an obligatory prayer for the sake of Allah the Exalted...."

This is a vile innovation and heinous negligence for intention is the desire and the conviction to do something. The place for this is the heart and it has no connection to the tongue whatsoever. This is why it is not reported anywhere that it should be articulated. This action arises from Shaytaan who whispers to those prone to his whispering—and refuge is sought from Allah. This occurs due to their being ignorant of the *Sharee'ah* or lacking in intellect, both being serious deficiencies.[1]

Another example is the saying of some people, "We have straightened our rows," after the Imaam says, "Straighten the rows."

Another example is the saying of some people, "Allah has spoken truthfully" after the Imaam has completed reciting a *Surah*. This is adding something to the prayer that is not part of it. Indeed, saying this statement outside of the prayer is a *bid'ah*, so how about within the prayer?

Another example is to pray optional prayers when the obligatory prayer has commenced. It is not permissible to commence an optional prayer after the obligatory prayer has started. If one is already praying an optional prayer, he should complete it with light *rak'ahs*, due to the saying of the Prophet (peace be upon him),

$$\text{إِذَا أُقِيمَتِ الصَّلَاةُ فَلَا صَلَاةَ إِلَّا الْمَكْتُوبَةُ}$$

"When the prayer is established, there is no prayer except the obligatory prayer."[2]

Ibn Abdul Barr, may Allah have mercy on him, said, "When there is a difference of opinion, the authority lies with the Sunnah and the one who clings to it has been successful. Leaving optional prayers when the obligatory prayer has commenced and praying them after one has finished praying the obligatory prayer is closer to following the Sunnah."

We have discussed this subject in detail previously.

Another example is betraying the right of the appointed Imaam by praying the prayer in congregation before the prayer has been pronounced for him. This subject has also been discussed previously.

Another example is the saying of some people, "We seek help with Allah," after the Imaam has said,

$$\text{إِيَّاكَ نَعْبُدُ وَإِيَّاكَ نَسْتَعِينُ}$$

---

[1] Refer to *an-Niyyah wa Atharuhaa fee al-Ahkaam ash-Shar'iyyah* (1/451).
[2] Reported by Muslim [Eng. Trans. 1/345 no. 1531].

"It is You Alone we worship and Your help Alone we seek"
[*al-Faatihah* (1):5].

The same goes for the saying of some people, "Our
Lord and to you belongs praise and thanks," adding the word
"thanks" after the Imaam has said (when rising from *ruku`*),
"Allah has heard the one who praised Him." The best course is
to restrict oneself to what occurs in the hadeeth.

**Another example is some people prostrating once
or twice** after the prayer has been completed. Imaam Abu
Shaamah said in his book *al-Baa`ith* concerning the innovation
of *Salaatul Raghaa`ib*, "The fifth aspect: Performing two
prostrations after completing the prayer is detestable for
indeed these two prostrations have no reason in the *Sharee`ah*
that would justify their performance. There is no text that
occurs with respect to performing prostrations in order to draw
close to Allah except when in prayer or for a specific reason,
such as the prostration of forgetfulness or recitation of
Qur`aan."

Al-Imaam al-Mutawallee, the author of *at-Tatimma*
said, "Some people have become accustomed to performing a
prostration after completing the prayer, supplicating in it. This
prostration has no known basis that would justify it. It is not
reported from the Messenger (peace be upon him) or the
Companions."

Reserving a Specific Place in the Mosque: Some of
the people who constantly attend the congregational prayer in
the mosque become accustomed to a specific place or area of
the mosque and reserve it for themselves, either directly
behind the Imaam or to one side of the *minbar* or the likes of
this, to the extent that they find no pleasure in worshipping
unless they be in that place.

Similar to this is what some people do in the Two
Holy Mosques and other Mosques in reserving a place for
themselves from one prayer to the next, a long time before it is
time to pray it.

Also in this vein is what some *Mu`adhdhins* do in
many of the Muslim lands in placing prayer mats on the
ground behind the Imaam in order to let people know that the
place is taken.

All of these matters have no precedent from our
righteous Salaf, may Allah be pleased with them, nor did they

know of this. It was not done during the time of the Prophet (peace be upon him), nor was it from the practice of the *Khulafaa ar-Raashideen al-Mahdiyyen* and those who came after them.

Some of the people who do this claim that their reason is their desire to attain the first row due to the great reward it has. To these people we say, "To desire the first row necessitates you staying in that place and sticking to that place waiting for the next prayer. It is in this way that you wait for the next prayer after having completed one prayer, not by leaving something that would indicate that the space is taken and then going away for a number of hours to return, step over the necks of people and sit in your reserved place."

Ibn Taymiyyah, may Allah have mercy upon him, was asked about one who reserved a place in the mosque by putting a prayer mat or rug, is such lawful or not. He replied, "It is not for anyone to reserve a place in the mosque, nor is it for him to place a prayer mat on the ground before his actually attending the congregation. It is not for anyone else to pray on that mat without the owner's permission but he can pick it up and pray in that place according to the most correct of the two opinions of the scholars. Allah knows best."[1]

It is important to note that this general rule finds exception in the case that a particular place is known to be specifically (and legitimately) appointed for a particular person. In that case, that person has most right to that place. Examples of this is the place on which the Imaam stands when leading the congregation, or the place in which he sits when giving lessons or passing rulings, or a place that has been appointed for an ill person in which he can pray and sit.

The Saying of One Who Wishes to Catch the Congregational Prayer When the Imaam is in *ruku`*, "Indeed Allah is with the patient," or his clearing his throat (to draw the attention of the Imaam) or his running in order to attain the *rak`ah.*

Seeking Forgiveness in Congregation in a Unified Voice after saying the *tasleem* [is an innovation]. The same applies to their saying, "O Most Merciful of those who show mercy, bestow Your Mercy upon us," as a group and in one

---

[1] *Majmoo` Fataawaa.*

voice after they have sought forgiveness. This is an innovation, misguidance and ignorance with regards to the religion.

Similarly, shaking hands (to those on the left and right) after completing the prayer is an innovation and evil.[1] This is because there is no evidence for this from the Sunnah and it is not affirmed from any of the Salaf, not to mention that doing this prevents one from performing the legislated *dhikr*.

And from the innovated acts is making supplication after the *iqaamah* but before the opening *takbeer*, such as their saying, "O Allah make good our standing before You and do not make the Day in which we stand before You a day of grief." And their reciting the verse,

رَبِّ اجْعَلْنِي مُقِيمَ الصَّلَاةِ وَمِنْ ذُرِّيَّتِي

"O my Lord make me one who is devout in prayer and my progeny…" [*Ibraaheem* (14):40]. This is a despicable innovation. The same applies to those who are prone to the whisperings of Shaytaan reciting *Surah an-Naas* before the opening *takbeer* in order to repress the whisperings. This is a *bid'ah*. This is regardless of whether any of this is done individually or in congregation for the Messenger of Allah (peace be upon him),

كَانَ يَفْتَتِحُ الصَّلَاةَ بِالتَّكْبِيرِ وَالقِرَاءَةِ بِالْحَمْدُ لِلَّهِ رَبِّ الْعَالَمِينَ

"Used to commence the prayer by saying the *takbeer* and reciting *al-Faatihah*."[2]

He (peace be upon him) said to the Bedouin,

إِذَا قُمْتَ إِلَى الصَّلَاةِ فَكَبِّرْ

"When you stand for prayer, say the *takbeer*…"[3] So anything that is additional to what has been legislated is to be rejected due to his (peace be upon him) saying,

---

[1] *Fiqh as-Salaah* (p. 564) by ibn Taymiyyah. [Refer to Appendix 2 for a detailed discussion concerning this – Trans.]

[2] *Saheeh Muslim* [Eng. Trans. 1/258 no. 1005].

[3] Ibid [1/218 no. 781].

239

$$\text{مَنْ عَمِلَ عَمَلاً لَيْسَ عَلَيْهِ أَمْرُنَا فَهُوَ رَدٌّ}$$

"Whoever does an action that we have not enjoined, it is rejected."[1]

Imaam Ahmad was asked, "Should something be said before (starting) the prayer?" He replied, "No, because there is nothing that is reported with regards to this from the Prophet (peace be upon him) or the Companions."

The same applies to supplicating in congregation after the prayer has been completed, such that the Imaam feels compelled to supplicate before standing from the place of prayer and the followers do not leave until the Imaam has completed the supplication. When the Imaam supplicates the followers say *aameen* aloud. This has occurred in most of the Muslim lands to the point that it has become a distinguishing sign, such that the people reject and severely censure the one who does not perform it—and the Aid of Allah is sought.

What is correct is that this act of supplicating in congregation after the completion of the prayer is a *bid'ah*, having no basis for it in the *Sharee'ah*. This is because performing supplication in this form and manner does not fall under the general texts that occur with regards to supplicating and it was not done by the Prophet (peace be upon him) nor by the Imaams who came after him.

Yes, in principle, the action of supplicating is sanctioned. But to actualize this in the form of a congregational supplication, after every prayer, continuously, with the followers saying *aameen*, is an innovated matter. Perhaps the Messenger of Allah (peace be upon him), after the obligatory and optional prayers, would perform the *dhikr* of Allah while the congregation had no part to play in that, unless they happened to say the same *dhikr* or perform the same supplication as he did, but this was not in congregation.[2]

Muslim reports in his *Saheeh* from Thawbaan that,

---

[1] Ibid [3/931 no. 4266].
[2] *al-Kashf al-Qinaa` min Mas'ala ad-Du'aa ba'd al-Maktoobah bi Hay'ah al-Jamaa'ah* (pp. 14-21).

إِذَا انْصَرَفَ مِنْ صَلَاتِهِ اسْتَغْفَرَ ثَلَاثًا وَقَالَ اللَّهُمَّ أَنْتَ السَّلَامُ
وَمِنْكَ السَّلَامُ تَبَارَكْتَ ذَا الْجَلَالِ وَالْإِكْرَامِ

"When the Messenger of Allah (peace be upon him) completed
the prayer he would seek forgiveness from Allah three times
and then say, 'O Allah, You are Peace and from you is peace.
Blessed are You, the Possessor of Majesty and Honor.'"[1]

Abu Daawood reports from Mu`aadh bin Jabal that the
Messenger of Allah (peace be upon him) took hold of his hand
and said,

يَا مُعَاذُ وَاللَّهِ إِنِّي لَأُحِبُّكَ وَاللَّهِ إِنِّي لَأُحِبُّكَ فَقَالَ أُوصِيكَ يَا
مُعَاذُ لَا تَدَعَنَّ فِي دُبُرِ كُلِّ صَلَاةٍ تَقُولُ اللَّهُمَّ أَعِنِّي عَلَى
ذِكْرِكَ وَشُكْرِكَ وَحُسْنِ عِبَادَتِكَ

"O Mu`aadh, by Allah, I love you. Do not leave saying, 'O
Allah help me to perform Your *dhikr* and give thanks to You
and worship You in the best of ways,' after every prayer."[2]

Muslim reports from Abdullaah bin Zubair that the
Messenger of Allah (peace be upon him) used to say after each
prayer,

لَا إِلَهَ إِلَّا اللَّهُ وَحْدَهُ لَا شَرِيكَ لَهُ لَهُ الْمُلْكُ وَلَهُ الْحَمْدُ وَهُوَ
عَلَى كُلِّ شَيْءٍ قَدِيرٌ لَا حَوْلَ وَلَا قُوَّةَ إِلَّا بِاللَّهِ وَلَا نَعْبُدُ إِلَّا
إِيَّاهُ لَهُ النِّعْمَةُ وَلَهُ الْفَضْلُ وَلَهُ الثَّنَاءُ الْحَسَنُ لَا إِلَهَ إِلَّا اللَّهُ
مُخْلِصِينَ لَهُ الدِّينَ وَلَوْ كَرِهَ الْكَافِرُونَ

"There is none worthy of worship except Allah, the One Who
has no partners. To Him belongs the Dominion and to Him

---

[1] *Saheeh Muslim* [Eng. Trans. 1/292 no. 1226].
[2] Abu Daawood [Eng. Trans. 1/396 no. 1517].

belongs all praise and He is Omnipotent over everything.
There is neither movement nor strength except with Allah and
we worship none save Him. To him belongs the favor and
beneficence and to Him belongs the best praise. There is none
worthy of worship save Allah, making the religion sincerely
for Him even though the disbelievers may detest this."[1]

Muslim also reports from Abu Hurayrah that the
Messenger of Allah (peace be upon him) said,

مَنْ سَبَّحَ اللَّهَ فِي دُبُرِ كُلِّ صَلَاةٍ ثَلَاثًا وَثَلَاثِينَ وَحَمِدَ اللَّهَ

ثَلَاثًا وَثَلَاثِينَ وَكَبَّرَ اللَّهَ ثَلَاثًا وَثَلَاثِينَ وَقَالَ تَمَامَ الْمِائَةِ لَا إِلَهَ

إِلَّا اللَّهُ وَحْدَهُ لَا شَرِيكَ لَهُ لَهُ الْمُلْكُ وَلَهُ الْحَمْدُ وَهُوَ عَلَى

كُلِّ شَيْءٍ قَدِيرٌ غُفِرَتْ خَطَايَاهُ وَإِنْ كَانَتْ مِثْلَ زَبَدِ الْبَحْرِ

"Whoever says 'SubhaanAllah' thirty three times after every
prayer, 'Alhumdolillaah' thirty three times, 'Allahu Akbar'
thirty three times, and completes one hundred by saying,
'There is none worthy of worship save Allah Who has no
partner. To Him belongs the Dominion and to Him belongs all
praise and He is Omnipotent over everything,'[2] will have all
his sins forgiven even if they be the extent of the foam on the
ocean."[3]

An-Nasaa'ee in *al-Kabeer* and at-Tabaraanee report
from Abu Umaamah that the Messenger of Allah (peace be
upon him) said,

مَنْ قَرَأَ آيَةَ الْكُرْسِيِّ عَقْبَ كُلِّ صَلَاةٍ لَمْ يَمْنَعْهُ دُخُولُ الْجَنَّةِ إِلَّا

أَنْ يَمُوتَ

---

[1] Muslim [Eng. Trans. 1/293 no. 1235].
[2] *Laa ilaaha illaAllah wahdahu laa shareeka lahu, lahul Mulku wa lahul hamdu wa huwa alaa kulli shayin qadeer.*
[3] Muslim [Eng. Trans. 1/294 no. 1243].

"For whoever recites *Aayah al-Kursee* [*al-Baqarah* 255] after every prayer, nothing prevents him from entering Paradise except his dying."[1]

Ibn Al-Qayyim said, "Meaning that there is nothing between him and entering Paradise except death."

So all of these *ahaadeeth* mention *dhikr* and supplication but not by way of doing them in congregation nor by way of doing them individually with raising the hands. Rather these *adhkaar* and supplications are to be done in the way the Prophet (peace be upon him) taught his Companions and in the way that he himself performed them. This is because *dhikr* is an action of worship. Therefore, it must be done as authentically reported from the Messenger of Allah (peace be upon him).[2]

When performing *dhikr* it is necessary to stick to the following matters:

Performing the *dhikr* with the words taught by the Prophet (peace be upon him).

Performing the *dhikr* in the time in which it is legislated to perform it.

Performing the number of the *dhikr* that has been legislated without adding or decreasing.

Performing the *dhikr* in the manner that it has been legislated, aloud, silently, individually or in congregation.

Sticking to the method of performing the *dhikr,* for example, by articulating the legislated *dhikr*.

Shaykh al-Islam ibn Taymiyyah said,

> There is no doubt that the *adhkaar* and supplications are from the best forms of worship. Worship is built upon *tawqeef* [sticking to what the texts state] and *ittibaa* [following]... Therefore, it is not allowed for anyone to legislate new *adhkaar* (words of remembrance) or supplications and take them as actions of worship that the people must

---

[1] *Amal al-Yawm wa al-Laylah* by an-Nasaa`ee, at-Tabaraanee (7532) and ibn al-Qayyim includes it in his *Waabil as-Sayyib* (p. 143-144). The hadeeth is *saheeh* when taking into account all of its routes of narration.
[2] [This does not negate the fact that generally speaking it is permissible to supplicate by raising ones hands - Trans.]

constantly perform, just as they constantly perform the five daily prayers. Rather this is innovating into the religion that for which Allah has not given permission. However, if a person were to supplicate with these new supplications on occasion and individually without making this supplication a Sunnah for the people, this would not be an innovation. As for the one who takes to a formula of *dhikr* (*wird*) that has not been legislated and makes this to be a Sunnah to be followed, then this is from those things that are forbidden.

Not only this but the legislated supplications and *adhkaar* contain all the correct goals and all the lofty intentions that a person could ever require and no one but an ignoramus or an extremist would turn away from these and recourse to these newly invented *adhkaar*. As for what is reported from the Prophet (peace be upon him) with regards to what is performed after the obligatory prayers, this is the well known *adhkaar* that can be found in the *Saheeh*s, the *Musnad*s and other books of hadeeth. As for the Imaam and the followers supplicating in congregation after the obligatory prayers, this is a *bid'ah* that did not exist at the time of the Prophet (peace be upon him). Indeed, his supplication used to be within the prayer. This is because the one who is praying is conversing with his Lord and supplicating at that time would be most fitting. As for supplicating after completing the prayer and the discourse with his Lord, such is not the most fitting time to supplicate.[1]

From the errors that some of the people who pray commit is their performing optional prayers before performing the legislated *adhkaar* (after the obligatory prayers). Muslim reports from ibn Umar bin `Ataa bin Abee al- Khawaar that

---

[1] *Majmoo` Fataawaa* (22/510, 595).

Naafi` bin Jubair sent him to as-Saa`ib, the son of Namir's sister, with a view to asking him about what he had observed of the prayer of Mu`aawiyah. He said, "Yes, I observed the *Jumu`ah* prayer with him in Maqsoorah and when the Imaam said the *tasleem,* I stood up in my place and observed (the *sunan* prayers). As he entered (his apartment), he sent for me and said, 'Do not repeat what you have done. Whenever you observe the *Jumu`ah* prayer do not observe (*sunan*) prayers till you have talked or gone out, for the Messenger of Allah (peace be upon him) ordered us to do this and not to combine (two types) of prayers without talking or going out.'"[1]

Imaam an-Nawawee said, "This hadeeth contains evidence for what our companions (the Shaafi`ees) say that it is recommended to pray the set optional prayers, and others, in a place different than the one in which the obligatory prayer was prayed. The best course is to pray the optional prayers in one's house and, if not, then at another place in the mosque or other than the mosque. This is so as to increase the number of places on which one makes prostration and to differentiate between the optional prayers and the obligatory prayers. His saying, 'Until we talk,' is proof that the prayers can be distinguished by talking as well, but moving from one place to another is better due to what we have mentioned and Allah knows best."[2]

Ibn Qayyim al-Jawziyyah said while mentioning the evidence that prohibits one from doing something that would lead to the unlawful, even if that thing in and of itself is permissible, "The fiftieth aspect: He forbade that the prayer of *Jumu`ah* be joined to another (optional) prayer until one talks or leaves. This is so that this is not taken as a means to making something which is optional obligatory, and so that one does not add into the obligation that which is not part of it."[3]

From the innovations and evil actions is to give the *salaam* to the Imaam. Meaning that one of the followers stands up after the *tasleem* and shakes the hand of the Imaam and those to his left and right, thereby disturbing their *dhikr* which was enjoined to be performed after the prayers. This is a

---

[1] *Saheeh Muslim* [Eng. Trans. 2/416 no.1921].
[2] *Sharh Saheeh Muslim* (6/170-171).
[3] *I`laam al-Muwaqqi`een `an Rabbil `Aalameen* (3/149-159).

bid`ah in the religion having no evidence for it—and the Aid of Allah is sought.[1]

---

[1] [Refer to Appendix 2 – Trans.]

Conclusion

This is what Allah has allowed me to gather together with regards the various aspects of this subject Alongwith new issues that I have explained and mentioned in some detail, I have also mentioned the various opinions of the scholars concerning them together with mentioning the strongest opinion. I added to this a number of beneficial observations. I have alerted the reader to errors, innovations and evils which are performed by some of those who pray in some of the Muslim lands, out of ignorance or blind following. I have argued against them and warned from them.

In conclusion, I ask Allah by His Beautiful Names and Lofty Attributes that He make our actions sincerely for His Noble Face and that He make them of benefit to us, indeed He is the One Who Hears and Responds.

Completed in Ramadaan in the year 1412H[1]
Dr. Saalih bin Ghaanim as-Sadlaan
Professor in the College of *Sharee`ah* in Riyaadh

---

[1] The editing was completed in Jamaadee al-Uolaa in the year 1414H and I rechecked it before the third edition was published on 1/11/1415.

APPENDIX 1¹

When the Imaam Prays Sitting, Does the Follower Pray Sitting?

(Note: Translated from *Fath al-Baaree* (2/224f) by al-Haafidh ibn Hajr al-Asqalaanee.)

From among the *ahaadeeth* concerning this issue are the three below quoted in *Saheeh al-Bukhaaree*:

On the authority of Aaʻishah that during the illness of the Prophet (peace be upon him) from which he died, he appointed Abu Bakr to lead the prayer. Then "when the Prophet (peace be upon him) felt a bit better, he came out for the *Dhuhur* prayer with the help of two people, one of whom was al-Abbaas, while Abu Bakr was leading the people in the prayer. When Abu Bakr saw him, he wanted to retreat but the Prophet (peace be upon him) beckoned him not to do so. He asked them to make him sit beside Abu Bakr and they did so. Abu Bakr was following the Prophet (peace be upon him) in the prayer, and the people were following Abu Bakr. The Prophet (peace be upon him) prayed sitting."

Aaʻishah, the mother of the believers reported, "Allah's Messenger (peace be upon him) prayed sitting in his house during his illness whereas some people prayed behind him standing. The Prophet (peace be upon him) beckoned them to sit down. On completion of the prayer he said, 'The Imaam is to be followed. Make *ruku* ` when he makes *ruku* `; raise your heads [from *ruku* `] when he raises his head; when he says, "*Sami Allahu liman hamida*," say, "*Rabbanaa wa laka al-hamd*"; and if he prays sitting, then pray sitting."

Anas bin Maalik reported, "Once Allah's Messenger (peace be upon him) rode a horse and fell down and the right side of his body was injured. He offered one of the prayers

---

¹ The translator has added all appendices and footnotes in them.

while sitting and we also prayed behind him sitting. When he completed the prayer, he said, 'The Imaam is to be followed...'" Al-Humaidee said: The saying of the Prophet (peace be upon him), "Pray sitting" was said in his former illness (during his early life) but the Prophet (peace be upon him) prayed sitting afterwards (in his last illness) and the people were praying standing behind him and the Prophet (peace be upon him) did not order them to sit. We should follow the latest actions of the Prophet (peace be upon him).

Ibn Hajr al-Asqalaanee says, "...Evidence is derived for the abrogation of the command—that the followers pray sitting behind a sitting Imaam—due to his (peace be upon him) endorsing the Companions' standing in prayer behind him when he was sitting. It was in this way that Imaam ash-Shaafi'ee endorsed the abrogation. Thus the author (al-Bukhaaree) quotes this opinion at the end of the chapter from his Shaykh, al-Humaidee who is the student of ash-Shaafi'ee. This was also the opinion of Abu Haneefah, Abu Yusuf and al-Awza'ee. Al-Waleed bin Muslim reports this saying from Maalik.

Ahmad rejected the abrogation of the aforementioned matter and reconciled the two hadeeth by saying that they were revealed with regards to two different situations.

The first is when the appointed Imaam starts the prayer sitting, due to an illness from which his recovery is hoped. IN this case, those behind him pray sitting. The second is when the appointed Imaam starts the prayer standing. In this case, it is necessary that the followers pray standing, even if it happens that it becomes necessary for the Imaam to pray sitting. This occurs in the hadeeth of the illness of the Prophet (peace be upon him) from which he died, for indeed his endorsing their standing indicates that he did not necessitate sitting for them in this situation because Abu Bakr started the prayer standing and they prayed [behind him] standing. This is contrary to the first situation in which he (peace be upon him) started the prayer sitting and when they prayed behind him standing, he prohibited it.

This reconciliation is strengthened because the basic principle is the absence of abrogation. This is especially true because in this situation it is necessary that the claim of abrogation occur on two occasions. This is because the basic principle for the ruling of the one who is capable of praying standing is that he does not pray sitting. So this principle was abrogated with regards to the one whose Imaam prays sitting. Now the claim of abrogating this sitting necessitates abrogation to have occurred a second time and this is far-fetched. What is even more far-fetched is what has preceded in the quotation from Qaadee Ayaadh for his words necessitate abrogation to have occurred on three occasions.

A group of the Shaafi`ee Hadeeth Scholars were of the same opinion as Imaam Ahmad, such as ibn Khuzaymah, ibn al-Mundhir, and ibn Hibbaan. They gave other replies to the hadeeth in this chapter. For example, ibn Khuzaymah said, 'Indeed, the hadeeth that occurs ordering the follower to pray sitting following his Imaam has no difference of opinion over it with regards to its authenticity and meaning. As for his (peace be upon him) praying sitting [and the followers standing], there is a difference of opinion over it as to whether he was the Imaam or the follower [of Abu Bakr]. That which is not differed upon should not be left for that which is differed upon. I reply by repressing the difference of opinion and take [the hadeeth] to mean that he (peace be upon him) was the Imaam on one occasion and the follower on the other.'

From among the replies is that some of them reconciled the narrations that the command for sitting was one of recommendation and his (peace be upon him) endorsing their standing behind him [while he was sitting] was to clarify its permissibility. Therefore, based on this opinion, the one who leads sitting due to a [valid] excuse should alternate the ones praying behind him between sitting and standing [in different prayers]. The followers' sitting takes precedence due to the establishment of the command to follow the Imaam and the many *ahaadeeth* that occur to do with this.

Ibn Khuzaymah replied to those who declared this reconciliation far-fetched by saying that the command emanated from the Prophet (peace be upon him) and the companions persisted in acting upon it during his life and after it. Abdur-Razzaaq reports with a *saheeh* chain from Qays bin Fahd al-Ansaaree that 'their Imaam fell ill during the lifetime of the Prophet (peace be upon him) and he used to lead us in prayer sitting and we would also pray sitting.'

Ibn al-Mundhir reported with a *saheeh* chain from Aseed bin Hadeer, 'that he used to lead his people, then he fell ill. He went to them while he was ill and they commanded him to pray with them. He said, "I am not capable of standing, so sit." So he prayed with them while sitting and they were sitting.'

Abu Daawood reports from another chain from Aseed bin Hadeer that he said, 'O Messenger of Allah, verily our Imaam is sick.' He said, "When he prays sitting, then pray sitting."' The chain is broken to that report.

Ibn Abu Shaybah reports with a *saheeh* chain from Jaabir, 'that he became ill, and the time for prayer came so he prayed with them sitting, and they prayed with him sitting.'

It is reported from Abu Hurayrah that he gave a *fatwa* with this meaning. The chain of that report is *saheeh* as well.

Ibn al-Mundhir enjoined those who follow the principle that a companion is most knowledgeable as regards to the explanation of what he narrates, that they follow this opinion. This is because Jaabir and Abu Hurayrah report the aforementioned matter and they persisted upon this opinion and gave a *fatwa* based upon it after the death of the Prophet (peace be upon him). Also, the one who follows the principle that when a companion narrates a hadeeth and then acts contrary to it, then that which is taken into consideration is what he acts on, has to follow this opinion because in this case [both these companions] are acting in conformity to what they narrate and this obviously takes greater precedence [in following].

Ibn Hibbaan claimed a consensus [of the Companions] of acting by this opinion [of sitting behind a sitting Imaam], and it is as of he means a consensus of silent approval (*ijmaa as-sukooti*). This was because he reports this opinion from four Companions whose mention has preceded and then he said, 'a contrary opinion is not preserved from any other Companion, neither via a *saheeh* route or a weak one.'

Likewise ibn Hazm said, 'There is nothing contrary to this opinion preserved from the Companions.' Then he contends with the certainty of the fact that the Companions prayed behind him (peace be upon him) standing while he was sitting and said, 'Because it does not occur clearly' and he extrapolates on this with a discussion of no consequence.

That which ibn Hazm negated, ash-Shaafi`ee affirmed and said, 'It is from the narration of Ibraaheem from al-Aswad from Aa`ishah.' Then I found a clarification to this hadeeth in the *Musannaf* of Abdur-Razzaaq from ibn Juraij that, `Ataa informed me' and he mentioned the hadeeth and its wording is, 'So the Prophet (peace be upon him) prayed sitting and he placed Abu Bakr behind him, between himself and the people. The people prayed behind him standing.' This is a *mursal* hadeeth supported by the narration that Imaam ash-Shaafi`ee links from [Ibraaheem] an-Nakha`i.

This is the hadeeth that necessitates investigation [into the claim of ibn Hazm], for they started the prayer standing with Abu Bakr, and there is no difference over this. So the one who claims that they sat afterwards [when the Prophet arrived], it is upon him to bring the proof. Then I saw ibn Hibban infer that they sat after they were standing with what Abu Zubair narrates from Jaabir, 'the Messenger (peace be upon him) fell ill so we prayed behind him standing and the people would hear the *takbeer* of Abu Bakr. Then he (peace be upon him) turned to us and saw us standing, so he motioned to us and we sat. So when he had said *tasleem* he said, "Verily you were doing what the Persians and Romans do, so do not do it."'

This is a *saheeh* hadeeth, reported by Muslim, but this did not occur at the illness from which he died. Rather this was when he fell from the horse as occurs in the narration of Abu Sufyaan from Jaabir as well who said, "The Messenger of Allah rode a horse to Madeenah and it threw him on a tree stump and he hurt his foot." Reported by Abu Daawood and ibn Khuzaimah with a *saheeh* chain.

Hence, there is no proof for what he claims due to this except that he clings to the saying in the narration of Abu az-Zubair, 'and the people heard Abu Bakr's *takbeer*.' He said, 'This did not occur except at the illness from which he died, because the prayer of his first illness took place in the room of Aa`ishah and there were a group of Companions with him and they did not need to hear the *takbeer* of Abu Bakr (his conveying the *takbeer* of the Prophet). This is contrary to the prayer at the illness from which he died for it was in the mosque with a large group of companions so Abu Bakr needed to convey his *takbeer*.'

There is no leeway for him in what he clings to because Abu Zubair was alone in reporting the hearing of this *takbeer*. Even if we accept that he preserved it, there is nothing preventing their hearing Abu Bakr's *takbeer* in this situation because it is possible that his (peace be upon him) voice was low due to pain, and it was his habit to raise his voice with *takbeer*, and so Abu Bakr used to raise his voice with the *takbeer* due to this.

Behind all this is that this [claim of ibn Hibbaan] is a possibility and the clear [meaning of the] narration is not to be left due to it. This being that they prayed behind him (peace be upon him) standing as has preceded in the *mursal* narration of `Ataa and others, indeed in the narration of `Ataa is that they persisted in standing until the prayer had been completed. Yes, there occurs in the aforementioned *mursal* narration of `Ataa an addition to the saying, 'and the people prayed behind him standing.' 'So the Prophet (peace be upon him) said, "If I had as much of my life left as has passed, you would not have prayed except sitting. So pray the prayer of your Imaam as it is. If he prays standing then pray standing, and if he prays sitting then pray sitting." '

So this addition strengthens what ibn Hibbaan said that the narration was at the time of the illness from which the Prophet (peace be upon him) died. The benefit gained from it is the abrogation of the obligation of the followers to pray sitting when their Imaam prays sitting because he (peace be upon him) did not command them on this last occasion to repeat the prayer. However, when the obligation is abrogated the permissibility still remains and permissibility does not negate desirability. So his last command is to be taken that they should pray sitting [when the Imaam prays sitting] due to the desirability of this because the obligation has been removed due to his endorsing their action [of standing] and the absence of his command to repeat the prayer. This accomplishes the reconciliation between the evidences.

Wa billaahil tawfeeq, wAllahu A'lam."

Appendix 2

The Innovations Related to Greeting After the Prayer

(Note: Translated in summarized form from *Al-Qawl al-Mubeen fee Akhta`i al-Musalleen* [pp. 290-295] by Shaykh Mashur Salmaan.)

Abu Hurayrah reported from the Messenger of Allah (peace be upon him) that he said, "When one of you meets his brother, let him give him the *salaam*. If a tree, wall or rock divides them, let them give the *salaam* upon meeting again."[1]

This hadeeth contains evidence for the Muslims to greet one another when they meet due to its benefits of inculcating unity, absence of hatred and mutual love. The command that is mentioned in this hadeeth is one of recommendation and not obligation.[2]

With respect to this, there is no difference between the one who is in the mosque or outside of the mosque. Indeed, the Sunnah proves that it is sanctioned to give the *salaam* to whoever is in the mosque, regardless of whether he is in prayer or not.

Ibn Umar reported that, "the Messenger of Allah (peace be upon him) went to Qubaa to pray there. The Ansaar came to him and greeted him while he was in prayer. I asked Bilaal, 'How did you see the Messenger of Allah (peace be upon him) replying to them when they greeted him while he was in prayer?' He replied, 'In this way.' Ja`far bin Awn

---

[1] *Sunan Abu Daawood* (Eng. Trans. 3/1435 no. 5181) and its chain is *saheeh* consisting of trustworthy and precise narrators. Refer to Muhammad Naasir al-Deen al-Albaani, *Silisilah as-Saheehah,* no. 186. Note: All footnotes in this section are by Shaykh Mashur.

[2] Refer to *Aqd az-Zabarjad fee Tahiyyah Ummah Muhammad* (p. 159).

demonstrated by extending his palm, keeping its inner side facing down and its back side facing up."[1]

Imaams Ahmad and Ishaaq bin Rahaawayah are of this opinion. Al-Marwazee said, "I asked Ahmad, 'Should one greet the people while they are in prayer?' He replied, 'Yes,' and he mentioned the story in which ibn Umar asked Bilaal how the Prophet (peace be upon him) replied to the *salaam* and his reply that he did so by indicating.' Ishaaq gave the same reply."[2]

This was also the opinion that Qaadee ibn al-Arabee chose saying, "It is possible that indicating in prayer occurs to reply to a *salaam*, just as it is possible that one indicates due to a need that presented itself to him. If it is to reply to the *salaam*, there are a number of authentic narrations concerning this, such as the action of the Prophet (peace be upon him) in Qubaa and other places."[3]

The evidence for the sanctioning of the *salaam* after completing the prayer in the mosque lies in the famous hadeeth of the man who prayed badly: Abu Hurayrah reported, "The Messenger of Allah (peace be upon him) entered the mosque and a man also entered and prayed and then came and greeted the Messenger of Allah (peace be upon him). The Messenger of Allah (peace be upon him) replied to the *salaam* and said, 'Return and repeat your prayer for you have not prayed.' The man returned as prayed as he had done on the first occasion and then came to the Messenger of Allah…(doing this three times)."[4]

Al-Albaanee said, "Through this hadeeth Siddeeq Hasan Khaan, in *Nuzul al-Abraar*[5], derived proof that 'if a person were to greet another and then meet him again shortly after, he should greet him again.'"

He also said, "This hadeeth also contains evidence towards the sanctioning of greeting those in the mosque. This

---

[1] Abu Daawood [Eng. Trans. 1/236 no, 927] and Ahmad (2/30) with a *saheeh* chain, meeting the conditions of al-Bukhaaree and Muslim. Refer to *Silsilah as-Saheehah* (no. 185).

[2] *Masaa`il al-Marwazee* (p. 22).

[3] *Aaridah al-Ahwadhee* (2/162).

[4] *Saheeh al-Bukhaaree* [Eng. Trans. 1/404 no. 724] and *Saheeh Muslim* [Eng. Trans. 1/218 no. 781].

[5] Pp. 350-351.

is also proven by the hadeeth that mentions the Ansaar greeting the Messenger of Allah (peace be upon him) in the Mosque of Qubaa as has preceded. However, despite this we find some of the partisans not attaching any importance to this Sunnah. So one of them enters the mosque and does not greet those there, thinking that it is disliked to do so. Maybe in what we have written, there serves a reminder to them and others; and admonition is of benefit to the believers."[1]

In conclusion, we learn that the *salaam* and shaking of hands is to be done upon meeting and upon leaving even if it be after a short time, regardless of whether this is in the mosque or outside of the mosque.

However, the matter that is distressful is that when you meet someone after completing the prayer and you say, '*as salaamu alaikum*' he promptly replies, '*taqabbalAllah*' and thinks that he has fulfilled what Allah has obligated in replying to the *salaam*. It is as if he has not heard the saying of Allah,

وَإِذَا حُيِّيتُمْ بِتَحِيَّةٍ فَحَيُّوا بِأَحْسَنَ مِنْهَا أَوْ رُدُّوهَا إِنَّ اللَّهَ كَانَ عَلَى كُلِّ شَيْءٍ حَسِيبًا

"When you are greeted with a greeting, greet in return with what is better than it, or at least return equally. Indeed Allah is Ever a careful account taker of all things" [*an-Nisaa`* (4):86].

The Messenger of Allah (peace be upon him) said, "Spread the *salaam* among you."[2] He did not say, 'Say *taqabbalAllah*.'

We do not know of a single Companion or Righteous Salaf, may Allah be pleased with them all, who used to shake hands with those on their left and right and give the tidings of the prayer being accepted after completing the prayer. If any one of them would have done this, it would have reached us, even it be via a weak chain, and the People of Knowledge would have quoted it—those who delved into every ocean and explored their deepest depths and derived from them many

---

[1] *Silsilah al-Ahaadeeth as-Saheehah* (1/314).
[2] *Saheeh Muslim* [Eng. Trans. 1/37 no. 96], Ahmad (2/391, 442, 447, 495) and others.

rules and regulations and did not neglect a single aspect of the Sunnah.[1]

Look and see how the Researching Scholars have quoted that the shaking of hands in the mannerism that has just been discussed is a *bid`ah*. Al-Izz bin Abdus Salaam said, "Shaking hands after praying the *Fajr* and *`Asr* prayers is a *bid`ah*. This does not hold for the one who has just arrived and shakes the hand of someone he meets before the prayer. Indeed, the shaking of hands is only sanctioned upon meeting and the Prophet (peace be upon him) used to follow up his prayer by saying the sanctioned *adhkaar*. He used to seek forgiveness three times and then turn. It is reported that he said (after the prayer), "O Lord save me from Your Punishment on the Day You resurrect Your servants."[2] All goodness lies in following the Messenger."[3]

This *bid`ah* that was confined to the *Fajr* and *`Asr* prayers in the time of the author has now spread to include all of the prayers—and there is no might or movement except with Allah.

Al-Luknawee said, "Two matters that should desired be abandoned have spread in our times and in many of the lands. The first is that the people do not greet those in the mosque upon entering the mosque at the time of the *Fajr* prayer. Instead, they enter, pray their *sunnahs* and then they pray their *fard*. Then they greet one another after completing the prayer and following on from it, and this is a vile state of affairs. The *salaam* is only a Sunnah when one meets as is established in the authentic Sunnah, it is not said at the end of a gathering. The second is that they shake each other's hands after completing the *Fajr*, *`Asr*, *Eed* and *Jumu`ah* prayers

---

[1] *Tamaam al-Kalaam fee Bid`iyyah al-Musaafaha ba`d as-Salaam* (pp. 24-25) and *al-Masjid fee al-Islam* (p. 225). Shaykh Abdullaah bin Abdurrahmaan al-Jibreen said, "Many of those who pray extend their hands to shake the hands of those around them after saying the *tasleem* of the obligatory prayers. They supplicate for them by saying, '*taqabbalAllah* (May Allah accept)' and this is an innovation and has not been reported from the Salaf." Refer to *Mujallah al-Mujtama`* (no. 855).
[2] Reported by Muslim [Eng. Trans. 1/345 no. 1529], at-Tirmidhee (no. 3398, 3399) and Ahmad (4/290).
[3] *Fataawaa al-Izz bin Abdis Salaam* (pp. 46-47) and refer to *al-Majmoo`* (3/488).

despite the fact that it is also only legislated to shake hands upon meeting the first time."[1]

After discussing the difference of opinion concerning shaking hands after completing the prayer, he said, "From those who forbade it were ibn Hajr al-Haythamee ash-Shaafi`ee and Qutub ad-Deen bin `Alaa ad-Deen al-Makkee al-Hanafee. Al-Faadil ar-Rumee declared it to be a vile *bid`ah* in *Majaalis al-Abraar* wherein he said, 'Shaking hands is commendable at the time of meeting. As for other than the time of meeting, such as after the *Jumu`ah* and *Eid* prayers, as is the habit of our times, the hadeeth is silent about this and, therefore, this action remains without any evidence. It is established that what has no evidence to support it must be rejected and it is not permissible to blindly follow it.'"[2]

Then he, may Allah have mercy upon him, proceeded to clarify his own *ijtihaad* and view saying, "As for what I say: They have agreed that this shaking of hands [in this manner] has no basis in the *Sharee`ah,* however they differed as to whether it was reprehensible or permissible. When a matter revolves around being reprehensible or permissible, it is desired to prohibit it because repressing the harm takes precedence over promoting that which is beneficial. Indeed, how is it not possible that it take precedence over an action that is permissible? Furthermore those who do shake hands [in this manner] see it as a good action and they go to great lengths in vilifying those who prohibit this and they stringently persist upon it. It has preceded that persisting upon something that is recommended can lead to it becoming disliked, so what then would be the case in persisting upon something that is a *bid`ah* having no basis in the *Sharee`ah*? Therefore, there is no doubt that such an action is reprehensible..."[3]

Finally, it is necessary to point out that it is not permissible for a Muslim to sever the *dhikr* of his brother

---

[1] *As-Si`aayah fee al-Kashf `ammaa fee Sharh al-Wiqaayah* (p. 264). From what has preceded it appears that there is no problem in two or more people shaking hands who have not previously met. Al-Albaanee said, "As for shaking hands after having completed the prayer, this is an innovation without doubt unless it be the case where two people meet not having previously met. In this case shaking hands is a Sunnah." (*Silsilah as-Saheehah* 1/23).

[2] Ibid. Refer also to *ad-Deen al-Khaalis* (4/314), *al-Madkhal* (2/84), *as-Sunan wa al-Mubtada`aat* (pp, 72-77).

[3] Ibid (p. 265).

Muslim unless it be for a valid valid reason. Also, it is not from wisdom that you retract your hand forcibly from the hand of the person next to you who is shaking it, nor is it from wisdom that you push back the hand that is extended to you, for this is harshness and rudeness which is alien to Islam. Instead, you should take his hand with gentleness and kindness and explain to him that this method of shaking is an innovation, for how many are the people who listen to exhortation and accept sincere advice and it was just ignorance that made them to fall into innovation. Therefore, it is upon the scholars and students of knowledge to explain the Sunnah in the best of ways. It is possible that a man or student of knowledge desire to put an end to an evil but he does so in a bad way and thereby falls into an evil greater than the one he wished to reject. So I enjoin you to gentleness. Gentleness, O callers to Islam, for then the called will love you and through your good morals and character you will attract their hearts and find them taking heed. Indeed, the nature of man is that he rejects what is presented to him in a severe and harsh way.[1]

---

[1] *Tamaam al-Kalaam fee Bid`iyyah al-Musaafaha ba`d as-Salaam* (p. 23).

BIBLIOGRAPHY

*Athar al-Ikhtilaaf fee al-Qawaa`id al-Usuliyyah fee Ikhtilaaf al-Fuqahaa.* Mustafaa al-Khann [Mu`assat ar-Risalaah, 1402H, 4th edition].

*al-Ahaadeeth al-Arba`een an-Nawawiyyah.* ibn Rajab al-Hanbalee [Tahqeeq Abdullaah Saalih al-Muhsin, Mataabi` as-Sa`aadah - Eqypt, 1390H].

*Arbah al-Bidaa`ah fee Fowaa`id Salaah al-Jamaa`ah.* Nabeel al-Basaarah [Daar ad-Da`wah - Kuwait].

al-Ashbaah wa an-Nadhaa`ir. al-Haafidh Jalaal ad-Deen as-Suyutee [Lebanon - Beirut, 1399H, 1st edition].

Bidaayah al-Mujtahid wa Nihaayah al-Muqtasid. ibn Rushd al-Qurtobee al-Maalikee [al-Istiqaamah edition - Cairo].

al-Bidaayah wa an-Nihaayah. Abu al-Fadaa` Ismaa`eel bin Katheer al-Qurashee [Tahqeeq Muhammad Abdul Azeez an-Najaar, Matba`a al-Fujaalah - Egypt].

Bida`u al-Qurraa` al-Qadeemah wa al-Mu`aasirah. Bakr bin Abdullaah Abu Zayd [Daar ar-Raayah - Riyaadh, 1408H, 2nd edition].

Basaa`ir Dhawee at-Tamyeez fee Tafseer al-Kitaab al-`Azeez. al-Fairoz Abaadee ash-Shayraazee [Maktabah al-`Ilmiyyah - Lebanon, distributed by Daar al-Baaz - Mecca].

Fadaa`il al-Qur`aan. al-Haafidh ibn Katheer [printed and added to the end of his tafseer].

Fath al-Baaree bi Sharh Saheeh al-Bukhaaree. al-Haafidh ibn Hajr al-`Asqalaanee [Mataabi` as-Salafiyyah, Cairo, 1381H].

Fath al-Qadeer. al-Kamaal ibn al-Hammaam al-Hanafee [Mataabi` `Eesaa al-Halabee, 1389H].

*Faydh al-Qadeer Sharh al-Jaami` as-Sagheer.* Abdur Ra`oof al-Munaawee [Lebanon, 2nd edition, 1396H].

Al-Fiqh al-Islamee wa Adillatuhu. Dr. Wahbah az-Zuhaylee [Daar al-Fikr edition, Lebanon].

*Al-Furoo` li ibn Muflih.* ibn Muflih al-Hanbalee [Mataabi` `Aalam al-Kutub, Lebanon, 4th edition].

Haashiyah ad-Dasooqee `alaa ash-Sharh al-Kabeer.
Muhammad `Arafah ad-Dasooqee [`Eesaa al-Halabee
edition - Egypt].

al-Hawaadith wa al-Bida`ah. Abu Bakr at-Turtooshee
[Tahqeeq Abdul Majeed at-Turkee, Daar al-Maghrib
al-Islamee - Morocco, 1410H, 1st edition].

Ihkaam al-Ahkaam Sharh `Umdah al-Ahkaam. ibn Daqeeq al-
`Eed [Mataabi` as-Sunnah - Cairo, 1342H].

Ihyaa `Uloom ad-Deen. Imaam Abu Haamid al-Ghazaalee
[Halabee print - Cairo, 1973CE].

al-Adhaan. Usaamah al-Quwsee with the introduction of
Muqbil bin Haadee al-Waadi`ee [Mu`assat at-Risaalah
- Lebanon, 1408H, 1st edition].

Irshaad a-Saaree bi Sharh Saheeh al-Bukhaaree in the margin
of which is *Sharh Saheeh Muslim* of an-Nawawee. al-
Qastalaanee [Daar Ihyaa at-Turaath al-Qawmee -
Lebanon].

Irwaa al-Ghaleel fee Takhreej Ahaadeeth Manaar as-Sabeel.
Muhammad Naasir ad-Deen al-Albaanee [Maktaba al-
Islamee - Lebanon, 1st edition].

al-Istidhkaar li Madhaahib Fuqahaa al-Amsaar. ibn `Abdul
Barr al-Qurtobee [al-Majlis al-A`laa li Shu`oon al-
Islamiyyah - Lebanon].

al-Istignaa fee al-Firaq wal Ististhnaa`. Muhammad al-Bakree
[Tahqeeq Dr. Sa`ood ath-Thabeetee - Jaami`a Umm al-
Qurra print].

I`laam al-Muwaqqi`een `an Rabb al-`Aalameen. Imaam Shams
ad-Deen ibn Qayyim al-Jawziyyah [Mataabi` Sa`aadah
- Egypt, 1394H].

al-Ifsaah `an Ma`aanee as-Sihaah. ibn Hubairah al-Hanbalee
[Dawjawee print - Cairo, 1978CE]

*Iqaamah al-Hujjah `alaa al-Musallee qabla al-Imaam ar-
Raatib min al-Kitaab wa as-Sunnah.* as-Sayyid Jamaal
ad-Deen al-Qaasimee [Mataabi` as-Sadaaqah -
Damascus, 1342H].

*al-Insaaf fee Ma`rifah ar-Raajih min al-Khilaaf.* `Alaa ad-
Deen al-Mardaawee [Tahqeeq Muhammad Haamid
Fiqee, Riyaadh 1374, 1st edition].

Jawaahir al-Ikleel Sharh Mukhtasar al-Khaleel. Saalih `Abd
as-Samee` al-Azharee [Daar al-Ma`rifah - Lebanon].

Al-Kaafee fee Fiqh Ahl al-Madeenah al-Maalikee. ibn Abdul Barr al-Maalikee [Tahqeeq Muhammad Ahmad, Riyaadh, 1st edition, 1398H].

Al-Kaafee fee Fiqh al-Imaam Ahmad bin Hanbal. ibn Qudaamah al-Maqidsee [Damascus].

*Kashshaaf al-Qinaa` `an Mas`alah ad-Du`aa ba`d al-Maktoobah bi Hay`ah al-Jamaa`ah.* Abu Muhammad Abdul Haqq al-Haashimee [Wizaarah al-I`laam as-Sa`udiyyah].

Kashshaaf al-Qinaa` `an Matn al-Iqnaa`. Mansoor al-Bahootee al-Hanbalee [1st edition, 1394H].

Al-Kitaab al-Musannaf fee al-Ahaadeeth wa al-Aathaar. al-Haafidh ibn Abee Shaybah [India, 2nd edition, 1399H].

Khabaaya az-Zawaayah. Badr ad-Deen az-Zarkashee [Wizaaraat al-Awqaaf - Kuwait].

Kitaab as-Salaah wa Hukm Taarikuhaa. al-Imaam ibn Qayyim al-Jawziyyah [contained within *Majmoo`ah al-Hadeeth an-Najdiyyah*, Mataabi` as-Salafiyyah, 1375H].

Al-Lu`lu` wa al-Marjaan feemaa Ittafaqa ash-Shaykhaan al-Bukhaaree wa Muslim. Muhammad Fo`aad Abdul Baaqee [al-Mataabi` al-`Asriyyah, Kuwait].

Al-Mabsoot. as-Sarkhasee al-Hanafee [Tahqeeq Shaykh Khaleel al-Mees al-Labnaanee, Daar al-Ma`aarif edition, Lebanon, 1406H].

Majmoo` Fataawaa ibn Taymiyyah.* [*Majmoo`ah Fataawaa ibn Taymiyyah al-Kubraa].

*Al-Majmoo` Sharh al-Muhadhdhab.* Muhiy ad-Deen an-Nawawee [al-`Aasimaa edition, Cairo].

*Al-Masaa`il al-Fiqhiyyah min Kitaab ar-Riwaayatain wa al-Wajhayn.* al-Qaadee Abu Ya`laa [Manuscript].

Mataalib Ulee an-Nahee Sharh Ghaayah al-Muntahaa. ar-Raheebaanee al-Hanbalee [al-Maktaba al-Islamee, Damascus, 1st edition, 1381H].

Al-Matla` Sharh al-Muqni`. ibn Muflih al-Hanbalee [1st edition, Lebanon, 1399H].

*Al-Mawsoo`ah al-Fiqhiyyah.* [Wizaarah al-Awqaaf bi al-Kuwait, Mataabi` Dhaat as-Salaasil, 2nd edition, 1410H].

Miftaah Daar as-Sa`aadah. al-Allaamah ibn al-Qayyim [Daar Najd edition, Riyaadh].

Al-Misbaah al-Muneer. Ahmad bin Muhammad al-Fuyumee [Daar al-Kutub al-Ilmiyyah, Lebanon].

Misbaah az-Zujaajah fee Zawaa`id ibn Maajah. Shihaab ad-Deen al-Busayree [Daar al-Janaan, Lebanon].

Misbaah az-Zujaajah ilaa Zawaa`id ibn Maajah. al-Kanaanee al-Busayree [Daar al-Janaan, Lebanon, 1st edition, 1406H].

Mu`aalim as-Sunan. Abu Sulaymaan al-Khattaabee al-Bustee [2nd edition, Lebanon, 1401H].

Al-Mubdi` Sharh al-Muqni`. ibn Muflih al-Hanbalee [al-Maktaba al-Islamee, Damascus, 1391H].

Al-Mudawwanah al-Kubraa Sahnoon al-Maalikee [Daar al-Fikr, Beirut, 1398H].

Al-Mughnee. ibn Qudaamah al-Hanbalee [Tahqeeq Dr. at-Turkee. 1st edition by Jaami`a al-Imaam, 2nd edition by Maytaabi` Hajar in Cairo].

Mughnee al-Muhtaaj ilaa Ma`rifah Ma`aanee Alfaadh al-Manhaj. ash-Sharbeenee al-Khateeb [Mataabib` Mustafaa al-Halabee, Cairo].

*Al-Muhadhdhab fee Fiqh ash-Shaafi`ee.* al-Fairozabaadee ash-Sheeraazee [`Eesaa al-Halabee edition, Cairo].

Al-Muhallah Sharh al-Mujallah. ibn Hazm adh-Dhaahiree [Daar al-Ittihaad al-Arabee edition, Egypt, 1387H].

*Mu`jam Lugha al-Fuqahaa.* Muhammad Saadiq Qaneebee [Daar an-Nafaa`is edition, Lebanon].

Mujma` az-Zawaa`id. al-Haafifh al-Haythamee.

*Al-Mukhtaaraat al-Jaliyyah fee Masaa`il al-Fiqhiyyah.* ash-Shaykh as-Sa`dee [Mu`assasah as-Sa`udiyyah, Riyaadh].

Mukhtasar al-Fataawaa al-Misriyyah. Badr ad-Deen Abu Abdullaah al-Ba`lee al-Hanbalee [Mataabi` at-Tunosee, Egypt].

Al-Mukhtasar fee Usool al-Fiqh. ibn al-Lahhaam [Daar al-Fikr, Lebanon, 1400H].

Mukhtasar al-Khaleel. Diyaa ad-Deen Khaleel al-Maalikee.

Al-Muntaqaa min Akhbaar al-Mustafaa. Majd ad-Deen Abu al-Barakaat ibn Taymiyyah al-Jadd [ar-Ri`aasah al-`Aamah li Idaarah al-Buhuth al-`Ilmiyyah wa al-Iftaa bi as-Sa`udiyyah].

Musannaf Abdur Razzaaq. al-Haafidh as-San`aanee [al-Maktabah al-Islamee, Lebanon, 1390H].

Musannaf ibn Abee Shaybah. ibn Abee Shaybah [2nd edition, 1399H].

Al-Musnad. al-Imaam Ahmad bin Hanbal [indexed by al-Albaanee, Maktbah al-Islamee, Damascus].

*Al-Mustadrak `alaa as-Saheehayn.* al-Haakim an-Naysaabooree [Daar al-Kitaab al-`Arabee, Lebanon].

Muwaahib al-Jaleel Sharh Mukhtsar al-Khaleel. al-Hitaab, [Daar al-Fikr edition, Lebanon, 1398H].

Nayl al-Awtaar. al-`Allaamah ash-Shawkaanee al-Yamaanee [Tahqeeq Rishdee Sulaymaan, Sabeeh edition, Cairo].

Nayl al-Maarib bi Sharh Daleel at-Taalib. Abdul Qaadir ash-Shaybaanee [Mataabi` Sabeeh, Egypt].

An-Nihaayah fee Ghareeb al-Hadeeth wa al-Athar. ibn Atheer al-Jazaree [Tahqeeq at-Tanaajee and az-Zawaawee, `Eesaa al-Halabee edition].

An-Niyyah wa Atharuhaa fee al-Ahkaam ash-Shar`iyyah. Dr. Saalih bin Ghaanim as-Sadlaan [Maktaba al-Khareejee, 1st edition, 1404H].

Qaamoos al-Fiqhee Lughatan wa Istilaahan. Sa`eedee Abu Jaib [Daar al-Fikr edition, Lebanon].

*Qawaaneen al-Ahkaam ash-Shar`iyyah wa Masaa`il al-Foroo` al-Fiqhiyyah.* ibn Juzzee al-Maalikee [Daar al-`Ilm, Lebanon, 1968H].

Al-Qiraa`ah Khalf al-Imaam. Abu Bakr ibn al-Husayn al-Bayhaqee [Idaarah Ihyaa as-Sunnah edition, Pakistan].

Radd al-Muhtaar `alaa ad-Darr al-Mukhtaar (Haashiyah ibn `Aabideen). ibn `Aabideen al-Hanafee [Daar Ihyaa Turaath al-`Arabee].

Rahmah al-Ummah Ikhtilaaf al-A`immah. Abu Abdurrahmaan ad-Dimishqee [Cairo print, 1386H, 2nd edition].

Rasaa`il ibn `Aabideen. ibn `Aabideen.

Ar-Rawd al-Anf. Imaam Abdurrahmaan as-Suhaylee [Tahqeeq Taa Haa AbdurRa`oof Sa`d, Daar al-Fikr al-`Arabee, Lebanon].

Ar-Rawd al-Marba` bi Haashiyah ibn Qaasim al-`Aasimee an-Najdee. ibn Qaasim an-Najdee [1st edition, Riyaadh, 1397H].

Rawdah at-Taalibeen. Yahyaa bin Sharf an-Nawawee [Maktabah al-Islamee edition, Beirut].

ar-Risaalah. Imaam Muhammad bin Idrees ash-Shaafi`ee [Tahqeeq Ahmad Shaakir, Daar Turaath, 1399H, 2nd edition].

ar-Risaalah as-Sanniyyah fee as-Salaah wa maa Yalzimu feehaa. Imaam Ahmad bin Hanbal [contained within *Majmoo`ah al-Ahaadeeth an-Najdiyyah*, Matba`a as-Salafiyyah, Egypt, 1386H].

*Saheeh al-Bukhaaree (al-Jaami` as-Saheeh).* Abu Abdullaah bin Muhammad bin Ismaa`eel al-Bukhaaree [al-Maktaba al-Islamee].

Saheeh ibn Khuzaymah. Abu Bakr Muhammad bin Ishaaq bin Khuzaymah an-Naysaabooree [Maktab al-Islamee, Lebanon, 1st edition].

Saheeh Muslim. Abu al-Husayn al-Qushayree an-Naysaabooree [ar-Ri`aasah al-Aamah lil Iftaa bi as-Sa`udiyyah, 1400H].

Saheeh at-Tirmidhee (or *Sunan at-Tirmidhee*). al-Haafidh Abu `Eesaa at-Tirmidhee [Daar al-Fikr edition, Lebanon].

Sayl al-Jarraar al-Mutadaffiq `alaa Hadaa`iq al-Azhaar. Muhammad bin `Alee ash-Shawkaanee [Mataabi` al-Baaz, Mecca, 1st edition].

Sharh al-Kabeer. ibn Qudaamah al-Hanbalee [Maktaba al-Islamee edition, Beirut].

*Sharh as-Sagheer `alaa Aqrab al-Masaalik ilaa Madhab Maalik.* Abu Barakaat Ahmad ad-Dardeer [Daar al-Ma`aarif edition, Egypt].

Sharh Saheeh Muslim. Muhiy ad-Deen bin Sharf an-Nawawee [Egyption edition].

Sharh as-Sunnah. Imaam al-Baghawee [1st edition, 1390H].

Shuroot as-Salaah wa Arkaanuhaa wa Waajibaatuhaa wa Aadaab al-Mashee ilayhaa. Imaam Muhammad bin Abdul Wahhaab [included among *Majmoo` Rasaa`il fee as-Salaah*, Ri`aasah al-`Aamah lil Iftaa edition, 1405].

Subul as-Salaam Sharh Bulugh al-Maraam. Muhammad Ismaa`eel as-Sana`aanee [Daar al-Kitaab al-`Arabee, Lebanon].

Sunan Abee Daawood. al-Haafidh Abu Sulaymaan bin al-Ash`ath as-Sijistaanee [Maktabaa al-Islamiyyah, 1388H].

Sunan al-Kubraa. Abu Bakr Ahmad bin al-Husayn al-Bayhaqee [Indian print, Majlis al-Ma'aarif al-'Umumiyyah, 1st edition].

Sunan Ibn Maajah. al-Haafidh Abu Abdullaah bin Yazeed al-Qazwaynee [ash-Sharikah at-Tibaa'ah as-Sa'udiyyah, 2nd edition, 1404H].

Sunan an-Nasaa'ee. al-Haafidh an-Nasaa'ee Ahmad bin Shu'ayb [al-Matboo'aat al-Islamiyyah, 1st edition, Lebanon].

Sunan at-Tirmidhee. al-Haafidh Abu 'Eesaaat-Tirmidhee [Daar al-Fikr edition, Lebanon].

As-Sunan wa al-Mubtada'aat fee al-Adhkaar wa as-Salawaat. Muhammad bin AbdusSalaam ash-Shuqayree [Mataabi' Yusufiyyah, Egypt].

at-Taaj al-Ikleel Sharh Mukhtasar al-Khaleel. Abu Abdullaah al-Mawwaaq [Daar al-Fikr, Beirut, 1398H 2nd edition].

Tabaqaat ash-Shaafi'iyyah al-Kubraa. Taaj ad-Deen Taqee ad-Deen as-Subkee [Daar al-Ma'rifah, Lebanon].

Tabsirah al-Hukkaam fee Usool al-Aqdiyyah wa Manaahij al-Ahkaam. ibn Firhawn al-Maalikee [Halabee edition, 1378H].

Tabyeen al-Haqaa'iq Sharh Kinz ad-Daqaa'iq. Fakhr ad-Deen az-Zaylafee al-Hanafee [Mataabi' al-Ameeriyyah - Egypt, 1313H].

at-Ta'leeq al-Mughnee 'alaa Sunan ad-Daaruqutnee. Imaam 'Alee bin 'Umar ad-Daaruqutnee [Faaliqin edition - Lahore].

at-Tamheed limaa fee al-Muwatta min al-Ma'aanee wa al-Asaaneed. ibn Abdul Barr al-Qurtobee [Morocco edition, 1402H].

at-Ta'reefaat. 'Alee bin Muhammad al-Jarjaanee [Maktaba al-Labnaan - Beirut, 1978CE].

at-Targheeb wa at-Tarheeb min Ahaadeeth ash-Shareef. al-Haafidh al-Mundhiree [Daar al-Fiqr - Lebanon, 1401H].

Tarh at-Tathreeb fee Sharh at-Taqreeb. al-Haafidh Zayn ad-Deen al-'Iraaqee [Daar Ihyaa at-Turaath edition, Lebanon].

Tuhfah al-Fuqahaa. 'Alaa ad-Deen as-Samarqandee [Daar Kutub al-'Ilmiyyah - Lebanon].

Al-Uddah Sharh al-Umdah. al-Ameer as-Sana`aanee [Maktaba ibn Taymiyyah, Cairo].

Al-Waabil as-Sayyib min al-Kalaam at-Tayyib. ibn Qayyim al-Jawziyyah [Daar al-Bayaan edition, Sa`udi, 1399H].

*Al-Wajeez fee Fiqh al-Imaam ash-Shaafi`ee.* Abu Haamid al-Ghazaalee [Daar al-Ma`rifah edition, Lebanon].

Al-Yaaqut an-Nafees fee Madh-hab ibn Idrees. as-Sayyid Ahmad ash-Shaatiree, [Mustafaa Halabee, 2nd edition, Egypt].

Az-Zawaa`id fee Fiqh al-Imaam Ahmad bin Hanbal. Shaykh Muhammad Aali Husayn [Daar al-Farzdaq edition, Riyaad].

Index of Verses Cited

Index of Hadeeth Quoted

'Whoever performs *wudu`* in an excellent way...' p. 33
'Whoever prays a prayer in which he does not recite...' p. 187
'Whoever prays during it out of faith...' p. 89
'Whoever prays *Ishaa* in congregation...' p. 42
'Whoever prays with the Imaam until...' p. 95
'Whoever recites *Aayatul Kursee...*' p. 243
'Whoever says *SubhaanAllah* thirty three times...' p. 242
'With the Name of Allah, I put my trust in Allah...' p. 48